John S. C. (John Stevens Cabot) Abbott, John Stevens Cabot Abbott

Miles Standish

Captain of the Pilgrims

John S. C. (John Stevens Cabot) Abbott, John Stevens Cabot Abbott

Miles Standish
Captain of the Pilgrims

ISBN/EAN: 9783742810243

Manufactured in Europe, USA, Canada, Australia, Japa

Cover: Foto ©ninafisch / pixelio.de

Manufactured and distributed by brebook publishing software (www.brebook.com)

John S. C. (John Stevens Cabot) Abbott, John Stevens Cabot Abbott

Miles Standish

Miles Standish

CAPTAIN OF THE PILGRIMS

By

JOHN S. C. ABBOTT

New York
Dodd, Mead and Company
1898

TO THE DESCENDANTS OF
CAPTAIN MILES STANDISH,
NOW NUMBERING THOUSANDS,
THIS VOLUME IS RESPECTFULLY INSCRIBED;
WITH THE HOPE THAT NO ONE OF THEM MAY EVER DIM
THE LUSTRE OF THAT NAME,
TO WHICH THE VIRTUES OF THEIR DISTINGUISHED ANCESTOR
HAVE ATTACHED IMPERISHABLE RENOWN.

JOHN S. C. ABBOTT.

PREFACE.

The adventures of our Pilgrim Fathers must ever be a theme of absorbing interest to all their descendants. Their persecutions in England, their flight to Holland, their passage across the stormy ocean, this new world, as they found it, swept by the storms of approaching winter, their struggles with the hardships of the wilderness, and conflicts with the ferocious savage,—all combine in forming a narrative replete with the elements of entertainment and instruction.

Fortunately, there can be no doubt in reference to the essential facts. All these events have occurred within the last three hundred years, a period fully covered by authentic historical documents. In giving occasional extracts from these documents, I have deemed it expedient to modernize the spelling, and occasionally to exchange an unintelligible, obsolete word for one now in use.

For a period of about forty years, Captain Miles Standish was intimately associated with the Pilgrims

His memory is inseparably connected with theirs. It has been a constant pleasure to the author to endeavor to rear a worthy tribute to the heroic captain and the noble man, who was one of the most illustrious of those who laid the foundations of this great Republic.

JOHN S. C. ABBOTT.

Fair Haven, Conn.

CONTENTS.

CHAPTER I.
PAGE

Elizabeth's Act of Uniformity.—Oppressive Enactments.—King James and his Measures.—Persecution of the Non-Conformists.—Plans for Emigration.—The Unavailing Attempt.—The Disaster near Hull.—Cruel Treatment of the Captives.—The Exiles at Amsterdam.—Removal to Leyden.—Decision to Emigrate to America.—The reasons.—Elder Brewster Selected as Pastor.—The Departure from Leyden.—Scene at Delft Haven.—The Embarkation............. 9

CHAPTER II.

The Departure from Southampton.—Hindrances.—Delay at Dartmouth and Plymouth.—Abandonment of the Speedwell.—Sketch of Miles Standish.—Death at Sea.—Perils and Threatened Mutiny.—Narrow Escape of John Howland.—Arrival at Cape Cod.—Testimony of Governor Bradford.—The Civil Contract.—John Carver Chosen Governor.—The First Exploring Tour.—The Sabbath 30

CHAPTER III.

Entering the Shallop.—The Second Exploring Tour.—Interesting Discoveries.—Return to the Ship.—A Week of Labor.—The Third Exploring Tour.—More Corn Found.—Perplexity of the Pilgrims.—The Fourth Expedition.—The First Encounter.—Heroism of the Pilgrims.—Night of Tempest and Peril.—A Lee Shore Found.—Sabbath on the Island... 44

CONTENTS.

CHAPTER IV.

The Voyage Resumed.—Enter an Unknown Harbor.—Aspect of the Land.—Choose it for their Settlement.—The Mayflower Enters the Harbor.—Sabbath on Shipboard.—Exploring the Region.—The Storm and Exposure.—The Landing.—View from the Hill.—Arduous Labors.—The Alarm.—Arrangement of the Village.—The Evident Hostility of the Indians. —Gloomy Prospects.—Expedition of Captain Standish.— Billington Sea.—Lost in the Woods.—Adventures of the Lost men.—The Alarm of Fire.................... 71

CHAPTER V.

Days of Sunshine and Storm.—Ravages of Pestilence.—A Raging Storm.—New Alarm of Fire.—Twelve Indians Seen.— Two Indians Appear on the Hill.—Great Alarm in the Settlement.—Measures of Defense.—More Sunny Days.- Humanity and Self-Denial of Miles Standish and Others.— Conduct of the Ship's Crew.—Excursion to Billington Sea. —The Visit of Samoset.—Treachery of Captain Hunt.—The Shipwrecked Frenchmen.—The Plague.—The Wampanoags.—More Indian Visitors.—Bad Conduct of the Billingtons.. 92

CHAPTER VI.

Two Savages on the Hill.—The Return of Samoset with Squantum.—The Story of Squantum.—The Visit of Massasoit and His Warriors.—Etiquette of the Barbarian and Pilgrim Courts.—The Treaty.—Return of the Mayflower to England.—A View of Plymouth.—Brighter Days.—Visit of Messrs. Winslow and Hopkins to the Seat of Massasoit.— Incidents of the Journey........................ 117

CHAPTER VII.

The Lost Boy.—The Expedition to Nauset.—Interesting Adventures.—The Mother of the Kidnapped Indians.—Tyanough.—

CONTENTS.

Payment for the Corn.—Aspinet, the Chief.—The Boy Recovered.—Alarming Intelligence.—Hostility of Corbitant.—The Friendship of Hobbomak.—Heroic Achievement of Miles Standish.—The Midnight Attack.—Picturesque Spectacle.—Results of the Adventure.—Visit to Massachusetts.—The Squaw Sachem.—An Indian Fort.—Charming Country.—Glowing Reports.................................... 145

CHAPTER VIII.

Arrival of the Fortune.—Object of the Pilgrims in their Emigration.—Character of the New-Comers.—Mr. Winslow's Letter.—The First Thanksgiving.—Advice to Emigrants.—Christmas Anecdote.—Alarming Rumor.—The Narragansets.—Curious Declaration of War.—The Defiance.—Fortifying the Village.—The Meeting in Council and the Result.—The Alarm.—The Shallop Recalled........................... 164

CHAPTER IX.

The Double-Dealing of Squantum.—False Alarm.—Voyage to Massachusetts.—Massasoit Demands Squantum.—The Arrival of the Boat.—The Virginia Massacre.—Preparations for Defense.—Arrival of the Charity and the Swan.—Vile Character of the Weymouth Colonists.—Arrival of the Discovery.—Starvation at Weymouth.—Danger of the Plymouth Colony.—Expeditions for Food.—Death of Squantum.—Voyage to Massachusetts and the Cape........................... 187

CHAPTER X.

Search for Corn.—Trip to Buzzard's Bay.—Interesting Incident.—Energy and Sagacity of Captain Standish.—Hostile Indications.—Insolence of Witeewamat.—The Plot Defeated.—Sickness of Massasoit.—The Visit.—Gratitude of the Chief.—Visit to Corbitant.—Condition of the Weymouth Colony.—The Widespread Coalition.—Military Expedition of Captain Standish.—His Heroic Adventures.—End of the Weymouth Colony............................... 209

CHAPTER XI.

Letter from Rev. Mr. Robinson.—Defense of Captain Standish.—New Policy Introduced.—Great Destitution.—Day of Fasting and Prayer.—Answer to Prayer.—The First Thanksgiving.--The Colony at Weymouth.—Worthless Character of the Colonists.—Neat Cattle from England.—Captain Standish Sent to England.—Captain Wollaston and His Colony. — Heroism of Captain Standish. — Morton Vanquished.—Difficulty at Cape Ann.—Increasing Emigration.—The Division of Property............................ 232

CHAPTER XII.

The Virginia Emigrants.—Humanity and Enterprise of the Governor.—Envoy Sent to England.—Trading-Posts on the Kennebec and Penobscot Rivers.—Capture by the French.—The Massachusetts Colony.—Its Numbers and Distinguished Characters.—Trade with the Indians.—Wampum the New Currency.—Trading-Post at Sandwich.—Sir Christopher Gardener.—Captain Standish Moves to Duxbury.—Lament of Governor Bradford............................ 257

CHAPTER XIII.

Removal to Duxbury.—Intercourse with the Dutch.—Trading-Posts on the Connecticut.—Legend of the Courtship of Miles Standish.—Personal Appearance of the Captain.—Proposition to John Alden.—His Anguish and Fidelity.—Interview with Priscilla.—The Indian Alarm.—Departure of Captain Standish.—Report of his Death.—The Wedding...

CHAPTER XIV.

Menace of the Narragansets.—Roger Williams.—Difficulty at the Kennebec.—Bradford's Narrative.—Captain Standish as Mediator.—The French on the Penobscot.—Endeavors to Regain the Lost Port.—Settlements on the Connecticut

CONTENTS.

River.—Mortality Among the Indians.—Hostility of the Pequots.—Efforts to Avert War.—The Pequot Forts.—Death of Elder Brewster.—His Character............ 301

CHAPTER XV.

Friendship Between Captain Standish and Mr. Brewster.—Character of Mr. Brewster.—His Death and Burial.—Mode of Worship.—Captain's Hill.—Difficulty with the Narragansets.—Firmness and Conciliation.—Terms of Peace.—Plans for Removal from Plymouth.—Captain Standish's Home in Duxbury.—Present Aspect of the Region................. 332

CHAPTER XVI.

The Will of Captain Standish.—His Second Wife.—Captain's Hill.—The Monument.—Letters from President Grant and General Hooker.—Oration by General Horace Binney Sargent.—Sketch of his Life.—Other Speakers.—Laying the Corner Stone.—Description of the Shaft............. 356

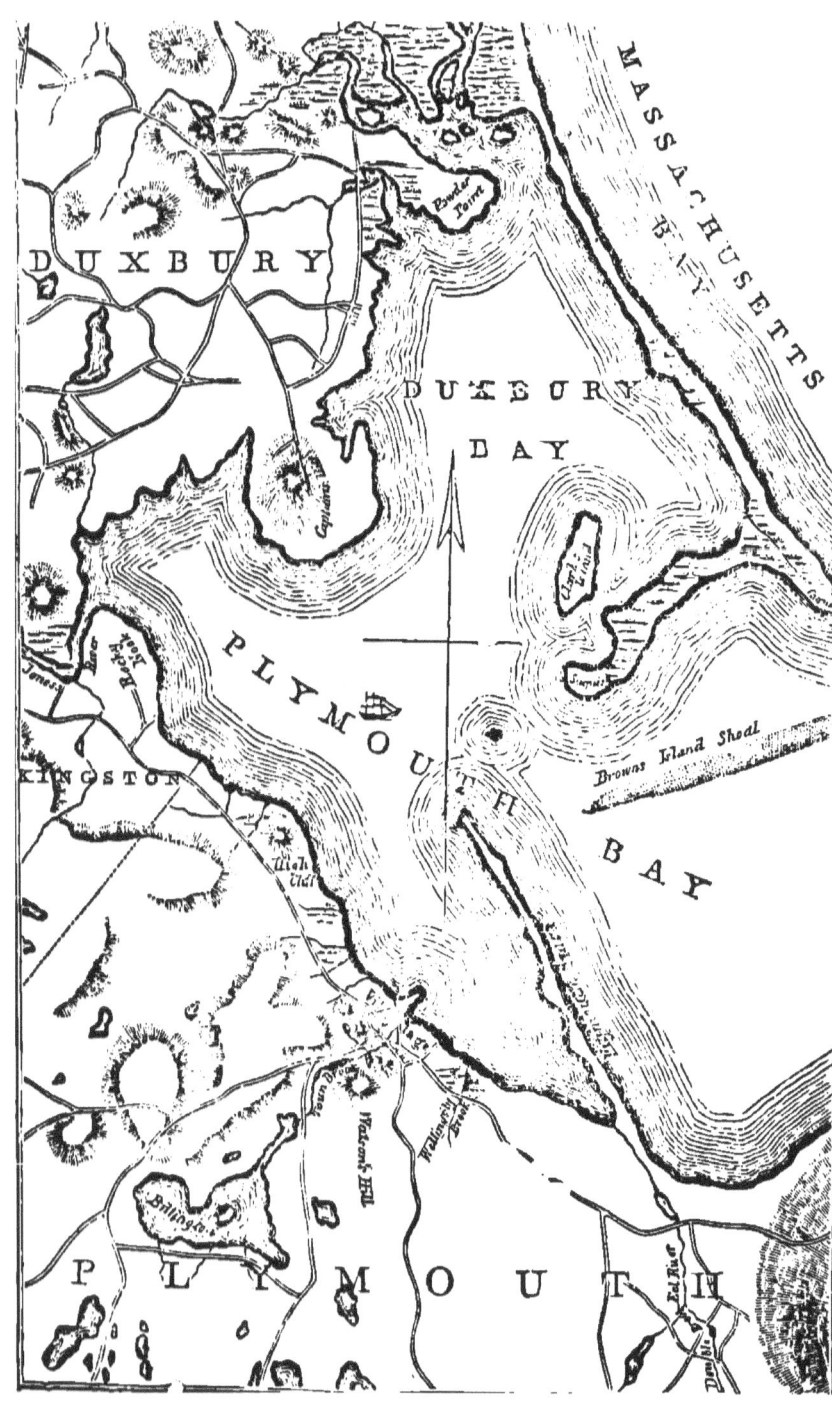

CHAPTER I.

The Pilgrims in Holland.

Elizabeth's Act of Uniformity.—Oppressive Enactments.—King James and his Measures.—Persecution of the Non-Conformists.—Plans for Emigration.—The Unavailing Attempt.—The Disaster near Hall.—Cruel Treatment of the Captives.—The Exiles at Amsterdam.—Removal to Leyden.—Decision to Emigrate to America.—The reasons.—Elder Brewster Selected as Pastor.—The Departure from Leyden.—Scene at Delft Haven.—The Embarkation.

Elizabeth, the maiden queen of England, commenced her long and eventful reign by issuing in May, 1659 a law concerning religion entitled the "Act of Uniformity." By this law all ministers were prohibited from conducting public worship otherwise than in accordance with minute directions for the Church of England, issued by Parliament. Any one who should violate this law was exposed to severe penalties, and upon a third offence to imprisonment for life.

England, having broken from the Church of Rome, and having established the Church of England, of which the queen was the head, Elizabeth and her counsellors were determined, at whatever cost, to enforce entire uniformity of doctrines and of modes of worship. In their new organization they retained many of the ceremonies and much of the imposing display of the Papal Church. There were very many of the clergy and of the laity who, displeased with the pageantry of the Roman Catholic Church, with its gilded robes and showy ceremonial, were resolved to cherish a more simple and pure worship. They earnestly appealed for the abolition of this oppressive act. Their petition was refused by a majority of but one in a vote of one hundred and seventeen in the House of Commons

The queen was unrelenting, and demanded uniformity in the most peremptory terms. Thirty-seven out of the ninety-eight ministers of London were arrested for violating this law. They were all suspended from their ministerial functions, and fourteen of them were sent to jail.

There were now three ecclesiastical parties in England—the Papal or Roman Catholic, the Episcopal, or Church of England, and the Presbyterian or Puritan party. The sympathies of the queen and of her courtiers was much more with the Papists than with the Presbyterians, and it was greatly feared that they would go over to their side The queen grew daily more and more determined to enforce the discipline of the English Church. The order was issued that all preachers should be silenced who had not been ordained by Episcopal hands or who refused to read the whole service as contained in the Prayer book, or who neglected to wear the prescribed clerical robes Under this law two hundred and thirty-three ministers, in six counties, were speedily deposed. A Court of High Commission was appointed invested with extraordinary powers to arrest and punish all delinquents.

Any private person who should absent himself from the Episcopal Church for a month, or who should dissuade others from attending that form of worship, or from receiving the communion from an Episcopal clergyman, or who should be present at any "conventicle or meeting under color or pretence of any exercise of religion," should be punished with imprisonment and should be held there until he signed the "Declaration of Conformity." Or in default of such declaration he was to be sent to perpetual exile under penalty of death if he were ever again found within the British realms.

Notwithstanding that many were banished, and some died in prison and several were hanged, the cause of dissent secretly gained ground. As they were deliberating in the House of Commons upon a more rigid law to compel all to adopt the same creed and the same modes of Worship. Sir Walter Raleigh said that he thought that there were then nearly twenty thousand dissenters in England. Many driven from their homes by this violent persecution emigrated to Holland where, under Protestant rule there was freedom of religious worship.

Upon the accession of James the Sixth of Scotland to the throne of England, eight hundred clergymen petitioned for redress. Among other things they prayed for the disuse of the cap and surplice in the pulpit, for an abridgement of the Liturgy, for the better observance of the Lord's day, and for a dispensation of the observance of other holy days; that none but pious men should be admitted to the ministry, and that ministers should reside in their parishes and preach on the Lord's day. To this appeal the king turned a deaf ear. In a conference which was held upon the subject, in Hampton court, the petitioners were received with contumely and insult. The king refused to pay any respect to private consciences, saying, 'I will have one doctrine, one discipline, one religion. And I will make you conform or I will harry you out of this land or else worse."

A book of Common Prayer was published as "the only public form established in this realm," and all were required to conform to its ritual and discipline as the king's resolutions were unchangeable. Ten of the petitioners for a redress of grievances were sent to jail. The king himself, a conceited pedant, drew up a Book of Canons consisting of one hundred and forty-one articles, expressed in the most arrogant style of pretensions to infallibility. The clergy and the laity were alike commanded to submit to them under penalty of excommunication, imprisonment and outlawry. The importation of all religious books from the Continent was prohibited. No religious book could be published in England unless approved by a court of Bishops. It is estimated that, at that time there were fifteen hundred Non-Conformist clergymen in England. Bishop Coverdale, with many others of the most prominent ecclesiastics of the Episcopal church, publicly announced their refusal to subscribe to the Liturgy or to adopt the ceremonies it enjoined. In their protest they declared that since "they could not have the Word freely preached, and the sacraments administered without idolatrous gear they concluded to break off from the public churches and separate in private houses."

The persecution of the Non-Conformists was continued with so much vigor, that the friends of religious reform became hopeless. Some sought refuge in concealment, while many fled from their country to Holland where, the principles of Protestantism prevailing, there was freedom of worship. In the county of Nottinghamshire, England, there was a small village called Scrooby, where there was a congregation o: Non-Conformists, meeting secretly from house to house. This was about the year 1606. A recent traveller gives the following interesting description of the present appearance of the little hamlet, which more than two and a half centuries ago was rendered memorable by the sufferings of the Puritans:

"The nearest way from Austerfield to Scrooby is by a path through the fields. Unnoticed in our history as these places have been till within a few years, it is likely that when, towards sunset on the 15th of September 1856, I walked along that path, I was the first person, related to the American Plymouth, who had done so since Bradford trod it last before his exile. I slept in a farm-house at Scrooby and reconnoitered that village the next morning. Its old church is a beautiful structure. At the distance from it of a quarter of a mile the dyke, round the vanished manor house, may still be traced; and a farmer's house is believed to be part of the ancient stables or dog kennels. In what was the garden is a mulberry tree so old that generations, before Brewster, may have regaled themselves with its fruit. The local tradition declares it to have been planted by Cardinal Wolsey, during his sojourn at the manor for some weeks after his fall from power."

The little church of Non-Conformists at Scrooby

had Richard Clifton for pastor and John Robinson for teacher. William Brewster, who subsequently attained to much distinction as pastor of the Puritan church in Plymouth, New England, was then a private member of the church. This little band of christians decided to emigrate in a body to Holland that they might there worship God in freedom.

It was a great trial to these christians to break away from their country, their homes, and their employments, to seek exile in a land of strangers. To add to their embarrassments cruel laws were passed forbidding the emigration of any of the Non-Conformists or Puritans as they began to be called. Bands of armed men vigilantly guarded all the seaports. Governor Bradford, who shared conspicuously in these sufferings, wrote:

"They could not long continue in any peaceable condition, but were hunted and persecuted on every side. Some were taken and clapped up in prison. Others had their houses beset and watched night and day, and hardly escaped capture. The most were fain to fly and leave their houses and habitations and the means of their livelihood. Yet seeing themselves thus molested, by a joint consent they resolved to go into the Low Countries where they heard was freedom of religion for all men; as also that sundry persons from London, and other parts of the land, had been exiled and persecuted for the same cause, and were gone thither, and lived at Amsterdam and other places of the land.

"Being thus constrained to leave their native soil and country, their lands and living, and all their friends and familiar acquaintance, it was much, and thought marvellous by many. But to go into a country they knew not except by hearsay, where they must learn a new language, and get their livings they knew not how, it being an expensive place and subject to the miseries of war, it was by many thought an adventure almost desperate, a case intolerable, and a misery worse than death. Especially seeing they were not acquainted with trades or traffic, by which the country doth subsist, but had been only used to a plain country life and the innocent trade of husbandry.

"But these things did not dismay them, though they did at times trouble them, for their desires were set on the ways of God and to enjoy his ordinances. But they rested on His providence and knew whom they had believed. Yet this was not all; for though they could not stay, yet were they not suffered to go; but the ports and havens were shut against them; so as they were fain to seek secret means of conveyance, and to bribe and fee the mariners, and give extraordinary rates for their passages. And yet they were

THE PILGRIMS IN HOLLAND.   17

often betrayed, many of them, and both they and their goods intercepted and surprised, and thereby put to great trouble."

The company at Scrooby however secretly chartered a vessel, at Boston, in Lincolnshire, about fifty miles south-east from Scrooby, the nearest port for their purpose. The peril of the enterprise was so great that they had to practise the utmost caution and to pay exorbitant passage money. They travelled by land to the appointed rendezvous, where to their bitter disappointment, they found neither captain nor vessel. After a long delay and heavy expenses, for which they were quite unprepared, the vessel made its appearance and, in the night, all were received on board. Then this infamous captain, having previously agreed to do so for his "thirty pieces of silver," betrayed them, and delivered them all up to the search officers.

Rudely they were seized, their trunks broken open, their clothing confiscated, and even the persons of their women searched with cruel indelicacy. Thus plundered and outraged they were placed in open boats and taken to the shore, where they were exhibited to the derisive gaze and the jeers of an ignorant and a brutal populace. A despatch was immediately sent to the Lords of the Council in London, and they were all committed to prison. After gloomy incarceration for a month, Mr. Brewster and six others of the most prominent men were bound over for trial, and the rest were released, woe-stricken, sick and impoverished, to find their way back, as best they could, to the Scrooby which they had left, and where they no longer had any homes. Oh man! what a fiend hast thou been in the treatment of thy brother man!

The next Spring a portion of these resolute men and women made another attempt to escape to Holland. They did not venture again to trust one of their own countrymen, but made a contract with a a Dutch shipmaster, from Zealand. He agreed to have his vessel, at an appointed day, in a retired spot upon the river Humber, not far from the seaport of Hull. Arrangements were made for the women and children, with their few goods, to be floated down the Humber in a barque, while the men made the journey by land. This was all done under the protection of night.

The Humber here swells into a bay, a long and wide arm of the sea. The wind was high, and the little barque, plunging over the waves, made the women and children deadly sea sick. Having arrived near their point of destination, before the dawn of the morning and the vessel not yet having arrived, the boatmen put into a little creek to find still water

Here the receding tide left them aground. In the morning came the ship. The captain, seeing the barque containing the women and children aground, and the men, who had come by land walking near by upon the shore, sent his boat to bring the men on board, that they might be already there when the returning tide should float the barque. One crowded boat load had reached the ship when a body of armed men, horse and foot, was seen rapidly approaching. The captain was terrified. Fine, imprisonment, and perhaps a worse fate awaited him. Uttering an oath, he weighed anchor, spread his sails, and a fresh breeze soon carried him out to sea.

Dreadful indeed was the condition of those thus abandoned to the insults and outrages of a brutal soldiery. Husbands and wives, parents and children were separated. The anguish of those, thus torn from their families, on board the ship, was no less than the distress of the mothers and daughters left upon the shore.

A storm soon rose—a terrific storm. For seven days and nights the ship was at the mercy of the gale, without sight of sun or moon or stars. The ship was driven near to the coast of Norway, and more than once the mariners thought the ship sinking past all recovery. At length the gale abated and, fourteen days after they had weighed anchor, the vessel reached Amsterdam, where from the long voyage and the fury of the tempest, their friends had almost despaired of ever again seeing them

But let us return to those who were left upon the banks of the Humber. They were all captured. Deplorable was the condition of these unhappy victims of religious intolerance, women and children weeping bitterly in their despair. Some of the men, who knew that the rigors of the law would fall upon them with the greatest severity, escaped. But most of those who had been left behind by the ship allowed themselves to be taken to share the fate of the destitute and helpless women and children, that they might if possible, assist them. The troops were very cruel in the treatment of their prisoners. They were roughly seized and hurried from one justice to another, the officers being much embarrassed to know what to do with them.

Governor Bradford, who witnessed these scenes, writes:—" Pitiful it was to see the heavy care of these poor women in this distress; what weeping and crying on every side; some for their husbands that were carried away in the ship; others not knowing what would become of them and their little ones; others melted in tears seeing their little ones hanging about them, crying for fear and quaking with cold."

In view of their sufferings general sympathy was

excited in their behalf. It seemed inhuman to imprison, in gloomy cells of stone and iron, women and innocent children, simply because they had intended to accompany their husbands and fathers to another land. It was of no use to fine them, for they had no means of paying a fine. Neither could they be sent to their former homes, for their houses and lands had already been sold, in preparation for their removal.

At last the poor creatures were turned adrift. No historic pen has recorded the details of their sufferings. Some undoubtedly perished of exposure. Some were kindly sheltered by the charitable, and some succeeded in various ways in crossing the sea to Amsterdam. There were similar persecutions in other parts of England. Quite a large company of pilgrims from various sections of England had succeeded, some in one way and some in another, in effecting their escape to Holland. They had nearly all taken up their residence in Amsterdam. This flourishing city was so called because it had sprung up around a *dam* which had been thrown across the mouth of the *Amstel* river. It was even then renowned for its stately buildings, its extended commerce and its opulence. Ships, from every clime, lined its wharfs; water craft of every variety and in almost countless numbers floated upon its canals, which took the place of streets

From many parts of Europe Protestants had fled to this city, bringing with them their arts, manufactures and skill in trade. The emigrants from Scrooby were nearly all farmers. They had no money to purchase lands, and they found it very difficult to obtain remunerative employment in the crowded streets of the commercial city. Governor Bradford writes, of his companions in affliction:

"They heard a strange and uncouth language and beheld the different manners and customs of the people with their strange fashions and attires; all so different from their plain country villages, wherein they were bred and had so long lived, as it seemed they were come into a new world. But these were not the things they much looked on, or which long took up their thoughts. For they had other work in hand and another kind of war to urge and maintain. For it was not long before they saw the grim and grisly face of poverty come on them, like an armed man, with whom they must buckle and encounter and from whom they could not fly."

The new comers did not find perfect harmony of agreement with those who had preceded them. After a few months tarry at Amsterdam they retired in a body to Leyden, a beautiful city of seventy thousand inhabitants, about forty miles distant. In allusion to this movemen' Governor Bradford writes :

"For these and some other reasons they removed to Leyden, a fair and beautiful city, and of a sweet situation; but made more famous by the university, wherewith it is adorned, in which of late had been so many learned men. But wanting that traffic by sea which Amsterdam enjoys, it was not so beneficial for their outward means of living. But being now established here, they fell to such trades and employments as they best could; valuing peace and their spiritual comfort above any other riches whatever.

"Being thus settled, after many difficulties, they continued many years in a comfortable condition, enjoying much sweet and delightful society, and spiritual comfort together in the ways of God, under the able ministry of Mr. John Robinson and Mr. William Brewster, who was an assistant unto him, in the place of an Elder, unto which he was now called and chosen by the church. So they grew in knowledge and other gifts and graces of God, and lived together in peace and love and holiness; and many came unto them from diverse parts of England so as they grew a great congregation.

" And if at any time any differences arose, or offenses broke out, as it cannot be but some time there will, even among the best of men, they were even so met with and nipped ir the head betimes, or otherwise so well composed as still love, peace and communion were continued."

The condition of the Pilgrims in Holland was a very hard one. They were foreigners; they found the language difficult to acquire. They were generally poor and notwithstanding their honesty and frugality, could obtain but a scanty support. Their sons were strongly tempted to enlist as soldiers, or to wander away as sailors. The future of their families seemed very gloomy.

"Lastly," writes Governor Bradford, "and which was not least, a great hope and inward zeal they had of laying some good foundation, or at least to make some way thereunto for propagating and advancing the kingdom of Christ, in those remote parts of the world,—yea, though they should be but the stepping stones unto others for the performing of so great a work."

"Their numbers assembled at Leyden can only be conjectured. It may, when at the largest, have counted between two and three hundred persons. Rev. John Robinson was chosen their pastor, and William Brewster their assistant pastor."

Thus gradually the Pilgrims came to the conviction that Holland was not a desirable place for their permanent home. Notwithstanding the oppression which they had endured from the British government, they were very unwilling to lose their native language or the name of Englishmen. They could not educate their children as they wished, and it was quite certain their descendants would become absorbed and lost in the Dutch nation. They therefore began to turn their thoughts to the New World, where every variety of clime invited them, and where boundless acres of the most fertile land, unoccupied, seemed to be waiting for the plough of the husbandman. " Hereby they thought they might more glorify God, do more good to their country, better provide for their posterity, and live to be more refreshed by their labors than ever they could do in Holland." *

Unsuccessful attempts had already been made to establish colonies in Maine and Virginia. They had also received appalling reports of the ferocity of the savages. Deeply, solemnly, they pondered the all important question with many fastings and prayers Bradford writes that,

" They considered that all great and honorable actions were accompanied with great difficulties, and must be both enterprised and overcome with answerable courages. The dangers were great, but not desperate ; the difficulties were many, but not invincible. For, though there were many of them likely, yet they were not certain. It might be, sundry of the things feared might never befall ; others, by provident care

---

* Winslow's Briefe Narrative, p. 31.

and the use of good means, might, in a great meas
ure, be prevented. And all of them, through the help
of God, by fortitude and patience, might either be
borne o. overcome. Their ends were good and honorable, and therefore they might expect the blessing
of God in their proceeding." *

The Dutch endeavored to induce them to join a
feeble colony which they had established at the mouth
of the Hudson river. Sir Walter Raleigh presented
in glowing terms the claims of the valley of the Ori-
noco, in South America, which river he had recently
explored for the second time.

"We passed," writes the enthusiastic traveller,
"the most beautiful country that my eyes ever beheld.
I never saw a more beautiful country or more lively
prospects. There is no country which yieldeth more
pleasure to its inhabitants. For health, good air,
pleasure, riches, I am resolved that it cannot be equal-
led by any region either in the east or west." †

There was a small struggling English colony in
Virginia which they were urged to join. But Bradford writes that they were afraid that they should be
as much persecuted there for their religion as if they
lived in England. After pondering for some time
these questions and perplexities, they decided to es-

---

* Bradford, 25, 26. † Works of Sir Walter Raleigh.

tablish a distinct colony for themselves, obtaining their lands from the Virginia Company in England. A delegation was sent to the king of England, soliciting from him a grant of freedom of worship. The Virginia Company gladly lent its co-operation to the emigrants. The king, however, was so unrelenting in his desire to promote religious uniformity throughout all his domains, that though the Secretary of State, and others high in authority, urged him to liberality, he could only be persuaded to give his reluctant assent to the assurance "that his majesty would connive at them, and not molest them, provided they carried themselves peaceably."

The very important question now arose, Who should go. Manifestly all could not be in a condition to cross a wide and stormy sea, for a new world, never to return. As only a minority of the whole number could leave, it was decided that their pastor, Mr. Robinson, should remain with those left behind, while Elder Brewster should accompany the emigrants as their spiritual guide. For nearly twelve years they had resided in Leyden. The hour of their departure was a sad one for all. Many very grievous embarrassments were encountered, which we have not space here to record.

A small vessel of but sixty tons burden, called the Speedwell, was purchased, and was in the harbor at

Delft Haven, twelve miles from Leyden, awaiting the arrival of the pilgrims. Their friends, who remained, gave them a parting feast. It was truly a religious festival.

' The feast," writes Winslow, " was at the pastor's house, which was large. Earnest were the prayers for each other, and mutual the pledges. With hymns prayers, and the interchange of words of love and cheer, a few hours were passed." The pilgrims, then, about one hundred and twenty in number, accompanied by many of their Leyden friends, repaired on board canal boats, and were speedily conveyed to Delft Haven. Here another parting scene took place. The description of it, as given by Bradford, in his " Brief Narration," is worthy of record :

" The night before the embarkation was **spent** with little sleep by the most; but with friendly entertainment and Christian discourse, and other real expressions of true Christian love. The next day, the wind being fair, they went on board, and their friends with them, where truly doleful was the sight of that sad and mournful parting. To see what sighs and sobs did sound among them ; what tears did gush from every eye, and pithy speeches pierced each heart ; that sundry of the Dutch strangers that stood on the quay as spectators, could not refrain from tears. Yet com**fortable** and sweet it was to see such lively and true expressions of dear and unfeigned love. But the tide, which stays for no man, calling them away that were thus loath to part, their reverend pastor falling down upon his knees, and they all, with him, with watery cheeks, commended them, with most fervent prayers to the Lord and His blessing. And then, with mutual embraces and many tears, they took their leaves one of another."

CHAPTER II.

The Voyage.

The Departure from Southampton.—Hindrances.—Delay at Dartmouth and Plymouth.—Abandonment of the Speedwell.—Sketch of Miles Standish.—Death at Sea.—Perils and Threatened Mutiny.—Narrow Escape of John Howland.—Arrival at Cape Cod.—Testimony of Governor Bradford.—The Civil Contract.—John Carver Chosen Governor.—The First Exploring Tour.—The Sabbath.

On the 22d of July, 1620, the Speedwell, with its little band of Christian heroes, left the haven of Delft for England.

Rev. Mr. Robinson and his friends returned sadly to Leyden. A prosperous wind rapidly bore the vessel across the channel to the British coast, and they entered the port of Southampton. Here they found a party of English emigrants who had chartered a vessel, the Mayflower, of one hundred and twenty tons. They were awaiting the arrival of the Speedwell, intending to unite with the Leyden band and sail in its company for the organization of a Christian colony in the New World.

Here, disappointed in some of their financial plans, it was found that they needed four hundred dollars to pay up sundry bills, before they could sail. To raise this money they were compelled to sell some of their provisions, including many firkins of butter, which luxury they thought they could best spare.

At length, all things being ready, both vessels weighed anchor and put to sea, from Southampton, on the 5th of August. In the two vessels there were about one hundred and twenty passengers. They had gone but about one hundred miles when Captain Reynolds, of the Speedwell, announced that his ship had sprung a leak, and that he did not dare to continue the voyage without having her examined and repaired. Both vessels, therefore, put into Dartmouth, losing a fair wind, and time which, with the rapidly passing summer weather, was invaluable to them. They were detained for more than a week, searching out the leaks and mending them. One of their number, Mr. Cushman, wrote from Dartmouth a doleful letter, full of anticipations of evil.

"We put in here," he wrote, "to trim our vessel; and I think, as do others, also, that if we had stayed at sea for three or four hours more she would have sunk right down. And, though she was twice trimmed at Southampton, yet now she is open and leaky as a sieve. We lay at Southampton seven days in fair weather waiting for her; and now we lie here in as fair a wind as can blow, and so have done these four days, and are like to do four days more; and by that time the wind will probably turn, as it did at Southampton Our victuals will be half eaten up, I think, before we go from the coast of England. And if our voyage last ong we shall not have a month's victuals when we come into the country.

"If I should write to you all things which promiscuously forebode our ruin, I should overcharge my weak head and grieve your tender heart. Only this I pray you, prepare for evil tidings of us every day. I see not in reason how we shall escape even the gaspings of hunger-starved persons. But God can do much, and His will be done."

Again the two vessels set sail, probably about the 21st of August.

They had been out but a day or two, having made about three hundred miles from Land's End, keeping close company, when the commander of the Speedwell hung out a signal of distress. Both vessels hove to and it appeared that the Speedwell had sprung a leak, of so serious a character that, though diligently plying the pumps, they could scarcely keep her afloat.

Nothing was to be done but to put back again to Plymouth, the nearest English port. Here the Speed well was carefully examined, and pronounced to be, from general weakness, unseaworthy. The disappointment was very great. The vessel was abandoned; twenty passengers were left behind, who could not be

THE VOYAGE. 33

"It was resolved," writes Governor Bradford, "to dismiss the Speedwell and part of the company, and proceed with the other ship. The which, though it was grievous and caused great discouragement, was put in execution. So, after they had taken out such provisions as the other ship could well stow, and concluded what number and what persons to send back, they made another sad parting, the one ship going back to London, the other proceeding on her voyage. Those who went back were, for the most part, those who were willing so to do, either out of some discontent, or from fear they conceived of the ill success of the voyage, seeing so many crosses befal, and the time of the year so far spent. But others, in regard to their weakness and charge of many young children, were thought least useful, and most unfit to bear the brunt of this hard adventure; unto which work of God and judgment of their brethren they were contented to submit. And thus, like Gideon's army, this small number was divided, as if the Lord, by this work of His providence, thought these few too many for the great work He had to do. But here, by the way, let me show, how afterwards it was found that the leakiness of this ship was partly caused by being overmasted and too much pressed with sails; for after she was sold and put into her old trim, she made many voyages and performed her service very sufficiently, to the great profit of her owners. But more especially by the cun ning and deceit of the master and his company, who were hired to remain a whole year in America; and now, fancying dislike, and fearing want of victuals, they plotted this stratagem to free themselves, as afterwards was known, and by some of them confessed."

Mr. Cushman, who wrote the doleful letter, was left behind at his own request. There was some excuse for his evil forebodings, for he was in a wretched state of health. He had written,

"Besides the imminent dangers of this voyage, which are no less than deadly, an infirmity of body hath seized me which will not, in all likelihood, leave me until death. What to call it I know not. But it is a bundle of lead, as it were, crushing my heart more and more these fourteen days; and, though I do the actions of a living man, yet I am but as dead."

The whole number of persons who took their departure from Dartmouth, in the one solitary vessel, the Mayflower, for the New World, amounted to one hundred and two.

Among these passengers there was a marked man, to whom we have already alluded, Captain Miles Standish. He was a native of Lancashire, England, a gentleman born, and the legitimate heir to a large estate. He had been for some time an officer in one of the British regiments, which had garrisoned a town

In the Netherlands. He was not a church member, and we know not what induced him to unite with the pilgrims in their perilous enterprise. Probably love of adventure, sympathy with them in their cruel persecution, and attachment to some of the emigrants, were the motives which influenced him. It is certain that he was very highly esteemed, and very cordially welcomed by the pilgrims. His military skill might prove of great value to the infant colony.

It is but little that we know of the early life of this remarkable man. He was born about the year 1584 and was, consequently, at this time, about thirty-six years of age. The family could boast of a long and illustrious line of ancestors. In the great controversy between the Catholics and the Protestants there was a division in the family, part adhering to the ancient faith, and part accepting the Protestant religion. Thus there arose, as it were, two families; the Catholics, who were of "Standish Hall," and the Protestants, who were of "Duxbury Hall." Both of these family seats are situated near the village of Chorley, in the county of Lancashire. The income of the whole property was large, being estimated at about five hundred thousand dollars a year.

It is probable that Miles Standish was the legal heir to all this property, and that, by gross injustice, he was defrauded of it. A few years ago the heirs of

Miles Standish, in this country, sent out an agent, Mr Bromley, to examine into the title. He thoroughly searched the records of the parish for more than a hundred years, embracing the period between 1549 and 1652. The result of this investigation was fully convincing, to the mind of Mr. Bromley, that Miles Standish was the rightful heir to the property, but that the legal evidence had been fraudulently destroyed. In reference to this investigation, Mr. Justin Winsor, in his History of Duxbury, writes:

"The records were all readily deciphered, with the exception of the years 1584 and 1585; the very dates about which time Standish is supposed to have been born. The parchment leaf, which contained the registers of the births of these years was wholly illegible; and their appearance was such that the conclusion was at once established that it had been purposely done with pumice stone, or otherwise, to destroy the legal evidence of the parentage of Standish, and his consequent title to the estates thereabout. The mutilation of these pages is supposed to have been accomplished when, about twenty years before, similar enquiries were made by the family in America."

Young Miles was educated to the military profession. England was then in alliance with the Dutch, in one of those wars with which the continent of Europe has ever been desolated. Miles was sent to the

Netherlands, commissioned as a lieutenant in Queen Elizabeth's forces. After peace was declared he remained in the country and attached himself to the English exiles, who, in Leyden, had found refuge from ecclesiastical oppression. He joined the first company of Pilgrims for America, and by his bravery and sagacity, contributed greatly to the success of their heroic enterprise.

Nothing of special moment occurred during the voyage, which was tedious, occupying sixty-four days. One event is recorded by Bradford as a special providence. One of the seamen, a young man of vigorous health and lusty frame, was a very vile fellow. As he went swaggering about the decks he lost no opportunity to insult the Pilgrims, ever treating their religious faith with contempt. When he saw any suffering from the awful depression of sea sickness, he would openly curse them, and express the wish that he might have the pleasure of throwing their bodies overboard, before they should reach the end of the voyage. The slightest reproof would only cause him to curse and swear more bitterly. Why the captain of the Mayflower allowed this conduct, we are not informed. But there are other indications that he was not very cordially in sympathy with his persecuted, comparatively friendless, but illustrious passengers. When about half way across the Atlantic, the dissolute young man was seized with sudden and painful sickness. Several days of severe suffering passed, as his ribald songs and oaths were hushed in the languor of approaching death. He died miserably, and his body, wrapped in a tarred sheet, was cast into the sea. "Thus," writes Bradford, "did his curses light upon his own head. And it was an astonishment to all his fellows, for they noted it to be the just hand of God upon him."

Very rough storms were encountered, often with head winds, and the frail Mayflower was sorely strained and wrenched by gale and surge. The shrouds were broken, the sails were rent, and seams were opened, through the oaken ribs, which threatened the engulfing of the ship in the yawning waves. Almost a mutiny was excited, as some, deeming the shattered bark incapable of performing the voyage, urged the abandonment of the expedition, and a return. After a careful examination, by the captain and the officers, of the injury the vessel had received, it was decided that the hull of the ship, under water, was still strong; that, to tighten the seam opened by the main beam, they had on board an immense iron screw, which the passengers had brought from Holland, which would raise the beam to its place; and that, by carefully calking the decks and upper works, and by the cautious avoidance of spreading too much sail, they might still, in safety, brave the perils of a stormy sea.

But we are told that many gales arose so fierce, and the sea ran so high, that for days together they could not spread an inch of canvass, but, in nautical phrase, were compelled to scud under bare poles. In one of these terrific storms a young man, John Howland, who ventured upon deck, was, by the sudden lurching of the vessel and the breaking of a wave, swept into the sea. He seemed to have been carried down fathoms deep under the raging billows. But, providentially, he caught hold of the topsail halyards, which happened to hang overboard. Though they ran out to full length, still, with a death gripe, he kept his hold until he was drawn up to the surface of the water, when, with boat hooks and other means, he was rescued.

The first land they made was Cape Cod. But it had been their intention to seek a settlement somewhere near the mouth of Hudson river. They therefore tacked about and stood for the southward. But after sailing with a fair wind for half a day, they found themselves becalmed in the midst of dangerous shoals and wild breakers. Alarmed by the perils which surrounded them in such unknown seas, they resolved to make their way back and seek the protection of the cape. A gentle breeze rose in their favor, and swept them away from the shoals before night came on. The next morning they anchored their storm-shattered vessel in a safe harbor at the extremity of Cape Cod.

Governor Bradford writes feelingly: "Being thus arrived in a good harbor, and brought safe to land, they fell upon their knees and blessed the God of Heaven, who had brought them over the vast and furious ocean, and delivered them from all the perils and miseries thereof, again to set their feet on the firm and stable earth, their proper element."

He continues in language which we slightly modernize: "But here I cannot but stay and make a pause, and stand half amazed at this poor people's present condition. And so I think will the reader too, when he well considers the same. Being thus past the vast ocean, and a sea of troubles before in their preparation, they had now no friends to welcome them, nor inns to entertain or refresh their weather-beaten bodies,—no houses, or much less, towns to repair to, to seek for succor.

"It is recorded in Scripture, as a mercy to the apostle and his shipwrecked company, that the barbarians showed them no small kindness in refreshing them; but these savage barbarians, when they met with them, as after will appear, were readier to fill their sides full of arrows than otherwise. And for the season, it was winter; and they that know the winters of this country, know them to be sharp and violent.

and subject to cruel and fierce storms, dangerous to travel to known places, much more to search an unknown coast. Besides, what could they see but a hideous and desolate wilderness, full of wild beasts and wild men? And what multitudes there might be of them they knew not. Neither could they, as it were, go up to the top of Pisgah to view, from this wilderness, a more goodly country to feed their hopes.

"For, which way soever they turned their eyes, save upward to the heavens, they could have little solace or content in respect of any outward objects. For, summer being done, all things stand upon them with a weather-beaten face, and the whole country, full of woods and thickets, presented a wild and savage view. If they looked behind them there was the mighty ocean, which they had passed, and which was now as a main bar and gulf to separate them from all the civil parts of the world. If it be said they had a ship to succor them, it is true; but what heard they daily from the master and company, but that with speed they should look out a place with their shallop, where they would be at some near distance; for the season was such that he would not stir from thence till a safe harbor was discovered by them, where they would be left, and where he might go without danger; and that victuals consumed apace, but that he must and he would keep sufficient for the crew and their return. Yea, it was muttered by some, that if the Pilgrims got not a place soon, they would turn them and their goods ashore and leave them."

It was in the morning of Saturday, November 11th, that the Mayflower, rounding the white sand cliffs of what is now Provincetown, on the extremity of Cape Cod, entered the bay on the western side of the Cape, where they cast anchor. Just before entering this harbor the Pilgrims had drawn up a brief constitution of civil government, upon the basis of republicanism, by which they mutually bound themselves to be governed. This was the germ of the American Constitution. John Carver they had unanimously chosen as their Governor for one year.

That afternoon a party of sixteen men, well armed, under Captain Miles Standish, was sent on shore to explore the country in their immediate vicinity. They returned in the early evening with rather a discouraging report. The land was sandy and poor, but covered with quite a dense forest of evergreens, dwarf oaks and other deciduous trees. They could find no fresh water, and met with no signs of inhabitants. The peninsula there seemed to be a mere sand bank, a tongue of barren land, about a mile in breadth. The water in the bay, however, abounded with fish and sea fowl. They brought on board much-needed fuel of the red cedar, which emitted, in burning, a grateful fragrance.

The next day was Sunday. These devout men, who had left their native land to encounter all the hardships and perils of the wilderness, that they might worship God freely, according to their own sense of duty, kept the day holy to the Lord. They had brought with them, as their pastor, as we have mentioned, the Rev. William Brewster. He was a gentleman by birth and in all his habits; a man of fervent piety and of highly cultivated mind, having graduated at Cambridge University, and having already filled several responsible stations in church and state. Mr. Brewster preached from the deck of the Mayflower. In their temple, whose majestic dome was the overarching skies, their hymns blended with the moan of the wintry wind, and the dash of the surge on the rockbound shore.

> "Amidst the storm they sang,
> And the stars heard, and the sea,
> And the sounding aisles of the dim woods rang.
> To the anthems of the free."

CHAPTER III.

Exploring the Coast.

Repairing the Shallop.—The Second Exploring Tour.—Interesting Discoveries.—Return to the Ship.—A Week of Labor.—The Third Exploring Tour.—More Corn Found.—Perplexity of the Pilgrims.—The Fourth Expedition.—The First Encounter.—Heroism of the Pilgrims.—Night of Tempest and Peril.—A Lee Shore Found.—Sabbath on the Island.

The next morning, refreshed by the repose of the Sabbath, the Pilgrims rose early to enter upon the arduous duties before them. The prospect of gloomy forests, barren sands and wild ocean, was any thing but cheerful. No alluring spot of grove or meadow or rivulet invited them to land. Weary as they were of their small and crowded bark, it was still preferable to any residence which the shore offered them. Still these heroic men indulged in no despondency. The martyr spirit of Elder Brewster animated his whole flock. Just before sailing for the New World, he had said to Sir Edward Sandys :

"It is not with us as with other men, whom small things can discourage, or small discontents cause to wish themselves home again. We believe and trust that the Lord 's with us, unto whom and whose service we have given ourselves, and that he will graciously prosper our endeavors according to the simplicity of our hearts therein."

The captain of the Mayflower was unwilling to leave the harbor at Cape Cod and peril his vessel by coasting about in those unknown seas in search for a suitable location for the colony. The Pilgrims had taken the precaution to bring with them a large shallop, whose framework, but partially put together, was stowed away in the hold of the vessel. They now got out these pieces, and their carpenter commenced vigorously the work of preparing the boat for service. It would require some days to put the shallop in order for a tour of exploration along the shore. There were twenty-eight females among the emigrants. Eighteen of these were married women, accompanying their husbands. These females, attended by a strong guard of armed men, were landed Monday morning to wash the soiled clothes which had accumulated through the long voyage. The weather was excessively cold, and the water so shoal that the boat could not come within several rods of the shore. The men were compelled to wade through the water, carrying the women in their arms; thus with many of them was laid the foundation of serious and fatal sickness.

In the meantime, while these labors were being

performed, Captain Miles Standish, on Wednesday morning, the 15th of November, set out with a party of fifteen men, well armed and provisioned, for a more extended tour of exploration. It was deemed rather a hazardous enterprise, as they knew not but that the woods were filled with savages, lying in ambush. The Mayflower was anchored, it is supposed, about a furlong from the end of what is now called Long Point, and at that place the men were probably set on shore.

Mourt writes: " The willingness of the persons was liked, but the thing itself, in regard to the danger, was rather permitted than approved. And so, with cautious directions and instructions, sixteen men were set out, with every man his musket, sword and corslet, under the conduct of Captain Miles Standish, unto whom was adjoined, for counsel and advice, William Bradford, Stephen Hopkins and Edward Tilley.'

The exploring party followed along the coast for the distance of about a mile, when they saw six or seven Indians, with a dog, approaching them. As soon as the savages caught sight of the party of white men, they seemed to be much terrified, and fled precipitately into the woods. The Pilgrims hotly pursued, hoping to open with them amicable relations. The Indians, seeing themselves thus followed, turned again from the woods to the sea shore, where, upon the beach, their flight would be unobstructed by tne bushes and branches, which impeded their flight in the forest. Their pursuers kept close after them, guided by the tracks of their feet in the sand.

Night now came on. The Pilgrims constructed a rude camp, with protecting ramparts of logs, built a rousing camp fire, for the night was cold as well as dark, and having established faithful sentinels, slept quietly until morning. The place of the bivouac, they supposed to be about ten miles from the vessel. The next morning, Thursday, November 16th, at the earliest dawn, the Pilgrims resumed their tour. They followed the track of the Indians from the shore into the woods. " We marched through boughs and bushes and under hills and valleys, which tore our very armor in pieces, and yet could meet with none of them, nor their houses, nor find any fresh water, which we greatly desired and stood in need of."

About ten o'clock in the morning they entered a deep valley, where they perceived tracks of deer, and found, to their great joy, a spring, bubbling cool and fresh from its mossy bed. Having refreshed themselves with a beverage which they pronounced to be superior to any wine or beer which they had ever drank, they pressed on their way, pushing directly south, and soon found themselves again upon the sea shore where they built a large fire that its smoke ascending through the silent air, might inform those on board the ship of the point which they had reached.

Then, continuing their journey, they soon entered another valley, where they found a fine clear pond of fresh water. This was undoubtedly the little lake which now gives name to the Pond Village in Truro. As they journeyed on they came to a plain of cleared land, consisting of about fifty acres, where the plough could be driven almost without obstruction. There were many indications that this land had formerly been planted with corn. Turning again into the interior, they came to several singular looking mounds, covered with old mats. Digging into one of these, they found decaying bows and arrows, and other indications that they were Indian graves. Reverently they replaced the weapons and again covered up the grave, as they would not have the Indians think that they would violate their sepulchres.

Further on they found an immense store of strawberries, large and very delicious. This seems very remarkable at that season of the year. Roger Williams writes: " This berry is the wonder of all fruits, growing naturally in those parts. In some places, where the natives have planted, I have many times seen as many as would fill a good ship within a few miles compass." They found, also, abundance of walnuts and grape vines, with some very good grapes. Coming upon a deserted dwelling, they found, to their astonishment, a large iron kettle, which must have been taken from some ship, wrecked upon the coast. Upon examining the remains of the hut more carefully, they became satisfied that it must have been erected by some sailors from Europe, who probably had been cast away upon the coast.

Here they came upon another mound, newly made, so different from the others that they were induced to examine it. "In it we found a little old basket, full of fair Indian corn, and digged further and found a fine, great new basket, full of very fair corn of this year, with some six and thirty goodly ears of corn, some yellow and some red, and others mixed with blue, which was a very goodly sight. The basket was round and narrow at the top. It held about three or four bushels, which was as much as two of us could lift from the ground, and was very handsomely and cunningly made." *

The Pilgrims had never seen corn before. Though they knew from its appearance that it must constitute an important article of food, they could have had no conception of the infinite value those golden kernels would contribute to the millions of inhabitants destined to throng this broad continent. These holes in

* Mourt's Narrative.

the earth were the Indian barns. They were constructed so as to hold about a hogshead each. The corn having been husked and thoroughly dried in the sun, was placed in baskets surrounded with mats, which were woven or braided with flags. As the provisions of the Pilgrims were nearly expended, from their unexpectedly long voyage, the sight of the golden ears of corn was more grateful to them than so many doubloons would have been.

"We were in suspense," writes one of these explorers, "what to do with it and the kettle. At length, after much consultation, we concluded to take the kettle and as much of the corn as we could carry away with us. And when our shallop came, if we could find any of the people, and come to parley with them, we would give them the kettle again, and satisfy them for their corn."

About eight months after this, as we shall have occasion hereafter to mention, they met the Indians and paid them to their "full content." The loose corn they put in the kettle, for two of the men to carry away on a staff. They also filled their pockets with the corn. The remainder they carefully buried again, "for we were so laden with armor that we could carry no more." It is worthy of note that the Pilgrims were cased in armor. One of the grandsons of Miles Standish is said to have in his possession the coat of mail which his illustrious ancestor wore upon this occasion. The Pilgrim Society of Plymouth claims also to have the identical sword blade used by Miles Standish.

Not far from this place they found the remains of an old fort, which had doubtless been built by the same persons who erected the hut and owned the kettle. This was near a spot which they at first supposed to be a river, but which proved to be an arm of the sea, and which was doubtless the entrance of what is now called Parmet River. They found here a high cliff of sand, since called Old Tom's Hill, after an Indian chief who had his wigwam upon its summit. They were, at this spot, about nine miles from Cape Cod harbor. Two birch bark canoes had been left here by the Indians, one on each bank of the creek. As the adventurers had received directions not to be absent more than two days, they had no time for extensive explorations. Returning to the fresh water pond, they established their rendezvous for the night. Building an immense fire, with the barricade to the windward, and establishing three sentinels, each man to take his turn as it came, they sought such sleep as could be found in a drenching rain, for the night proved dark and stormy.

In the morning they set out on their return home and lost their way. As they wandered along they entered a well-trodden deer path in the entangled forest. Here they came upon a singular contrivance, apparently some sort of a trap, which they were carefully examining, when Mr. Bradford, subsequently Governor, found himself suddenly caught by the leg and snapped up into the air. As he experienced no serious injury, the incident afforded only occasion for merriment. It was a deer trap, ingeniously constructed by bending a strong sapling to the earth, with a rope and noose concealed under leaves covered with acorns.

"It was a very pretty device," writes Mourt, "made with a rope of their own making, having a noose as artificially made as any roper in England can make." These traps were so strong that a horse would be tossed up if he were caught in one of them. "An English mare," writes Wood, "having strayed from her owner, and grown wild by her long sojourning in the woods, ranging up and down with the wild crew, stumbled into one of these traps, which stopped her speed, hanging her, like Mahomet's coffin, betwixt earth and heaven."

Toiling along through the wilderness, they saw three bucks and a flock of partridges, but could not get a shot at them. "As we came along by the creek we saw great flocks of wild geese and ducks, but they were very fearful of us, so we marched some while in the woods, some while on the sands, and other while in the water up to the knees, till at length we came near the ship, when we shot off our pieces, and the long boat came to fetch us " * Those familiar with the locality can trace their route as they passed round the head of East Harbor Creek, and went down on the north side of it. They then waded through Stout's Creek, near Gull Hill, and passed on to the end of Long Point, near which the ship was anchored

It was Friday afternoon, November 17th, when the expedition returned, with rent clothes and blistered feet, and with a discouraging report; for they had found no place suitable for the location of their colony.

Another Sunday came, and this little band of exiles was again assembled, on the deck of the Mayflower, to attend to their accustomed worship. The whole of the ensuing week was employed in refitting the shallop, which required the labor of seventeen days, and in making preparation for another and more extensive tour along the coast.

On Monday of the next week, the 27th of November, twenty-four of the colonists and ten of the seamen, in the shallop, all under command of Captain Jones, of the Mayflower, again set out in search of a spot where they might commence their lonely settle-

* Mourt's Narrative.

ment in the wilderness. It was a dreary winter's day, with clouds, a rough sea, freezing winds and flurries of rain and sleet. The sand hills, whitened with snow swept by the wind and covered with a stunted growth of oaks and pines, presented nothing alluring to the eye. As the day wore away and the storm increased in violence, they ran in towards the shore for security. Here the shallop cast anchor, under the lee of the sand hills, in comparatively smooth water. The crew passed the night in the boat, which probably afforded shelter for a few persons. A party landed, and following along the beach about six miles, encamped, with a glowing fire at their feet.

The next morning, the storm still continuing, the shallop reached them about eleven o'clock, and taking them on board, continued their voyage until they arrived at Pamet Creek, which the previous expedition had visited. Here they found a sheltered cove, which they called Cold Harbor. It afforded a safe refuge for boats, but was not a suitable harbor for ships, as it had a depth of but twelve feet of water at flood tide The creek here separates into two streams, running back about three and a half miles into the country, and separated by the high cliff of which we have spoken, called Tom's Hill.

A party landed at the foot of the cliff and marched into the interior, between the streams four or five miles. The country was broken with steep hills and deep valleys, and there was six inches of snow upon the ground. As night darkened over them they entered a small grove of pine trees, where they built their camp and kindled their fire, and established their sentinels for the night. They supped luxuriously upon three fat geese and six ducks, which they had shot by the way.

It was their intention in the morning to follow up this creek to its head, supposing that they should there find emptying into it a river of fresh water. But in talking the matter over, it seemed to the majority that the region was very undesirable. It was rough, hilly, with poor soil, and a harbor fit only for boats. n the morning, consequently, the shallop returned to its anchorage at the mouth of the creek, while the party on land crossed over to the other stream to get the rest of the corn which they had left behind. Here they found one of the canoes, of which we have previously spoken, which was sufficiently capacious to carry seven or eight over at a time. Here they found several other depositories of corn, so that they obtained seven or eight bushels.

"And sure it was God's good providence," writes Mourt, "that we found this corn, for else we know not how we should have done; for we knew not how we should find or meet with any of the Indians, except it be to do us a mischief. Also we had never, in all likelihood, seen a grain of it if we had not made our first journey; for the ground was now covered with snow, and so hard frozen that we were fain, with our cutlasses and short swords, to hew and carve the ground a foot deep, and then wrest it up with levers, for we had forgot to bring other tools."

Captain Jones, satisfied that there was no place here for the location of the colony, was quite discouraged and wished to return to the ship. Several others were quite sick from exposure and fatigue. They therefore returned to the shallop, while eighteen remained to continue their exploration until the next day, when the shallop was to come to take them. Several Indian trails were discovered, leading in various directions into the woods. One of these they followed five or six miles without finding any signs of inhabitants. Returning by another route, they came to a plain which had been cultivated, where they found several Indian graves, and among them manifestly the grave of a white man. In it they found fine yellow hair, some embalming powder, a knife, a pack-needle, and two or three iron instruments, bound up in a sailor's canvas coat. It was supposed that the Indians had thus buried the man to honor him.

While thus ranging about, some of them came upon two deserted Indian huts. They were made round, like an arbor, of long saplings, each end being stuck into the ground. The door was about three feet high, protected by a mat. The chimney was a hole in the top. In the centre of them, one could easily stand upright. The fire was built in the centre, around which the inmates slept on mats. The sides and roof were warmly sheathed, as a protection from wind and rain, with thick mats. A few very mean articles of household furniture were found within, such as bowls, trays and earthen pots. There were also quite a variety of baskets, some of them quite curiously wrought. Some of these baskets were filled with parched acorns, which it subsequently appeared they often used instead of corn.

During the day the shallop arrived. The latter part of the afternoon they hastened on board, with their treasures, and, it is supposed, reached the Mayflower that evening. In Mourt's narrative it is recorded: "We intended to have brought some beads and other things, to have left in the houses in sign of peace, and that we meant to truck with them. But it was not done, by means of our hasty coming away from Cape Cod."

The question was then very earnestly and anxiously discussed, whether they should decide upon Cold Harbor for their settlement, or send out another expedition on an exploring tour. Those who were in favor of Cold Harbor for their settlement, wished to locate their dwellings upon the bluff, at the entrance of Pamet River, now called Old Tom's Hill. The arguments they urged were, that there was there a convenient harbor for boats; convenient corn land ready to their hands; that Cape Cod would be a good place for fishing, as they daily saw great whales swimming about; that the place was healthy and defensible, and most important of all, that the heart of winter had come, and that they could not embark on more exploring tours without danger of losing both boat and men. The question, however, was settled in the negative, in view of the shallowness of the harbor, the barrenness of the land, and the inadequate supply of fresh water.

But very little was then known of Massachusetts Bay. But the second mate of the ship, Robert Coppin, had been in that region before. He said that upon the other side of the Bay, at a distance of about twenty-five miles, in a direct line west from Cape Cod, was a large navigable river with a good harbor. It was decided immediately to fit out another expedition to explore the whole coast of Massachusetts Bay, as far as the mouth of that fabulous river, but not to go beyond that point. A party of ten picked men, among whom were Governor Carver and William Bradford, set out in the shallop in the afternoon of the

6th of December, upon this all-important expedition, in which it seemed absolutely necessary that they should select some spot on which to establish their colony. They were well armed and provisioned, and it was certain that they would leave nothing untried which human energy could accomplish. It was a perilous enterprise in the dead of winter, in a comparatively open boat upon a storm-swept sea.

A cold wind ploughed the bay, raising such waves that many of the voyagers were deathly sick. It was late in the afternoon before they succeeded in clearing the harbor. The severity of the winter weather was such that the spray, dashing over them, was immediately frozen, covering them with coats of ice. They ran down the coast in a southerly direction, about twenty miles, when, doubling a point of land, they entered a small shallow cove, where they discovered twelve Indians on the beach, cutting up a grampus. As they turned their bow towards the land the Indians fled, and soon disappeared in the stunted growth behind the sand hills. The water in the little bay was so shallow that they found it difficult to approach the shore. At last they effected a landing about three miles from the point where they had seen the Indians, but even then they had to wade several yards through the water up to their knees. As the weather was intensely cold, this caused much suffering.

It was quite dark before they reached the land With considerable difficulty they constructed a barricade of logs, to shelter them from the wind, and also to protect them from the arrows of the natives, should they be attacked. Sentinels were stationed to keep a vigilant guard, a roaring fire was built, and our weary exiles, wrapped in their cloaks and with their feet to the fire, soon forgot, for a few hours, all their troubles in the oblivion of sleep. During the night the sentinels could see, at the distance of but a few miles, the gleam of the camp fire of the Indians.

In the morning the company divided, a part to follow along the shore through the woods to see if they could find any suitable place for their settlement, while the rest sailed along slowly in the boat, noticing the depth of water and watching for harbors. Thus the day passed without any successful results. Those on the shore followed an Indian trail for some distance into the woods. They came to a large burying place, surrounded with a palisade and quite thickly filled with graves. As the sun of the short winter's day was sinking, and the shades of another night were coming on, the boat put into a small creek, where its inmates were soon joined by the party from the woods. They met joyfully, for they had not seen one another since the morning, and some anxiety was felt for the safety of those upon the shore.

Governor Bradford, who was of the party, says that they made a barricade, as they were accustomed to do every night, of logs, stakes and thick pine boughs, the height of a man, leaving it open to the leeward, partly to shelter it from the cold and winds, making their fire in the middle and lying round about it, and partly to defend them from any assaults of the savages, if they should attack them. So, being very weary, they betook themselves to rest.

"But about midnight they heard a hideous and great cry, and their sentinel called 'arm! arm!' So they bestirred themselves and stood to their arms and shot off a couple of muskets, and then the noise ceased. They concluded that it was a company of wolves, or such like wild beasts; for one of the seamen told them that he had often heard such a noise in Newfoundland. So they rested till about five of the clock in the morning, for the tide and their purpose to go from thence made them bestirring betimes.

"After prayer they prepared for breakfast, and it being day-dawning, it was thought best to be carrying things down to the boat. But some said that it was not best to carry the arms down; others said they would be the readier, for they had wrapped them up in their coats, from the dew. But some three or four would not carry theirs until they went themselves; yet, as it fell out, those who took their arms to the boat, the water not being high enough for the boat to come to the shore, they laid them down upon the bank and came back to breakfast.

"But presently, all on the sudden, they heard a great and strange cry, which they knew to be the same voices which they heard in the night, though they varied their notes; and one of their company being abroad, came running in and cried, 'Indians! Indians!' Immediately a shower of arrows fell upon the encampment. Then men ran with all speed to recover their arms, as by the good providence of God they succeeded in doing.

"In the mean time, Captain Miles Standish, having a snaphance * ready, made a shot, and, after him, another. After they two had shot, other two were ready; but Captain Standish wished us not to shoot till we could take aim, for he knew not what need we should have. Then there were four only of us which had their arms there ready, and stood before the open side of our barricade which was first assaulted. They thought it best to defend it lest the enemy should take it and our stuff, and so have the more vantage against us."

From the hideous yells of the Indians it seemed as though the woods were full of them. There might

---

* A musket with a flint lock.

be ten or twenty Indians to one white man. It was greatly to be feared that they might, by a sudden rush, seize the shallop, and thus cut off all possibility of retreat. Captain Standish, therefore, immediately divided his little army of ten men, leaving five to defend the barricade and five to protect the boat. In the midst of the terrific turmoil and storm of Indian missiles, the two divisions, separated but by a distance of a few yards, cheered each other by encouraging words. Most of the guns were matchlocks. Those by the shallop called for a firebrand to light their matches. One seized from the fire a burning log and carried it to them. The Indians seemed to understand the act, for they redoubled the fury of their yells.

The thick winter garments of the Pilgrims and their coats of mail effectually protected a large portion of their bodies from the arrows of the natives. The arrows as, unlike bullets they could be seen in their flight, could also be dodged. There was one Indian, of gigantic stature, apparently more brave than the rest, who seemed to be the leader of the band. He was in advance of all the other Indians, and, standing behind a large tree, within half musket shot of the encampment, let fly his arrows with wonderful strength and accuracy of aim, while his voice, rising above the din of the conflict, animated them to courage and exertion. Three arrows which he shot were avoided by stooping. Three musket shots, which were aimed at him, struck the tree, causing the bark and splinters to fly about his ears, but he was unharmed. Captain Standish devoted his special attention to this chief. Watching his opportunity, when the arm of the savage was exposed, in the attempt to throw another shaft, he succeeded in striking it with a bullet. The shattered arm dropped helpless. * The savage gazed for a moment in apparent bewilderment and dismay, upon the mangled and bleeding limb, and then, as if conscious that he had fought his last battle, uttered a peculiar and distressing cry, which was probably the signal for retreat, and dodging from tree to tree, disappeared.

His warriors followed his example, and were speedily lost in the solitude and silence of the forest. Their flight was so instantaneous into the glooms which surrounded them, that scarcely one moment elapsed ere not an Indian was to be seen, and the demoniac clamor of war gave place to the sacred quietude of the untenanted wilderness. Captain Standish led his heroic little band, driving before them they knew not how many hundreds of Indians, nearly a quarter of a mile. Then they shot off two muskets

* Johnson's Wonder Working Providence.

and gave three loud cheers, "that they might see," Governor Bradford writes, "that we were not afraid of them, nor discouraged. Then the English, who more thirsted for their conversion than their destruction, returned to their boat without receiving any damage."

The first act of these devout men, upon returning to their encampment, was to give thanks to God for their great deliverance. There was a sublimity in this *Te Deum*, from the lips of these exiles, as in the twilight of the wintry morning, exposed to wind and rain, they bowed reverently around their camp fire, which never could have been surpassed by peals from choir and organ, resounding through the groined arches of the cathedrals of Saint Peter, Notre Dame or Saint Paul

The escape of the Pilgrims, unharmed, from this shower of missiles, was indeed wonderful. The arrows of the Indians were thrown with great force, and being pointed with flint and bone, would, when hitting fairly, pierce the thickest clothing. Some of them were barbed with brass, probably obtained from some fisherman's vessel. When striking any unprotected portion of the body, they would inflict a very dangerous and painful wound. But no one was hurt. Some overcoats which were hung up in the barricade were pierced through and through. Arrows were sticking in the logs, and many were found beneath the leaves. They collected quite a number of them and sent them back to England as curiosities.

It is supposed that the scene of this conflict, was at what is now called Great Meadow Creek, in Eastham, about a mile northeast from Rock Harbor. The Pilgrims named the place The First Encounter.

It was indeed a gloomy morning of clouds and rain and chill wind which now opened before these stout-hearted wanderers. The surf dashed sullenly upon the shore. The gale, sweeping the ocean, and moaning through the sombre firs and pines, drove the sheeted mist, like spectral apparitions of ill omen over the land and the sea. As the Pilgrims re-embarked the rain changed to sleet. A day of suffering and of great peril was manifestly before them The gale rapidly increased in violence. The billows dashed so furiously upon the beach there was no possibility of again landing unless they should find some sheltered cove. The waves frequently broke into the boat. Their garments were drenched, and clothing and ropes were soon coated with ice. Anxiously, hour after hour, as they were buffeted by the storm, they searched the dim shore hoping to find some bay or river in which they could take refuge.

The short winter's day was soon drawing to a close. Night was at hand,—night long, dark and stormy, in an unknown sea. They were numbed and nearly frozen with the cold. To many of them it seemed not improbable that before the morning they would all find a grave in the ocean. As twilight was darkening into night, a huge billow, chasing them with gigantic speed, broke into the boat, nearly filling it with water, at the same time unshipping and sweeping away their rudder. They immediately got out two oars, and with exceeding difficulty succeeded in steering their tempest-tossed bark. To add to their calamities, and apparently to take from them their last gleam of hope, just then a sudden flaw of wind snapped their mast into three pieces, dashing their sail into the foaming sea, and they were left at the mercy of the billows.

Their pilot, who had been upon the coast before, and who had thus far cheered them with the assurance that there was a harbor at hand, now lost all presence of mind, and throwing up his arms, exclaimed, "The Lord have mercy upon us. I was never in this place before. All that we can do is to run the boat ashore through the breakers." It was insane counsel which, being followed, involved almost certain death.

Some one of their number, was it their gallant leader Miles Standish, remonstrated, shouting out in the darkness, "If ye be men, seize your oars or we are all cast away." They did so, and, with lusty arms on a flood tide, still guided their boat along the shore which was dimly seen as the breakers dashed high over sand and rock. At last they discerned land directly before them. Whether it were an island or a promontory they knew not. By great exertions they succeeded—though it was very dark and the rain fell in torrents—in gaining the lee of the land. Here they cast anchor in comparatively still water. But they were afraid to leave the boat. The experience of the past night had taught them that the woods might be full of savages.

Their sufferings however from the cold, the wind and the rain, became unendurable. A few of their number, feeling that they should certainly perish in the open boat, ventured ashore, where after much difficulty they succeeded in building a fire. Though its blaze illumining the forest, might be a beacon to point them out to their savage foes, they piled upon it branches and logs and, forgetting their danger, rejoiced in the cheerful flame and the warmth. Those in the boat could not long resist the aspect of comfort which the fire presented. They soon also landed, and with their axes, speedily constructed a camp to shelter them from the rain, and a rampart of logs, behind which, with their guns, they could protect themselves from a large number of natives armed only with bows and javelins.

Thus ere long they found themselves in what might be deemed, under the circumstances, comfortable quarters. During the night the clouds were dispersed. The morning dawned, serene and bright, but cold. It was the morning of the Sabbath. And these remarkable men, notwithstanding the importance of improving every moment of time, decided, apparently without hesitation or thought of doing otherwise, to remain quietly in their encampment in the religious observance of the Lord's day. Some may say that this was fanaticism; that a more enlightened judgment would have taught them that the Sabbath was made for man, and not man for the Sabbath; and that situated as they then were, it was a work of necessity and mercy to prosecute their tour without delay.

But these men believed it to be their duty to sanctify the Sabbath by resting from all but necessary abor. Thus believing, their decision could not but be pleasing in the sight of God. Captain Miles Standish, as we have mentioned, was the leader of this expedition. The decision must have been consequen ly in accordance with his views.

Governor Bradford, describing this painful and perilous dventure, writes: "And though it was very dark and rained sore, yet in the end they got under the lee o, a small island and remained there all night in safety. But they knew not this to be an island til morning, but were divided in their minds. Some would keep the boat for fear they might be among the Indians. Others were so weak and cold, they could not endure, but got ashore and with much ado got a fire, all things being so wet, and the rest were glad to come to them; for after midnight the wind shifted to the northwest and it froze hard.

"But though this had been a day and night of much trouble and danger unto them, yet God gave them a morning of comfort and refreshing, as He usually does to His children; for the next day was a fair, sunshining day, and they found themselves to be on an island, secure from the Indians, where they might dry their stuff, fix their pieces and rest themselves, and give God thanks for his mercies in their manifold deliverances. And this being the last day of the week they prepared to keep the Sabbath."

In their frail camp they spent the sacred hours of the Lord's day, in thankgivings and supplications and in hymning the praises of God. They named this spot, where they had found brief refuge from the storm, Clark's Island, in honor of the captain of the Mayflower.

CHAPTER IV.

The Landing.

The Voyage Resumed.—Enter an Unknown Harbor.—Aspect of the Land.—Choose it for their Settlement.—The Mayflower Enters the Harbor.—Sabbath on Shipboard.—Exploring the Region.—The Storm and Exposure.—The Landing.—View from the Hill.—Arduous Labors.—The Alarm.—Arrangement of the Village.—The Evident hostility of the Indians.—Gloomy Prospects.—Expedition of Captain Standish.—Billington's Sea.—Lost in the Woods.—Adventures of the Lost Men.—The Alarm of Fire.

The Pilgrims, having passed the Sabbath in rest and devotion upon the island, early the next morning repaired their shattered boat and spreading their sails again to the wintry winds continued their tour. Soon a large bay opened before them, partially protected by a long sand bar from the gales and the billows of the ocean. It was but a poor harbor at the best. The low and dreary sand bar broke the fury of the waves, but afforded no protection against the fierce gales which swept the seas.

Cautiously our adventurers sailed around the point of sand, every few moments dropping the lead that they might find a channel of sufficient depth of water to allow their vessel to enter the bay. Having found this passage, they steered for the shore and landed.

They found here one or two streams of pure water, several corn fields which had evidently, in former times been cultivated by the Indians, in their rude style of agriculture, but which, for some reason they had abandoned. Eagerly they looked for some navigable river, but could find none. The soil, though not so rich as they could wish, seemed promising. The landscape was pleasingly diversified with hills and valleys, while the forest, in its mysterious gloom, spread far away to unknown regions in the west.

The location was by no means such as they had hoped to find. But it was far superior to any other which had as yet presented itself. As winter was approaching and time pressed they decided to look no further. A party of them, well armed, marched along the shore for a distance of eight miles, in search of a suitable spot for their village. They selected a spot, but saw no natives, no wigwams, and no signs that the region had recently been inhabited.

Having, in their own minds, settled the important question they spread their sails and, instead of returning by the long circuit of the shore, which they had traversed, pushed boldly across the bay, and in a few hours reached the ship with their report. Without loss of time the Mayflower weighed anchor on the 15th of December, and crossing the bay anchored on the 16th in the shallow water of the harbor about a mile and a half from the shore. The next day was the Sabbath. Strong as was the temptation to land, they all remained on board the vessel, and their hymns of thankfulness blended with the moan of the wintry gale as it swept through the icy shrouds.

Early Monday morning Miles Standish set out with a small but well armed party to explore that part of the country which immediately surrounded the harbor, to decide upon the spot where they should rear their little village of log huts. They traversed the coast for a distance of several miles. Several brooks of crystal water were found, but to their disappointment no navigable river rolling down its flood from the unknown interior. They scarcely knew whether to be glad or sorry that they found no Indians and no indications that the Indians then occupied the region. Several quite extended fields were found, where the heavily timbered forest had disappeared and where it was evident that the Indians, in former years, had raised their harvests of corn. At night the party returned to the ship not having fixed upon any spot for their settlement.

"The next day, the 19th, another exploring party set out moving in an opposite direction. They divided into two companies, one to sail along the coast in the shallop, hoping to find the mouth of some large river. The other party landed and marched along the shore, examining the lay of the land, the streams, the soil, and the timber of the forests. At night they returned to the ship, still somewhat undecided. They had however found one spot where there was a small stream of very clear, sweet water, which seemed to be well stocked with fish, and a high hill, a little back from the shore, which could be easily fortified, and which commanded a very extensive view of the surrounding country and the ocean. "It had clay, sand and shells," writes Bradford, "for bricks, mortar and pottery, and stone for wells and chimneys. The sea and beach promised abundance of fish and fowl, and four or five small running brooks brought a supply of very sweet, fresh water."

The next morning, after earnest and united prayer for divine guidance, a still larger party of twenty was sent on shore, more carefully to examine the spot which had been suggested for their village. Though it was not all they could desire, it still presented many attractions. It was a cold December day. They climbed the hill, and gazed with pleasure upon a prospect which was sublime and beautiful even on that bleak and windy day, when the boughs of the trees were naked and when the withered leaves were borne like snow flakes on the wintry air. They tried to imagine its loveliness in the luxuriance and bloom of a June morning.

THE LANDING.   75

While they stood upon the hill, the clou s, which all the morning had been darkening the sky, began to increase in density and gather in blackness. The wind rose to a gale, and the windows of heaven seemed to be opened, as the rain fell upon them in torrents. All unsheltered they found themselves exposed to the fury of a New England northeast storm. Huge billows from the ocean swept the poorly protected harbor and broke in such surges upon the beach that it was impossible for them to return to the ship. They were totally unprepared for an emergency so unexpected. Night came, a long, dark, cold, stormy night. They sought shelter in the forest, constructed a rude camp which but poorly sheltered them from wind and rain, and building a large fire, found such comfort as they could in the imperfect warmth which it afforded. All the night of Wednesday and all day Thursday the northeast storm raged with fury unabated. Towards the evening of Thursday the 21st there was a lull in the tempest, so that the weary adventurers succeeded in working their way back to the ship.

The next day was the ever-memorable Friday, December 22d. A wintry storm, with its angry billows, still swept the bay. The day opened upon the Pilgrims cold, cloudy and dreary. The long and anxiously looked for hour had now come, when the Mayflower, the only material tie which bound them to the Old World, was to be abandoned, and these bold men were to be left three thousand miles from their native shores, to struggle with all the known and unknown perils and hardships of the wilderness. Familiar as are the graphic words of Mrs. Hemans, the first verse of her memorable hymn so truthfully describes the scene which that morning was presented to the Pilgrims, as to be worthy of transcript here.

> "The breaking waves dashed high
> On a stern and rock-bound coast,
> And the woods against a stormy sky,
> Their giant branches toss'd."

At an early hour all the passengers of the Mayflower were assembled upon the deck of their little ship, bowed down by emotions not easily described Men, women and children, all were there, oppressed by thoughts too deep for utterance. Elder Brewster conducted their morning devotions as the wintry gale breathed forth its requiem through the icy shrouds. Sublime as was the hour, not one of those men of martyr spirit could have had any true conception of its grandeur. They could not have been conscious that then and there they were laying the foundations of one of the mightiest empires upon which the sun has ever shone.

Their devotions being ended, boat load after boa

THE LANDING.

load left the ship which, in consequence of the shallowness of the water, was anchored at the distance of a mile and a half from the shore. There was a large and jagged rock projecting into the sea, upon which a landing was with difficulty effected. Those who first we e placed upon shore marked out a street from their point of landing directly westward to the hill, upon each side of which street their log huts were to be reared.

One of the first things, however, to be done, was to erect a log store-house, about twenty feet square, where they could deposit their effects, which were immediately to be landed from the ship, and where the women and the children could find a temporary shelter from wind and rain.

In the old style of computing time, the day of their landing was the 11th of December. For many years the 22d day of September, new style, has been observed as "Forefather's Day." It is said, however, that December 11th, O. S., corresponds with December 21st, N. S. But when the anniversary was instituted at Plymouth, in 1769, *eleven* days were added for difference of style, instead of *ten*, the true difference.

The common house, to which we have alluded, it is supposed was erected on the south side of what is now called Leyden street, near the declivity of the hill. All hands working energetically, this building was speedily put up, with a thatched roof.

Though the situation for their colony was not every thing they could desire, yet, as they prosecuted their labors, they became better and better satisfied with the choice which they had made. One of their number wrote;

"There are here cleared lands, delicate springs, and a sweet brook running under the hill side, with fish in their season, where we may harbor our shallops and boats. On the further side is much corn ground. There is a high hill on which to plant our ordnance. Thence we may see into the bay, and far out at sea, and have a glimpse of the distant cape. Our greatest labor will be the bringing of wood. What people inhabit here we know not, as we have yet seen none.'

All the day of Saturday every able-bodied man of the Pilgrims was on the shore laboring with all possible diligence, felling trees, hewing them, and dragging them with their own hands to the building lots, for they had no horses or oxen. The women also were diligently at work cooking at camp fires and helping to stow away their goods as they were brought on shore.

The whole company was divided into nineteen families, each family to build its own log hut. For protection against the Indians it was needful that these huts should be clustered near together. The captain of the Mayflower brought all the energies of

THE LANDING.

his crew into requisition in transporting the luggage to the shore, for his provisions were fast disappearing, and he was exceedingly anxious to set out on his return. The distance of the ship from the land caused much time to be lost in going and coming. For several days a portion of the Pilgrim band remained to lodge in the ship, while others were on the shore. The labors of all were rendered painful and much impeded by cold and stormy weather. Often the bay, swept by the wintry gale, was so rough that no boat could leave the ship, and there could be no communication between the two parties.

Sunday was again with them all a day of rest and devotion, though they were divided, some being still on board the ship, while others were in their frail shelters on the land. Those on shore assembled, for their devotions, in their partially finished store-house. Their harps must have been hung upon the willows, and pensive must have been the strains which were breathed from their lips as they endeavored to sing the Lord's songs in a strange land. As with firm but saddened voices they sang, they were startled by the war-whoop of the Indians in the forest. They knew those fearful cries too well which many of them had heard at the First Encounter.

Their efficient military commander, Miles Standish, had everything arranged for such an emergency

Instantly every man seized his musket and was at his post. Behind their barricade of logs, they could, with their deadly fire arms, repel almost any number of savages approaching over the open fields with only bows and arrows. The Indians, who had been already taught to dread these weapons, after carefully reconnoitering the position of the Pilgrims, vented their rage in a few impotent yells, and, without any exposure of their persons to the bullet, retreated into the wilderness.

The next day was Christmas. With renewed diligence the Pilgrims plied their labors. "We went on shore," writes Mourt, "some to fell timber, some to saw, some to rive, and some to carry. So no man rested all that day."

As we have mentioned, there were nineteen families, but they differed considerably in size. The single men joined themselves to some of these families. The lots of land assigned to these families differed in size, according to the number of the household. To each individual person there was allotted about eight feet in breadth by fifty in length. This would make but about four hundred square feet for each one. Thus, a family of six persons would have a lot but forty-eight feet wide by fifty deep. This seems an incredibly small amount of land for each homestead, when the Pilgrims had the whole continent of North

America before them. The explanation is probably
to be found in the fact that it was necessary for them
to place their houses as near together as possible;
that, with neither horses, oxen, or any other beasts of
burden, it was but a small portion of land which any
one man could cultivate; and, again, if any one wished
for more land, there were fields all around him, entirely free, and no one would dispute his title deed
The homestead lots were so arranged as to make the
little cluster of huts a fortress, protected by their cannon, where their whole force could be instantly rallied for the public defense. Towards night of Christmas day, the yells of evidently unfriendly savages
were heard in the depths of the forest. This caused
every man to seize his musket and place himself in
the attitude of defense. The wary savages, however
while uttering these impotent menaces, still kept themselves carefully concealed.

Tuesday, the 26th of December, ushered in such
a storm of rain that those on shore could do no work,
and the gale so roughened the bay that those on board
the ship could not venture an attempt to land. The
next day the storm abated, and every available men
was at work As it seemed very evident that the
savages were hostile, and it was apprehended that
they might be gathering for a general assault, it was
deemed necessary, notwithstanding the pressing need

of dwellings, that all should go to work upon the hill, in the construction of a rude fort and platform for their ordnance. The vestiges of this fortification are still visible on the Burial Hill, where the guns could sweep with grape shot the approaches to their village. It was hoped that the thunders of these formidable weapons of war, followed by the carnage they could inflict, should the savages approach in great numbers, would overwhelm them with terror.

The weather, during the remainder of the week, continued very unfavorable, it being cold, wet and stormy. Still the works on the land slowly advanced The savages, without showing themselves, continued to hover around, and the smokes of great fires were seen, apparently at the distance of about six or seven miles, indicating that the Indians, in large numbers, were gathering around them.

The last day of the year 1620 came, sombre and sad. It was the Sabbath. Many were sick. All were dejected. Wintry dreariness frowned over earth and sea. Howling savages filled the forest. The provisions of the Pilgrims were very scanty. The Mayflower was soon to leave them, to contend, a feeble band, against apparently nostile elements, and against the far more formidable hostility of savage men. To meet these perils the Pilgrims could number but forty-one men. Sickness had already commenced its ravages, and of these men, within three months, twenty-one died. The chances that such a colony could long be preserved from extinction, must have seemed almost infinitely small. As usual, the Pilgrims rested from labor, and devoted the day, some on shore, some in the ship, to prayer and praise. On this day the Pilgrims solemnly named their little village Plymouth, in grateful remembrance of the kindness which they had received from the people of Plymouth, in England.

Monday morning, the first day of the new year dawned propitiously upon these bold-hearted exiles. A cloudless sky and genial atmosphere invited them to labor. It was still necessary to be ever prepared for an attack from their unseen foes. With no little solicitude, while urging forward their work, they watched the moving columns of smoke, which day by day rose from the distant wilderness, and the gleam of the fires, which by night illumined the horizon, indicating the movement and position of the Indians. During Tuesday and Wednesday these fires seemed to increase in numbers. They were thus led to infer that the savages were collecting in large numbers from distant parts, and were making careful preparation for a general and simultaneous assault upon the feeble colony.

On Thursday morning, the 4th of January, Captain Miles Standish, who might be truly called the "bravest of the brave," took with him four men, well armed, and boldly plunged into the forest, intending to find the Indians at their rendezvous, and if possible, to open friendly relations with them. Adopting every precaution to avoid falling into an ambuscade, he rapidly pushed forward several miles into the pathless wilderness, threading gloomy ravines, crossing rivulets, and traversing sublime forests. The wary Indians had undoubtedly their scouts stationed to give warning of any approach of the white men ; for Captain Standish could not catch sight of a single one of the savages, though he found several of their deserted wigwams, and even the still glowing embers of their camp fires. The adventurers were also disappointed in finding that the woods seemed destitute of game. Upon their return, at the close of the afternoon, they shot one solitary eagle, whose flesh the Pilgrims, in their half famished state, pronounced to be "excellent meat, hardly to be discerned from mutton."

Friday and Saturday passed away without any event of importance occurring, while all hands were diligently at work. Another Sabbath of rest, the 7th of January, dawned upon these toil-worn men and women. The sun, of Monday, the 8th, rose in a cloudless sky. All bent themselves eagerly to work. By some unaccountable oversight no small fishhooks had been brought with them. Thus, though the harbor and the brook apparently abounded with fishes, they could not be taken. The shallop, however, was sent out to explore the coast, ascertain where fishes could be found, and supplied with apparatus for taking seals, which were seen in large numbers In the evening the boat returned, a gale having in the mean time arisen which greatly endangered its safety. The crew had taken three large seals, and in some way, perhaps by spearing, had got an excellent codfish.

One of their number, Francis Billington, had, a few days before, climbed a tree upon the top of a hill, whence he saw, about two miles southwest from the town, a large body of water, which was either a lake or an arm of the sea, he could not tell which. He started to-day, with a companion, to visit it, and found two large lakes of crystal water, nearly connected together. One was about six miles in circuit, embellished with a small, luxuriantly wooded island. The other they estimated to be about three miles in circumference. They both abounded with fish and water fowl, and apparently an unfailing stream of water, which is now called Town Brook, issued from one of the lakes and emptied into the harbor a little south of the rock upon which the Pilgrims landed. Several Indian houses, but all uninhabited, were found upon the margin of these sheets of water, which were essentially one lake.

"This beautiful pond, so accurately described, bears the appropriate name of Billington Sea. In the first century it was called Fresh Lake. It is about two miles southwest from the town, and in it are two small islands. It is now, as at first, embosomed in a wilderness of woods. The eagle still sails over it, and builds in the branches of the surrounding forest. Here the loon cries, and leaves her eggs on the shore of the smaller island. Here too, the beautiful wood-duck finds a sequestered retreat; and the fallow deer, mindful of their ancient haunts, still resort to it to drink and to browse on its margin." *

On Tuesday, Wednesday and Thursday all hands were busy in their out-door work. The store-house, or, as they called it, the Common House, was nearly finished and thatched. The cold, damp weather hindered them very much, so that they could seldom work more than half of the time. Friday morning dawned pleasantly, but about noon the clouds gathered, and the chill rain began to fall, and an increasing gale moaned through the tree tops. Four men had gone out into the woods in the morning to gather tall dry grass for thatching. In the afternoon two of

---

* Note to Young's Chronicles of the Pilgrims.

them returned, and said that in some way they had lost sight of their companions. They had searched for them in vain; and though they had hallooed and shouted as loud as they could, they could hear nothing from them. Intense solicitude was felt for them, and a party of four or five men were immediately dispatched to search in the direction in which they were last seen. After an absence of a few hours they returned, at the close of the day, not having been able to discover any traces of the lost, though they found many indications that the Indians were lurking around The long, stormy wintry night passed slowly away, and still there were no tidings of the wanderers. In the morning twelve men, well armed, probably under the leadership of Captain Miles Standish, set out for a more extended exploration. It was well known that Captain Standish would fail in nothing which mortal energy or courage could accomplish. The prayers of the sorrowing band accompanied them as they plunged into the forest. After a long and careful search, in which they could find no trace whatever of the lost men, they returned at night in deep dejection to their companions. All the Pilgrims gathered around them, men, women and children, to hear the account of their unsuccessful search.

While thus assembled they were startled by a shout in the distance, and looking up, to their inexpressible joy, saw the two men emerging from the forest. They ran to meet the wanderers, John Goodman and Peter Brown, whose apparition was as life from the dead. Their tattered garments and emaciate cheeks testified to the hardships which they had endured. The following was the account which they gave of their adventure:

As they were gathering some long grass, for thatching, about a mile from the village, probably on the banks of Town Brook, they saw a pond in the distance, perhaps Murdock's Pond, and repaired to it. Upon the margin of the pond they found a deer drinking. Two dogs they had with them sprang after the deer, and pursued it eagerly into the forest. The men followed, hoping that the dogs would seize the deer, and that thus they might be able to capture so rich a prize. As, led by the baying of the hounds, they followed the deer in its windings and turnings, they became bewildered and lost in the pathless wilds which they had penetrated. All the afternoon they wandered in vain seeking some clew to lead them back to their home.

Night, dismal night, lowered over them with clouds, a rising gale, and snow mingled with rain. They had no axes with which to construct a shelter. They could find no cave or hollow tree in which to take refuge. Weary, foot-sore and starving, and with no weapon but a small sickle with which they had been cutting thatch, they heard the howling of wolves around them, and other strange cries from wild beasts, of they knew not what ferocity. Their only protection seemed to be to climb into a tree. They tried it. The keen wintry blast so pierced their thin clothing that they could not endure the cold. Death by freezing would be inevitable.

The blackness of Egyptian darkness was now around them. They also heard a fearful roaring of wild beasts, which was undoubtedly the howling of wolves, but which they supposed to be the roar of lions. They stood at the root of the trees all the night long, exercising as they could to keep themselves warm, ever ready to spring into the branches should danger approach. They were compelled to hold one of their dogs by the neck, he was so eager to rush in pursuit of the beasts whose cries excited him.

The long winter night at length gave way to the gloom of a stormy morning. Half frozen and starving, and expecting to perish in the wilderness, these lost men resumed their search for home. They waded through swamps, forded streams, encountered ponds, struggled through thickets which tore clothing and skin. At last they came to a hill. Climbing one of the tallest trees, they saw the ocean in the distance, and, to their inexpressible joy, recognized the harbor of Plymouth, by two little islands which dotted its surface. The sight reanimated their drooping minds and bodies. All day long, in the extreme of exhaustion, they tottered on their way, until just before nightfall they reached their home. The feet of one of these men, John Goodman, were so swollen that they were compelled to cut off his shoes.

The work of building had advanced slowly. The days were short, cold and stormy. Nearly all were enfeebled by toil and exposure, while some were seriously sick. Both Governor Carver and Mr. Bradford, his successor in office, were prostrate with fevers. They were on beds in the Common House, where cots had been arranged on the floor for the sick, as near one to another as they could be placed. Though many of the Pilgrims were still in the Mayflower, the majority lodged on shore.

The Common House was so far finished, nearly all of its roof being thatched, that it afforded protection from the snow and rain, while its thick walls of logs shut off the piercing wind, and a cheerful fire blazed upon the stone hearth.

On Sunday morning, January 14th, about six o'clock, the wind blowing almost a gale, they were appalled by the cry of "fire." The thatch of grass, dry as tinder, touched by a spark, was in a blaze. All the ammunition and most of the arms had been brought on shore and deposited in the store-house. Its loss would expose them, defenceless, to the tomahawk of the Indian. Nearly all of their scanty supply of food was there. Without it starvation was inevitable. The people in the ship saw the smoke and the flame, but the tide was out, and they could not reach the shore. Soon, however, the tide came in, the gale abated, and a boat load cautiously advanced to the land, where they had all proposed to pass the Sabbath together, the majority of the company being then on shore. Upon landing they were cheered with the tidings that the lost men were found, and that **the fire, which had been extinguished, was accidental.**

CHAPTER V.

Life On Shore.

Days of Sunshine and Storm.—Ravages of Pestilence.—A Raging Storm.—New Alarm of Fire.—Twelve Indians Seen.—Two Indians Appear on the Hill.—Great Alarm in the Settlement.—Measures of Defense.—More Sunny Days.—Humanity and Self-Denial of Miles Standish and Others.—Conduct of the Ship's Crew.—Excursion to Billington Sea.—The Visit of Samoset.—Treachery of Captain Hunt.—The Shipwrecked Frenchmen.—The Plague.—The Wampanoags.—More Indian Visitors.—Bad Conduct of the Billingtons.

Monday, the 15th of January, opened upon the way-worn exiles with another storm of wind and rain, so that those on shipboard could not leave the vessel, and those on shore could do no work. The next three days, however, were pleasant, each morning dawning upon them with rare loveliness. Their hearts were cheered, and they pressed forward in their labors with great vigor. The terrible fright which the fire caused taught them that they must place their store-house apart from the other buildings, and where there would be no exposure to conflagration. They, therefore, went immediately to work to put up a shed for this purpose, intending to reserve the building already erected as a common lodging house until the separate huts could be reared.

Friday opened pleasantly; but at noon it began to rain, which prevented any out-door work. Towards evening the storm abated, and John Goodman, whose feet had been sadly crippled by his exposure in the woods, hobbled out a little way from the village for exercise, accompanied by a small spaniel. Two half famished wolves came leaping from the forest in pursuit of his dog. The terrified animal ran between his master's legs for protection. Mr. Goodman caught up a heavy stick, and for some time kept the ferocious beasts at bay. They kept at a little distance, just out of reach of his club, gnashing upon him with their sharp and glistening teeth in most dramatic style. But ere long the wolves, to Mr. Goodman's intense relief, turned away and rushed howling into the woods.

The next day, Saturday the 20th of January, they completed their shed for a store-house, and nearly all of their company came to the land. On Sunday, 21st, there was a general assembling of the Pilgrims in the Common House, as their temple, where their revered and beloved pastor, Rev. Mr. Brewster, conducted divine worship. This was the first Sabbath on which the Pilgrims as a body had been able to meet together in their new home.

Monday, 22d, was a fair day, and during the whole week the weather continued propitious. All were busy, bringing boat loads of freight from the ship, and packing away their provisions and other goods in the store-house. Two boats were employed in bringing the luggage on shore, but it was slow work, in consequence of the distant anchorage of the Mayflower As they had neither ox, mule nor horse, all the articles had to be carried by hand from the landing-place to their destination many rods distant from the shore.

The next week was ushered in by a storm of piercing wind and sleet. To add to its gloom, on its first day, Rose, the young and beautiful wife of Captain Standish, died. But care, sickness, death now came in such swift succession as to leave the survivors but little time to weep over the dead. The two succeeding days the weather was so inclement that no work could be done. Not very far from the ship's place of anchorage there was a small island. On Wednesday morning those on board the ship saw two savages walking upon the island. What they were doing no one could tell. They were seen but for a few moments, when they retired out of sight in the forest.

On Sunday morning, February 4th, a fearful gale swept the bay. It was the most severe storm the Pilgrims had yet encountered. For some time great apprehensions were felt lest the ship should be torn from her moorings and dashed upon the shore. The huts, which they were erecting for their dwellings, were of unhewn logs, the interstices being filled with clay. The wind and the rain washed out this clay, causing very serious damage. Much of the thatching also, as yet but insecurely fastened, was whirled into the air by the tempest, like autumn leaves. During the whole of the week the weather continued so cold and stormy that but little work could be done.

In consequence of the increasing sickness, it had been found necessary to put up a small house for a hospital. On Friday, the 9th, the thatched roof of this building took fire from a spark. Fortunately the wet weather had so dampened the straw that the fire was extinguished without doing much damage. Where wood was the only fuel, ever throwing up a shower of sparks, a thatch of straw, often as dry as tinder, seemed to invite conflagration. Thus their little hamlet, of clustered log houses, was peculiarly exposed to the peril of fire. That afternoon five wild geese were shot, which afforded a very grateful repast to the sick people. A good fat deer was also found, which had just been killed by the Indians, and which, for some inexplicable reason they had left, having cut off its horns. It is possible that the wary savages, keeping a sharp look out, had seen some of the white men approaching, and had fled. A wolf had, however, anticipated the Pilgrims, and was daintily feeding upon the tender venison.

Another week came, with great discouragement of stormy weather, and with increasing sickness. The men worked to much disadvantage, everything having to be done with their own hands. The logs, generally about a foot in thickness and nearly twenty feet long, had often to be dragged from very inconvenient distances. This was labor which could not safely be performed with clothing drenched with rain and pierced with the wintry gale. Often whole days were lost in which no work could be done.

Friday, February 16th, was a fair day. It was however, very cold, and the ground was frozen hard. In the afternoon one of the company took his gun and went into the woods a fowling. He had gone about a mile and a half from the plantation, and had concealed himself in some reeds, which fringed a creek, watching for wild geese or ducks, when, to his astonishment, twelve Indians appeared, walking towards the plantation, in single file and in perfect silence. Almost breathless he crouched down beneath his covert until they had disappeared, and then, with the utmost caution, hastened back to give the alarm.

The Indians, it would seem, were out upon a reconnoitering tour. They were very careful not to show themselves at the settlement, though they came sufficiently near to take some tools which Captain Standish and Francis Cooke, who had been at work in the woods, had left behind them, with no apprehension that there were any prowlers so near. The alarm caused the whole Pilgrim band immediately to rally under arms. There was, however, nothing more seen of the savages. But that night a large fire was discovered near the spot where the twelve Indians had made their appearance.

It was now deemed important to have a more perfect military organization, to meet the dangers impending from the manifestly unfriendly spirit of the Indians. The Pilgrims, in their weakened state, were but poorly prepared for any general assault. On Saturday morning, the 19th of February, they all assembled in council, and Captain Standish was invested with almost dictatorial powers as military commander. With characteristic sagacity and energy he undertook the responsible duties thus devolving upon him While they were assembled in consultation, two Indians appeared upon a small eminence, then called Strawberry Hill, on the other side of Town Brook, about a quarter of a mile southwest from the village, and made signs to the Pilgrims to come to them.

It was not improbable that they were a decoy, and that hundreds of armed warriors were concealed in the forest behind, ready, at a concerted signal, to raise the terrible war-whoop and rush upon their victims with javelin and tomahawk. There were not a score of Pilgrims able to bear arms. What could they do to repel such an onset. It was an awful hour, in view of the possibilities which were before them. The women and children huddled together in terror. It seemed probable to them that the Indians had long been gathering and making preparations for this assault, and that within an hour their husbands and fathers would be slain, and that they would be at the mercy of the savages.

The perilous duty of advancing to meet the savages, and of thus being perhaps the first to fall into the ambush, Captain Standish took upon himself. Selecting Mr. Stephen Hopkins, one of the most illustrious of the Pilgrims, and a man alike distinguished for his prudence and his bravery, to accompany him, he advanced, entirely unarmed, in token of his friendly disposition, across the brook. Mr. Hopkins carried his gun. When they reached the foot of the eminence the gun was laid upon the ground, as an additional sign of peace, and they both moved forward to meet the tufted warriors. The conduct of the savages was often quite inexplicable. They were as capricious as children. On this occasion, as Captain Standish and Mr. Hopkins slowly ascended the hill, the two Indians upon the summit suddenly turned and fled precipitately down the other side of the hill into the dense forest.

It was a very bold act, it seems to us now a very imprudent one, for these two unarmed men, still to advance to the summit of the hill, thus exposing themselves to fall into an Indian ambush. They however cautiously moved on ; when they reached the top of the hill not an Indian was in sight, but they heard the noise of a great multitude retreating through the forest. They were of course greatly perplexed to judge what all this senseless conduct could mean. One thing, however, was certain ; the Indians were not disposed to establish friendly relations with the new comers.

Captain Standish made immediate and vigorous preparation for a war of defense. It was very evident to him that, though they might be surrounded by cruel, treacherous and inveterate foes, they had but little to fear from the intelligence or military ability of their enemies. He had immediately brought on shore, and mounted on the platform, which he had arranged for them on the hill, three guns. One was called a minion, with a bore three and a quarter inches in diameter. Another was a saker, about four inches in bore. The third, called a base, was but little larger than a musket, having a bore but one and a quarter inches in diameter. The heaviest gun weighed about a thousand pounds, and carried a ball about four pounds in weight. This important work was all accomplished by Wednesday, February 21st. It ap pears that the officers of the Mayflower assisted efficiently in the operation. The united company then dined luxuriously upon a very fat goose, a fat crane, a mallard, * and a dried neats tongue. And so we were kindly and friendly together. †

Sunday, the 3d of March, came. It was a lovely day. The severity of winter had passed. A dreadful winter to the Pilgrims, indeed it had been. During the month of February seventeen of their number had died. Eight had died during the month of January. In burying the dead it had been deemed necessary carefully to conceal their graves lest the Indians, in counting them, should ascertain how greatly they had been weakened. Governor Bradford, in recording these disastrous events, writes:

"After they had provided a place for their goods, or common store, which were long in unlading for want of boats, foulness of winter weather and sickness of divers, and begun some small cottages for their habitation, they met, as time would admit, and consulted of laws and orders, both for their civil and military government, as the necessities of their occasion did require.

'In these hard and difficult beginnings they found some discontents and murmurings arise among some,

---

* A Duck. † Mourt's Relation.

and mutinous speeches and carriage in others. But they were soon quelled and overcome by the wisdom, patience, and just and equal carriage of things, by the Governor and better part, which clave faithfully together in the main. But that which was most sad and lamentable was that, in two or three months' time half of their company died; especially in January and February, being the depth of winter, and wanting houses and other comforts; being infected with scurvy and other diseases, which their long voyage and inaccommodate condition had brought upon them; so as there died sometimes two or three of a day, that of one hundred and odd persons, scarce fifty remained.*

"And of these, in the time of most distress, there were but six or seven sound persons who, to their great commendation be it spoken, spared no pains, night nor day, but with abundance of toil and hazard of their own health, fetched them wood and made them fires, dressed their meat, made their beds, washed their loathsome clothes, clothed and unclothed them; in a word, did all the homely and necessary offices for them which dainty and quesie stomachs cannot endure to hear named; and all this willingly and cheerfully, without any grudging in the least, shewing

---

* The bill of mortality, according to Prince, which he copied from Bradford, was as follows: In December, six died; in January, eight in February, seventeen; in March, thirteen; total, forty-four.

herein their true love unto their friends and brethren
A rare example, and worthy to be remembered.

"Two of these seven were Mr. William Brewster, their reverend Elder, and Miles Standish, their Captain and military commander, unto whom myself and many others were much beholden in our low and sick condition.

"And yet the Lord so upheld these persons as, in this general calamity, they were not at all infected with sickness or lameness. And what I have said of these I may say of many others who died in this general visitation, and others yet living, that whilst they had health, yea or any strength continuing, they were not wanting to any that had need of them. And I doubt not but that their recompense is with the Lord.

"But I may not here pass by another remarkable passage, never to be forgotten. As this calamity fell among the passengers that were to be left here to plant, and were hasted ashore and made to drink water, that the seamen might have the more beer. And one (Mr. Bradford) in his sickness desiring but a small can of beer, it was answered that if he were their own father he should have none. The disease began to fall amongst them also, so as almost half of their company died before they went away, and many of their officers and lustiest men, as the boatswain, gunner, three quartermasters, the cook and others At which the Master was somewhat strucken, and sent to the sick, on shore, and told the Governor he would send beer for them that had need of it, though ıe drank water, homeward bound.

"But now amongst his company there was far another kind of carriage in this misery than among the passengers. For they that beforetime had been boon companions in drinking and jollity in the time of their health and welfare, began now to desert one another in this calamity, saying that they would no. hazard their lives for them; they should be infected by coming to them in their cabins. And so, after they came to die by it, would do little or nothing for them, but if they died, let them die.

"But such of the passengers as were yet aboard shewed them what mercy they could, which made some of their hearts relent, as the boatswain, who was a proud young man, and would often curse and scoff at the passengers. But when he grew weak they had compassion on him and helped him. Then he confessed he did not deserve it at their hands; he had abused them in word and deed. 'O,' saith he, 'you, I now see, show your love, like Christians indeed, one to another. But we let one another lie and lie like dogs.'

"Another lay cursing his wife, saying if it had not

been for her he had never come this unlucky voyage, and anon cursing his fellows, saying he had done this and that for some of them ; he had spent so much and so much amongst them, and they were now weary of him, and did not help him having need Another gave his companion all he had, if he died, to help him in his weakness. He went and got a little spice, and made him a mess of meat once or twice; and because he died not as soon as he expected, he went among his fellows and swore the rogue would cozen him ; he would see him choked before he made him any more meat ; and yet the poor fellow died before morning."

As we have mentioned, the third of March dawned beautifully, sunny and mild, upon the weary Pilgrims. The birds sang sweetly, and everything indicated the speedy return of the much-longed-for summer weather. But towards noon the clouds gathered, the rain fell in torrents, and they were visited with one of the severest tempests, accompanied by the loudest thunder, any of them had ever witnessed.

On Wednesday, the 7th of March, a company of five, all well armed, accompanied Governor Carver to the great lakes, to which they had given the name of Billington Sea. These waters abounded with fish, and it would seem that by this time they had devised some plan by which to take them. They found the woods through which they passed filled with well beaten deer tracks, indicating the presence of large numbers of that species of game, though they did not chance to meet with any. Many water fowl were also disporting upon the placid waters of the lake, some of very beautiful plumage. The weather was so warm and the season so advanced that some garden seeds were sown on this day.

Another week passed, during which their work proceeded very slowly in consequence of their enfeebled numbers and the claims of the sick on the services of the few who were well. Friday, the 16th, was a fair, warm day. Every one felt the situation of the colony to be perilous in the extreme. The sailors of the Mayflower were suffering alike with the Pilgrims on the land. There were but seven men who, in case of an attack, which was hourly anticipated, could present any efficient resistance. The onset of a hundred armed warriors (and a thousand might come) would sweep away their little village like an Alpine avalanche. The responsibility for the public defense thus resting upon Captain Standish, was very weighty. Every individual had his post of duty assigned him, that there should be no confused or embarrassed action in the alarm. Captain Standish had this morning assembled all who were capable of bearing arms in the northern part of their little street, to complete their military preparations, when, to their surprise, they saw a solitary savage approaching from the south.

Without the slightest indication of embarrassment or hesitation he strode along, entered the street, and advancing boldly to the rendezvous, saluted the Pilgrims with the words, " Welcome Englishmen." His only clothing consisted of a leather belt around his waist, to which was attached a fringe, about ten inches long. He had a bow and two arrows. He was a powerful man, tall and straight, with very black hair, long behind, but cut short over the forehead. In broken English he told them that his name was Samoset, and that he came from the Island of Monhegan, between the Kennebec and Penobscot rivers, about twelve miles from the shore.

This island had for many years been a favorite resort for the English fishermen. From them he had learned a little English, and knew the names of many of the captains who annually visited those waters. Seeing the Mayflower in the harbor, he supposed it to be a fishing vessel, and thus, without any fear, approached the men.

Samoset affected to be very free and unembarrassed in his carriage. He declared himself to be one of the chiefs of the tribe, and assumed to be perfectly informed respecting the whole adjacent country, its tribes and their strength. He called for beer, and seemed disposed to make himself very much at home, entering the houses and spying out with an eagle eye all the works around him. Captain Standish was not disposed to have his weakness exposed to this perhaps wary and treacherous savage, who might have entered the village merely as a spy, in the interest of the Indian warriors who were lurking in the woods around. To make him a little more presentable to the families, a large horseman's coat was placed upon him. Instead of being allowed to wander about at will, he was entrusted to the keeping of Mr. Hopkins, who took him to his hut and fed him with the utmost hospitality.

From Samoset they learned three very important facts. The first was that the Indians, all along the coast, were greatly and justly exasperated against the white men, by the treachery of one Captain Hunt. This infamous man, while trading with the Indians, had inveigled twenty-seven men on board his ship, and then, closing the hatches upon them, had carried them off where most of them had never been heard of more. The wretch took these poor kidnapped Indians to Spain, and sold them as slaves, for one hundred dollars each. The untutored savages who, before this, were friendly, being thus robbed of their kindred, knew no better than to wreak their vengeance upon any white man whom they might en counter.

Not long after this a French ship was wrecked on Cape Cod. The savages, burning with a desire for vengeance, massacred all but three or four of the crew, whom they reserved as prisoners. Everything that had been saved from the wreck they divided among themselves. Hence, perhaps, the iron kettle which the Pilgrims had found in one of their exploring tours. The captives were sent from one tribe to another, into the interior, that there might be no possibility of a rescue. One of these captives, probably a thoughtful, perhaps a religious man, learned their language, and told them that " God was angry with them, and in punishment would destroy them and give their country to another people." They replied that "they were so numerous that God would not be able to destroy them."

But it so happened that ere long a terrible plague, resembling the yellow fever, broke out among the Indians, sweeping them off by thousands. The whole country became nearly depopulated. In these disastrous days the Indians remembered the words of the Frenchman, and began to fear that the white man's God was really taking vengeance upon them. When the Mayflower arrived they feared that another people had come to take possession of their lands. Hence

LIFE ON SHORE.

the hostile attitude which had been assumed, and the attack at the First Encounter. Samoset seemed to know all about this attack, and said that it was made by a tribe on the Cape called Nausites.

It appears that the plague, above referred to swept the whole seaboard, from the mouth of the Penobscot River to Narraganset Bay. Some tribes became nearly extinct. The Massachusetts tribe was reduced, it is said, from thirty thousand to three hundred fighting men. Captain Dermer, who visited the coast a year before the landing of the Pilgrims, writes:

"I passed along the coast where I found some ancient plantations, not long since populous, now utterly void. In other places a remnant remains, but not free of sickness. Their disease was the plague, for we might perceive the sores of some that had escaped, who described the spots of such as usually die."

Morton writes in his New English Canaan: "Some few years before the English came to inhabit in New Plymouth, the hand of God fell heavily upon the natives, with such a mortal stroke that they died on heaps. In a place where many inhabited there hath been but one left alive to tell what became of the rest. And the bones and skulls upon the several places of their habitations made such a spectacle, after my coming into these parts, that as I travelled in that forest, near the Massachusetts, it seemed to me a new-found Golgotha."

In view of these facts it was stated, in the Great Patent of New England, granted by King James, on the 3d of November, 1820, "We have been further given certainly to know, that within these late years there hath, by God's visitation, reigned a wonderful plague amongst the savages there heretofore inhabiting, in a manner to the utter destruction, devastation and depopulation of that whole territory, so as there is not left, for many leagues together, in a manner, any that do claim or challenge any kind of interest therein. Whereby we, in our judgment, are persuaded and satisfied that the appointed time is come in which Almighty God, in his great goodness and bounty towards us and our people, hath thought fit and determined, that these large and goodly territories, deserted as it were by their natural inhabitants, should be possessed and enjoyed by such of our subjects and people as shall, by his mercy and favor, and by his powerful arm, be directed and conducted thither."

All the afternoon was spent in earnest communication with Samoset. He told them that the Nausites, by whom they had been attacked, numbered about one hundred souls. There was a powerful tribe, called the Wampanoags, upon the shores of what is now called Bristol Bay. Their chief, Massasoit, was so powerful that he exercised a sort of supremacy over many of the tribes in the vicinity. There was another numerous tribe, not far from the Wampanoags, called the Narragansets. Samoset does not seem to have known, or if so, was not willing to tell the number of Indians lurking in the woods around the Pilgrim settlement. The mystery of their conduct was, however, in some degree revealed, when the Pilgrims were informed that the Indians, with their priests, had met in a dark swamp, in a general pow-wow, hoping by their curses and incantations to destroy the white men.

On the whole, the information communicated by Samoset was encouraging. It led them to hope that their foes were not so numerous as they feared, that they regarded, with superstitious dread, the God of the white man, and that they were rather disposed to rely upon witchcraft and incantations, in their warfare upon the new-comers, than upon more material and dangerous weapons. Had the Indians known what ravages death was making in the huts of the Pilgrims, they would have felt assured that their magic arts were signally successful.

As night approached, Captain Standish was quite anxious to get rid of his suspicious guest. But Samoset manifested no disposition to leave. He however consented to go on board the ship to pass the night. They went down to the shallop. But the wind was so high that it was not deemed prudent to encounter the high sea, and they returned to Mr. Stephen Hopkins' house, where Samoset was lodged, and carefully though secretly watched.

The next day, Saturday, the 17th, early in the morning, Samoset withdrew, to go, as he said, to visit the great sagamore, Massasoit. He received a present of a knife, a bracelet and a ring, promising to return in a few days, bringing with him some of Massasoit's people, and some beaver skins to sell.

Sunday, the 18th, was another mild and lovely day. As the colonists were assembling for the Sabbath devotions, Samoset again made his appearance, with five tall Indians in his train. They were all dressed in deer skins, fitting closely to the body. The most of them had also a panther's skin, or some similar furs on his arm, for sale. As Captain Standish did not deem it safe to allow any armed savages to enter the town, he made a previous arrangement with Samoset, that whoever of the Indians he might bring with him, should leave their bows and arrows a quarter of a mile distant from this village. This arrangement was faithfully observed. Samoset also brought back the tools, which, it will be remembered, had been carried away by the Indians. Mourt, in his Relation, describes, in the following language, the appearance of these strange visitors:

"They had, most of them, long hosen (leggins) up to their groins, close made; and above their groins to the waist, another leather. They were altogether like the Irish trousers. They are of complexion like our English gipseys; no hair, or very little, on their faces; on their heads, long hair to their shoulders, only cut before; some trussed up before with a feather, broadwise like a fan; another a fox tail hanging out. Some of them had their faces painted black, from the forehead to the chin, four or five fingers broad; others after other fashions, as they liked."

The Pilgrims, anxious to win the confidence and friendship of the natives, received these savages with the utmost kindness, and very hospitably entertained them. They seemed to relish very highly the food which was set before them, and manifested their satisfaction and friendship by singing hilariously, and performing the most grotesque antics in a dance. It was Sunday, and this was not pleasing to these devout exiles. They told Samoset that they could not enter into any traffic on that day; but that if he and his companions would withdraw and return upon the morrow, or any other day of the week, they would purchase, not only all the furs they had with them, but any others which they might bring. Each one was made happy with a present of some article which to him was of almost priceless value. They all retired except Samoset. He refused to go, asserting, and as the Pilgrims thought, feigning, that he was sick. He therefore remained until Wednesday. Each of these men carried his commissariat stores with him, consisting of a small bag of the meal of parched corn. Mr. Gookin, in an article in the Massachusetts Historical Collection, writes:

"The Indians make a certain sort of meal of parched maize, which they call *nokake*. It is so sweet, toothsome and hearty that an Indian will travel many days with no other food but this meal, which he eateth as he needs, and after it drinketh water. And for this end, when they travel a journey or go a hunting, they carry this *nokake* in a basket or bag, for their use."

Roger Williams says, "Nokake, or parched meal, is a ready, very wholesome food, which they eat with a little water, hot or cold. I have travelled with near two hundred of them at once, near a hundred miles through the woods, every man carrying a little basket of this at his back, and sometimes in a hollow leather girdle about his middle, sufficient for a man three or four days. With this ready provision and their bows and arrows, they are ready for war or travel at an hour's warning."

The corn was usually parched in hot ashes, and then, after having the ashes carefully brushed off, was beat to powder. About a gill of this mixed with water, taken three times a day, gave them sufficient nourishment. With no other food than this, a man would often travel through the woods four or five days, carrying a very heavy burden upon his back.

When the Mayflower was leaving England, a man by the name of John Billington, uninvited, with two ungovernable boys, joined the company. He proved to be a very uncongenial companion. Governor Bradford, writing of him, said: "This Billington was one of the profanest among us. He came from London, and I know not by what friends, was shuffled into our company." Again, Governor Bradford wrote to Mr. Cushman, in June, 1625, "Billington still rails against you, and threatens to arrest you, I know not wherefore. He is a knave, and so will live and die." In "Mourts' Narrative," under date of December 5th he writes:

"This day, through God's mercy, we escaped a great danger by the foolishness of a boy, one of Billington's sons, who, in his father's absence, had got gunpowder, and had shot off a piece or two and made squibs; and there being a fowling-piece charged in his father's cabin, shot her off in the cabin." There was half a keg of powder in the cabin, with many grains scattered over the floor; also flints and pieces of iron strowed about. It was a very narrow escape from an explosion which might have blown the Mayflower, with all its occupants, into the air. This John Billington, "a mischievous and troublesome fellow, was dissatisfied with the authority with which Captain Standish was invested. He endeavored to undermine his influence by assailing him with insulting and opprobrious language. This was a very serious offense, since, in their perilous position, it was a matter of infinite moment that the orders of their military commander should be implicitly obeyed. The whole company was convened to try the culprit and pass sentence upon him. "He was adjudged to have his neck and heels tied together. But upon humbling himself and craving pardon, and it being the first offense, he was forgiven."

CHAPTER VI.

The Indians.

Two Savages on the Hill.—The Return of Samoset with Squantum.—The Story of Squantum.—The Visit of Massasoit and His Warriors.—Etiquette of the Barbarian and Pilgrim Courts.—The Treaty.—Return of the Mayflower to England.—A View of Plymouth.—Brighter Days.—Visit of Messrs. Winslow and Hopkins to the Seat of Massasoit.—Incidents of the Journey.

Several days passed, and the Indians, who had retired into the forest, did not return. The cottages of the Pilgrims, each man building his own, had now become habitable, and Monday and Tuesday, the weather being fair, they were busy digging the ground and sowing their garden seeds. On Wednesday morning, the 21st of March, Samoset was sent into the woods to ascertain why the Indians did not come back according to their promise. He had but just disappeared in the forest when two savages, in war costume and thoroughly armed, appeared upon the hill, on the other side of Town Brook—the same eminence upon which the two Indians had appeared on the 17th of February—and brandishing their weapons, with every demonstration of hostility, seemed to bid the new-comers defiance. This was probably one of the acts in their drama of incantation.

Captain Standish, who was ever prompt to assume any office of danger, took a companion with him and advanced to meet the challengers. They both took their muskets, but carefully avoided any attitude of menace. Two other Pilgrims followed, at a little distance, also with their muskets, to render aid should there be any rush of the Indians from an ambush. But before Captain Standish had arrived within arrow-shot of the natives they both turned, as before, and fled.

In consequence of sickness and the imperfect accommodations on the shore, several of the Pilgrim company had thus far remained on board the Mayflower. To-day, however, the shallop brought them all to the land, and their colonizing became complete One-half of the crew of the ship had already died; and so many of the remainder were enfeebled by sickness that Captain Jones did not deem it safe to undertake his return voyage in so crippled a condition. A month passed before the sick and his diminished crew were so far recovered as to allow him to venture to set sail.

The sun of Thursday morning, with healing in its beams, rose bright and warm over the busy little village of the exiles. The dreary winter had manifestly passed. The sick were generally recovering, and there was presented a very cheering scene of peace, industry and happiness. At noon all the men had met upon some public business, when, in the midst of their deliberations, they saw Samoset returning, accompanied by three other Indians. The name of one was Squantum, and it was said that he was the only surviving member of the Patuxat tribe, who had formerly occupied the territory upon which the Pilgrims had now settled.

His story, undoubtedly truthful, was that he was one of the men whom Captain Hunt had so infamously kidnapped. He had been carried to Spain and sold there as a slave. A humane Englishman, whose name we love to perpetuate, Mr. John Slaney, chanced to meet the poor fugitive. He liberated him, took him to England, and treated him with that truly fraternal kindness which Christianity enjoins upon all men. At length he had an opportunity to send Squantum back to his native land.

Good deeds and bad deeds ever bear their corresponding fruit. As the treachery of the miserable Hunt caused the hostility of the Indians, the massacre of the shipwrecked Frenchmen, and the attack at the First Encounter, so did the brotherly kindness of good John Slaney secure for the Pilgrims, in their hour of need, a permanent and influential friend

Squantum, forgetting the outrage of the knave who had kidnapped him, remembered only the kindness of his benefactor. His residence in England had rendered him quite familiar with the English language, and he became invaluable to the Pilgrims as an interpreter. He attached himself cordially to them, and taught them many things of great value in their new life in the wilderness. And when, after many years, he died, the good old man was heard praying that God would take him to the heaven of the white men.

Squantum had joined the powerful tribe of the Wampanoags, his own tribe having become extinct. These Indians brought with them a few skins to sell, and some dried red herrings; and they also announced the rather startling intelligence that their great Sagamore, or King Massasoit, accompanied by his brother Quadequina and a retinue of sixty warriors, was near at hand to pay the Pilgrims a friendly visit.

After the lapse of an hour Massasoit appeared on the top of Watson's Hill with his plumed warriors. From that eminence, distant about a quarter of a mile, they had a perfect view of the little village, and were conspicuously exposed to the view of the Pilgrims. Under the circumstances, knowing not what might be the treachery of the Indians, Captain Standish did not deem it safe to allow so powerful a band of armed savages to enter the village, or to allow any considerable band of his weak force to withdraw from behind the intrenchments which they had reared, and to go out to meet the royal retinue. Neither did Massasoit deem it prudent to place himself in the power of the white men, whom the treachery of Hunt had caused him to dread.

After several messages had passed to and fro between the two parties, through Squantum, their interpreter, Massasoit, who, though unlettered, proved himself to be a man of much sagacity, proposed that the Pilgrims should send one of their men to his encampment to communicate to him their designs in settling upon ands which had belonged to one of his vassal tribes. Mr. Edward Winslow consented to go upon this important and somewhat hazardous mission. He took, as a present to the barbarian monarch, two skins and a copper necklace, with a jewel attached to it. He also took to Quadequina a knife, an ear-ring, consisting of a pendent jewel, some biscuit and butter, and, we are sorry to add, a jug of rum; but those were the days of ignorance which God winked at.

Mr. Winslow, accompanied by Squantum, as his interpreter, crossed the brook, ascended Watson's Hill, and presented himself before the Indian chief. "Our messenger,' writes Mourt, "made a speech unto him, that King James saluted him with words of love and peace, and did accept him as his friend and ally; and that our Governor desired to see him, and to truck with him, and to confirm a peace with him, as his next neighbor."

Massasoit listened attentively to the speech, as communicated to him by the interpreter, and seemed much pleased with it. In token of amity, they had a little feast together. Massasoit seemed much impressed with the long and glittering sword which hung by the side of Mr. Winslow, and expressed a strong desire to purchase it; but Mr. Winslow could not consent to part with the weapon.

After a pleasant and very friendly interview, Massasoit, cautiously leaving Mr. Winslow as a hostage in the custody of his brother Quadequina, came down to the brook with twenty men, as his retinue, all unarmed. Six of them were sent into the village, as hostages in exchange for Mr. Winslow.

Then Captain Standish, with one companion, probably Mr. Thomas Williams, and followed by half a dozen musketeers, advanced to the brook to meet the royal guest and to escort him, with all due honor, to the presence of their Governor. A salute of six muskets was fired, and the monarch with his Indian band was led to an unfinished house which had been hastily decorated for their reception. It was deemed important to arrange something of an imposing pageant to impress the minds of their barbarian visitors. Two or three cushions were laid down, covered with a green carpet, as seats for the Indian chief and for the Governor in this important interview. As soon as Massasoit was seated the music of drums and of a trumpet was heard, and Governor Carver, with a suitable retinue, entered. Gracefully he took the hand of Massasoit and kissed it. In accordance with the mistaken views of hospitality in those days, ardent spirits were brought forward to regale the guests. This was probably the first time Massasoit had ever seen the accursed liquid, and he was entirely unacquainted with its fiery nature. The Indian chieftain, deeming it a part of politeness to partake generously of the entertainment provided for him, when the goblet was presented, "drunk a great draft which made him sweat all the while after."

Massasoit was a remarkable man. He was of majestic stature, in the prime of life, of grave and stately demeanor, reserved in speech, and ever proving faithful to all his obligations. He wore a chain of white bone beads about his neck, and a little bag of tobacco, from which he smoked himself and presented to Governor Carver to smoke. His face was painted of a deep red color, and his hair and face so oiled as to present a very glossy appearance. His followers were also all painted, in various styles and of various colors. Some were partially clothed in skins, others were nearly naked. They were all tall, powerful men. After much friendly deliberation, the Governor and Massasoit entered into the following very simple, but comprehensive treaty of peace and alliance :

1. The Sagamore pledged himself that none of his men should do any harm to the Pilgrims ; and that, if any harm were done, the offender should be sent to them that they might punish them.

2. That, if any property belonging to the white men should be taken away, it should be restored, Governor Carver agreeing to the same in reference to his party.

3. The Governor agreed that if any Indian tribe should wage an unjust war against Massasoit, he would help him ; Massasoit agreeing in the same way to aid the Pilgrims, should they be assailed.

4. Massasoit pledged himself to send word to all his confederate tribes that he had entered into this alliance with the white men, and to enjoin its faithful observance upon them.

5. Finally, it was agreed that whenever any of the Indians visited the settlement of the white men, they should leave their arms behind them. The Pilgrims were also bound always to go unarmed whenever they should visit the residence of the Indian chief.

As evening approached, Massasoit and his followers withdrew. The Governor accompanied him to the brook, where they embraced and separated. The six Indian hostages were retained until Mr. Winslow should be returned. But soon word was brought that Quadequina wished to make them a short visit. He soon appeared, with quite a troop around him. He was a young man, tall, modest and gentlemanly. He was also conducted, with music of drum and fife, to the Governor. He seemed very much afraid of the muskets; and to calm his manifest fears they were laid aside. After a short interview he returned to the hill, and Mr. Winslow came back to the camp. The Indian hostages were also then released. The scenes of the day had inspired them with so much confidence in the Pilgrims that two of them wished to remain all night. But Captain Standish did not deem it prudent to grant their request.

Samoset and Squantum remained with the Pilgrims. Massasoit withdrew his party from the hill, about half a mile south into the forest, and there they encamped for the night. Their wives and children were with them there. During the night both parties kept up a vigilant watch, for neither had, as yet, full confidence in the other. In the morning several of the Indians came into the settlement, according to their agreement, unarmed. They said that in a few days they should come to the other side of the brook and plant corn, and remain there with their families al summer. The king sent an invitation to have some f the Pilgrims visit him.

"Captain Standish and Israel Alderton," writes Mourt, " went venturously, who were welcomed of him after their manner. He gave them three or four ground nuts and some tobacco. We cannot yet conceive but that he is willing to have peace with us, for they have seen our people sometimes alone, two or three in the woods, at work and fowling, when they offered them no harm, as they might easily have done, and especially as he has a potent adversary in the Narragansets, that are at war with him, against whom he thinks we may be some strength to him, for our pieces are terrible unto them."

The English visitors remained in the encampment of Massasoit until about eleven o'clock. Governor Carver sent by them to the chief a kettleful of peas, which the Indians seemed to regard as truly a princely gift. The next day, Friday, it was again pleasant. Squantum, who with Samoset, still remained with the Pilgrims, went to a neighboring creek, since appropriately called Eel River, and at night came home with as many eels as he could carry. "They were fat and sweet. He trod them out with his feet, and so caught them with his hands, without any other instrument." In a comparatively recent history of Plymouth, it is stated that a hundred and fifty barrels of eels are annually taken from that creek. The Pilgrims on that day held a general meeting, to conclude some military arrangements, to enact certain needful laws, and to choose a Governor for the year. The choice fell, with apparently great unanimity, upon the then incumbent, Mr. John Carver.

In Young's Chronicle of the Pilgrims we find a note containing the following statement: "It will be recollected that Carver had been chosen Governor on the 11th of November, the same day on which the Compact was signed. It was now the 23d of March, and the new year commencing on the 25th, according to the calendar then in use, Carver was re-elected for the ensuing year."

Pleasant summer days now came, and glided rapidly away, with nothing occurring of essential importance. Friendly relations were established with the Indians, and the affairs of the colony seemed as prosperous as, under the circumstances, could be expected On the 5th of April the Mayflower weighed anchor and set sail on her return voyage to England. She had but one-half of the crew with which she had sailed from Old Plymouth. The rest had fallen victims to the winter's sickness. It is remarkable that, notwithstanding the hardships to which the Pilgrims were exposed, not one was disposed to abandon the enterprise and return in the ship. When the May flower left, there remained in the colony but fifty-five persons. Of these, nineteen only were men. The remaining thirty-six were women, children and servants.

Scarcely had the ship disappeared over the distant horizon, ere Governor Carver, "oppressed by his great care and pains for the common good," on one hot April noon returned from the field, complaining of a severe pain in his head, probably caused by a sunstroke. He soon became delirious, and, in a few days, died. It was a severe loss to the colony, and they mourned over him with great lamentation and heaviness. He was buried with all the imposing ceremonies of sorrow which the feeble colony could arrange. His wife, overwhelmed with grief in view of her terrible loss, in a few weeks followed her husband to the grave. Soon after, Mr. William Bradford, who was then in a state of great debility from his recent sickness, was chosen his successor.

The settlers, having no animals to draw the plough, were laboriously opening the ground near their dwellings with the spade. Six acres they sowed with barley and peas. Fortunately they had ten bushels of corn for seed. With this they planted twenty acres, Squantum showing them how to plant and hill it.

Berries were found in abundance in the woods, as the season advanced, and a very grateful supply of grapes

Mr. Palfrey, in his admirable History of New England, writes very pleasantly, " A visitor to Plymouth during this summer, as he landed, on the southern side of a high bluff, would have seen, standing between it and a rapid little stream, a rude house of logs, twenty feet square, containing the common property of the plantation. Proceeding up a gentle declivity, between two rows of log cabins, nineteen in number, some of them, perhaps, vacant since the death of their first tenants, he would have come to a hill surmounted with a platform for cannon. He might have counted twenty men at work with hoes, in the enclosures about the huts, or fishing in the shallow harbor, or visiting the woods or beach for game; while six or eight women were busy in household affairs, and some twenty children, from infancy upwards, completed the domestic picture."

All fears of famine seem now to have passed away In addition to the stores which they brought with them they had an abundant supply of fish, wild fowls and native fruits. On the 18th of June two of the servants of Mr. Hopkins undertook to fight a duel with sword and dagger. Both were wounded. The Pilgrims met in a body to adjudge the penalty for so serious an offense. They were sentenced to be tied together, by their head and feet, and thus to lie twenty-four hours, without meat or drink. The punishment was begun to be inflicted, "But within an hour, because of their great pains, at their own and their master's humble request, upon promise of better carriage, they are released by the Governor."

Early in July, Governor Bradford decided to send a deputation to visit Massasoit. There were several objects he wished to accomplish by this mission. First, it was desirable to ascertain where he lived and what his strength was. He also wished to honor Massasoit by paying him a friendly visit. Another consideration of no little importance which influenced him was, that vagabond Indians were increasingly in the habit of coming with their wives and children loitering about the village to the great annoyance of the settlers, and clamoring for food, which they devoured with the voracity of famished wolves.

Mr. Winslow and Mr. Hopkins, accompanied by Squantum as their interpreter, were appointed for this important mission. Mr. Winslow has transmitted to us a minute account of the interesting adventure They left the village, probably on Tuesday morning, July 3d, bearing the following message to Massasoit with the present of a brilliant horseman's coat, of red cotton, gaudily laced.

"Inasmuch as your subjects come often and without fear, upon all occasions amongst us, so we are now come unto you. In witness of the love and good will the English bear you, our Governor has sent you a coat, desiring that the peace and amity between us may be continued; not that we fear you, but because we intend not to injure any one, desiring to live peaceably, as with all men, so especially with you our nearest neighbors.

"But whereas your people come very often, and very many together, unto us, bringing for the most part their wives and children with them, they are welcome. Yet we being but strangers, as yet, at Patuxet, or New Plymouth, and not knowing how our corn may prosper, can no longer give them such entertainment as we have done, and as we desire still to do. Yet if you will be pleased to come yourself, or any special friend of yours desires to see us, coming from you, they shall be welcome.

"And to the end that we may know them from others, our Governor has sent you a copper chain, desiring that if any messenger should come from you to us, we may know him by his bringing it with him, and may give credit to his message accordingly.'

They then added the following, which we record with pleasure, as showing the conscientiousness of these remarkable men:

"At our first arrival at Paomet, called by us Cape

Cod, we found there corn buried in the ground, and finding no inhabitants, but some graves of the dead newly buried, took the corn, resolving that if ever we could hear of any that had right thereunto, to make satisfaction to the full for it. Yet since we understand the owners thereof had fied, for fear of us, our lesire is either to pay them with the like quantity of corn, or with English meal, or any other commodities we have, which they may desire. We request that some of your men may signify so much unto them, and we will content him for his pains.

"Last of all, our Governor requested one favor of him, which was that he would exchange some of their corn for seed, with us, that we might make trial which was best agreed with the soil where we live."

It was a warm and sunny day when the two Pilgrims, with their Indian guide, set out on their adventurous journey through the forest. The Indians. in their movements from place to place, however nu merous the party, always went, with moccasined feet, in single file, one following after the other. The forests were threaded with many of these narrow paths, or trails, which had thus been trodden by them through countless generations. These paths were as well known by them, and almost as distinctly marked, as the paved roads of the Old World which had resounded with the tramp of the Roman legions. Indian in stinct had, ages ago, selected these routes, often through glooms which no rays of the sun ever penetrated, and again through scenes of marvelous picturesque beauty, beneath frowning mountains, along the margin of crystal lakes, and upon the banks of sparkling rivulets.

Much to the annoyance of the two Pilgrims appointed upon this mission a party of ten or twelve lazy Indians, men, women and children, uninvited, persistently tagged after them, often very vexatiously intrusive, and ever clamorous to share their food.

The first day they travelled about fifteen miles, to an Indian village called Namasket. It was situated upon a branch of what is now called the Taunton River, within the limits of the present town of Middleborough.

"Thither we came," writes Mr. Winslow, "about three o clock after noon; the inhabitants entertaining us with joy, in the best manner they could, giving us a kind of bread called by them *maizium*,* and the spawn of shads, which they then got in abundance, insomuch that they gave us spoons to eat them. With these they boiled musty acorns; but of the shads we ate heartily.

These Indians had probably all heard of the won-

---

* Made of maize or Indian corn.

derful power of the muskets of the white men, though, perhaps, none of them had ever seen the effects accomplished by powder and ball. The crows troubled their corn fields, and it was almost impossible for the Indians to get near enough to these wary animals to hit them with the arrow. They begged their guests to show them the power of their guns by shooting some of these crows. There was one upon a tree at the distance of about two hundred and forty feet. With intense interest the Indians watched as they saw one of the Pilgrims take deliberate aim at the bird, and when they heard the report, and saw the bird fall dead, struck by an invisible shaft, their astonishment passed all bounds. Several crows were thus shot, exciting the admiration and awe of all the savage beholders.

As Squantum told the Pilgrims that it was more than a day's journey from Namasket to Pokanoket, or Mount Hope, where Massasoit resided, and that there was a good place to pass the night about eight miles further on their way, they decided to resume their journey. About sunset they reached a small group of Indians at a place now called Titicut, on Taunton River, in the northwest part of Middleborough, adjoining Bridgewater.

Here quite an attractive region presented itself to their eyes. The land on both sides of the river had

THE INDIANS. 135

long been cleared, being entirely free from trees or stumps, and had evidently waved with cornfields There were many indications that the place had formerly been quite thickly inhabited. The plague, of which we have spoken, it is said, had swept every individual into the grave. A few wandering outcast Indians had come to this depopulated region to take fish. By means of a wear in the river, which consisted of a sort of net or fence, constructed of branches of trees and twigs, they caught an abundance of bass. They had not erected any shelter for themselves, but were sleeping, like the cattle, in the open air. These wretched savages had no food but fish and roasted acorns. Very greedily they partook of the stores which the Pilgrims brought with them. Liberally they were fed, "we not doubting," writes Mr. Winslow, "but that we should have enough where'er we came."

The Pilgrims lodged that night in the open fields. The next morning, at an early hour, after such frugal breakfast as the occasion could furnish, they set out again upon their journey. Six savages followed them Having travelled about six miles, following down the banks of the river, they came to a shoal place, where the stream could be forded. This was undoubtedly at a spot now called Squabetty, three and a half miles from Taunton Green.

"Here," writes Mr. Winslow, "let me not forget the valor and courage of some of the savages on the opposite side of the river; for there were remaining alive only two men, both aged, especially the one being about threescore. These two, espying a company of men entering the river, ran very swiftly, and low in the grass, to meet us at the bank, where, with shrill voices and great courage, standing, they charged upon us with their bows, demanding who we were, supposing us to be enemies, and thinking to take advantage of us in the water. But seeing we were friends, they welcomed us with such food as they had, and we bestowed a small bracelet of beads upon them."

Here, after refreshing themselves, they continued their journey down the western banks of the river. It was a very sultry July day, but the country was beautiful, and abundantly watered with innumerable small streams, and cool, bubbling springs. The savages would never drink of the flowing brooks, but only at the spring heads. Very pleasantly Mr. Winslow writes in reference to the amiability and obliging disposition of these savages:

"When we came to any brook where no bridge was, two of them desired to carry us through, of their own accord. Also, fearing that we were or would be weary, they offered to carry our pieces. If we would lay off any of our clothes, we should have them carried. And as the one of them had found more special kindness from one of the messengers, and the other savage from the other, so they showed their thankfulness accordingly, in affording us all help and furtherance in the journey."

It was very manifest to the travellers, as we have said, that they were passing through a country which once had been crowded with a population which but recently had been swept away. There were widely extended fields, which had formerly been planted with corn, where there was then to be seen but a rank growth of weeds, higher than a man's head. The region was pleasantly diversified with hills and plains, often presenting extended forests of the most valuable timber. It was a very noticeable and beautiful feature in these forests, that they were entirely free of underbrush, presenting the aspect of the most carefully-trimmed English park. Mr. Wood, who visited this region in year 1633, writes:

"Whereas it is generally conceived that the woods grow so thick that there is no more clear ground than is hewed out by labor of men, it is nothing so; in many places divers acres being clear, so that one may ride a hunting in most places of the land. There is no underwood, saving in swamps and low grounds; for, it being the custom of the Indians to burn the woods in November, when the grass is withered and leaves dried, consumes all the underwood and rubbish, which otherwise would overgrow the country, making it impassable, and spoil their much-affected hunting. So that in these places there is scarce a bush or bramble or any cumbersome underwood to be seen in the more champaign ground."

Hour after hour they journeyed on through these lonely fields, without meeting an individual. At length one solitary Indian was espied in the distance The Indians, who accompanied the Pilgrims, seemed much alarmed, from fear that he might be one of the Narraganset tribe, with whom Massasoit was then at war, and that there might be more of the Narragansets near at hand. The Pilgrims, however, bade them not to fear, assuring them that, with their guns, they should not hesitate to meet twenty of the foe. The savage was hailed. He proved to be a friend, having two women with him. The two parties interchanged courtesies, ate and drank together, and separated, well pleased with each other.

Soon after this they met another Indian, also accompanied by two women. They had been at a rendezvous, by a salt water creek, and had some baskets full of roasted crabs and other small shell fish. They, also, in oriental fashion, ate and drank together, in token of friendship. The women were made very happy by a present each of a string of beads, as bril-

THE INDIANS. 139

liant in their eyes as the priceless jewels of the crown to any European queen. "There is but one step between the sublime and the ridiculous." The step is equally short between the court-dress of an European monarch and his jeweled queen, and that of the feathered Indian warrior and his beaded squaw.

Continuing their journey, they soon reached one of the small towns of Massasoit. This was probably Mattapoiset, now known as Gardner's Neck, in Swansey. They were hospitably received here, and fed with oysters and other fish.

The latter part of the afternoon they reached Pokanoket, on the northern shore of Narraganset Bay. The capital of the Indian monarch, which they had thus entered, was about forty miles from Plymouth. The spot where the little cluster of wigwams stood was probably Sowams, in the present town of Warren. We cannot better describe the interview which took place, than in the language of Mr. Winslow:

"Massasoit was not at home. There we stayed he being sent for. When news was brought of his coming, our guide, Squantum, requested that, at our meeting, we would discharge our pieces. But one of us going about to discharge his piece, the women and children, through fear to see him take up his piece, ran away, and could not be pacified till he laid it down again; who afterwards were better informed by our interpreter.

"Massasoit being come, we discharged our pieces and saluted him; who, after their manner, kindly welcomed us, and took us into his house and set us down by him; where, having delivered our foresaid message and presents, and having put the coat on his back, and the chain about his neck, he was not a little proud to behold himself, as were his men also, to see their king so bravely attired.

"In answer to our message, he told us we were welcome, and he would gladly continue that peace and friendship which was between him and us. As for his men, they should no longer pester us as they had done. He would also send us corn for seed, according to our request.

"This being done, his men gathered near to him, to whom he turned himself and made a great speech; they sometimes interposing, and, as it were, confirming and applauding him in that he said."

In this harangue the king enumerated thirty towns or villages over which his sovereignty was recognized; and enjoined it upon his people ever to live in peace with the white men, and to carry to them furs for sale.

"This being ended he lighted tobacco for us, and fell to discoursing of England and of the King's Maj-

esty, marvelling that he would live without a wife.*
Also he talked of the Frenchmen, bidding us not to
suffer them to come to Narraganset, for it was K.ng
James's country, and he was King James's man.
Late it grew, but victuals he offered us none; for, indeed, he had not any, he being so newly come home.
So we desired to go to rest. He laid us on the bed
with himself and his wife, they at the one end and
we at the other, it being only planks laid a foot from
the ground, and a thin mat upon them. Two more
of his chief men, for want of room, pressed by and
upon us, so that we were worse weary of our lodging
than of our journey.

"The next day being Thursday, many of their
sachems, or petty governors, came to see us, and many
of their men also. There they went to their manner
of games for skins and knives. We challenged them
to shoot with us for skins, but they durst not; only
they desired one of us to shoot at a mark, who, shooting with hail-shot, they wondered to see the mark so
full of holes.

"About one o'clock Massasoit brought two fishes
that he had shot. They were like bream, but three
times as big, and better meat. † These, being boiled,

* James I., then King of England, had been a widower for about a
year
† This was probably the fish called *tautaug*.

there were at least forty looked for share .. ..
The most ate of them. This meal only we had in
two nights and a day. And had not one of us bought
a partridge we had taken our journey fasting.

Very importunate he was to have us stay with
him longer. But we desired to keep the Sabbath at
home, and feared that we should either be light-
headed for want of sleep, for what with bad lodging,
the savage's barbarious singing, for they use to sing
themselves asleep, lice and fleas within doors, and
mosquitoes without, we could hardly sleep all of the
time of our being there; we much fearing that if we
should stay any longer we should not be able to recover home for want of strength. So that on Friday
morning, before sun-rising, we took our leave and departed, Massasoit being both grieved and ashamed
that he could no better entertain us."

Their journey home was a weary one. They commenced it hungry, and without any supply of food for
the way. Squantum and five other Indians accompanied them, who were accustomed to the hardships
of the wilderness, and knew how to obtain food if there
were roots or berries, game or fish anywhere within
reach. When they arrived at Mattapoiset, the friendly
but half-starved Indians there refreshed them with a
small fish, a handful of parched corn, and a few clams.
The clams they gave to their six Indians, reserving

for themselves only the little fish and the handful of meal which by no means satiated their craving appetites. The Indians led them five miles out of their way, with the hope of obtaining food, but they found the place abandoned and no food there.

Hungry and weary they toiled along, and that night reached the wear at Titicut, on Taunton River. Here again they found famine. But one of the hospitable savages, who had speared a shad, and shot a small squirrel, gave half to the nearly famished travellers. In this starving condition they sent one of the Indians forward to Plymouth, imploring their brethren immediately to send an Indian runner to meet them at Namasket with food. Fortunately that evening a large number of fishes were caught in the wear, so that they feasted abundantly upon roasted fish, and their fatigue enabled them to sleep soundly in the open air. In the morning, after another ample breakfast of roasted fish, which their good appetites rendered palatable, they set out again upon their journey.

About two o'clock in the morning it had commenced raining with great violence, accompanied with thunder and lightning. The fire which the Pilgrims had built to keep their feet warm was extinguished, and, drenched with the rain and shivering with cold, they must have suffered severely had not their great fatigue rendered them almost insensible to the exposure. The storm of wind and rain raged unabated through the day. But they toiled on, wet and weary until, a little after noon, they reached Namasket. Here they found the provisions which their companions had sent them from Plymouth. Liberally they rewarded all who had shown them any kindness by the way. At night they reached home, wet, weary and footsore. They had been absent five days, leaving Plymouth Tuesday morning, and returning home Saturday evening, having spent Thursday with the renowned Indian monarch Massasoit.

CHAPTER VII.

Exploring Tours.

The Lost Boy.—The Expedition to Nauset.—Interesting Adventures.—The Mother of the Kidnapped Indians.—Tyanough.—Payment for the Corn.—Aspinet, the Chief.—The Boy Recovered.—Alarming Intelligence.—Hostility of Corbitant.—The Friendship of Hobbomak.—Heroic Achievement of Miles Standish.—The Midnight Attack.—Picturesque Spectacle.—Results of the Adventure. Visit to the Massachusetts.—The Squaw Sachem.—An Indian Fort.—Charming Country.—Glowing Reports.

We have before spoken of the notorious John Billington and his ungovernable family. His boy John, the same one who came so near causing the Mayflower to be blown up with gunpowder, got lost in the woods. The search to find him was unavailing. At last news came that he had, after wandering five days in the woods, living upon berries, been picked up by the Nauset Indians, the same who had attacked the Pilgrims at the First Encounter. Following an Indian trail he had reached a small Indian village, called Manomet, in the present town of Sandwich, about twenty miles south of Plymouth. The Indians treated him kindly, and took him with them still further down the Cape to Nauset, in the present town of Barnstable.

Massasoit sent word to Governor Carver where he was, and an expedition of ten men was immediately fitted out, in the shallop, to bring him back. It was a beautiful day, the latter part of July, when the boat sailed from Plymouth harbor on this short trip. They had not, however, been many hours at sea ere a tempest arose with vivid lightning and heavy peals of thunder. They ran, for shelter, into a place called Cummaquit, which was doubtless Barnstable harbor. Squantum and another Indian, by the name of Tokamahamon, accompanied them, as interpreters and aids.

It was night before they reached the harbor and cast anchor. The receding tide left them dry upon the flats. In the morning they saw several savages, on the shore, seeking for shell-fish. The two Indian interpreters were sent to communicate with them. They returned stating that the boy was well, but that he was several miles further down the Cape, at Nauset. The Indians also invited the white men to come on shore and eat with them. As soon as the returning tide floated the boat they drew near to the shore, and, cautiously taking four unarmed Indians on board as hostages, six of the voyagers landed. Here they had a very pleasant interview with the sachem, or chief of the tribe, a young man, by the name of Tyanough, but twenty-six years of age. He was very hospitable, and seemed to have but little of the savage in his nature. They describe him as "very personable, gentle, courteous and fair conditioned."

They met here with an aged Indian woman whom they judged to be not less than one hundred years old. She had never before seen a white man. As soon as she saw the English she burst into a convulsive fit of weeping. It appeared that she had three sons who had been lured on board the ship of the infamous Captain Hunt and kidnapped. They were carried off to Spain, and she had never heard any tidings from them. The Pilgrims spoke all the words of comfort to the poor bereaved mother which they could, assuring her that Captain Hunt was a very wicked man, whom God would punish; that all the English condemned him for his crime, and that they would not be guilty of the like wickedness for all the skins the country could afford. They made her some presents which quite cheered her.

After dinner they re-embarked, on such friendly terms with the natives that the chief and two of his men went on board with them to accompany them on the way. It was in the evening twilight when they reached Nauset, and the tide was out. The savages here seemed to be very numerous, and they crowded the shore. It is supposed that the point which they had reached here was in the present town of Eastham. The shallop touched the flats at quite a distance from the land. Tyanough, the chief of the Cummaquit Indians, and his two men, waded over the wet and sandy flats to the beach. Squantum accompanied them, to inform Aspinet, the chief of the Nauset Indians, of their object in coming. The savages manifested great eagerness of cordiality, flocked out to the boat, and expressed more than willingness to drag it over the flats to the shore. But the Pilgrims would not allow this. They had not full confidence in their sincerity. This was the same tribe which had so fiercely assailed them in the First Encounter.

They, therefore, warned the Indians off, and with their weapons stood guard, allowing but two to enter the boat. One of these was from Manamoick, now Chatham, and was one of the owners of the corn which the Pilgrims had taken. The Pilgrims received him with great kindness, and assured him that if he would come to Plymouth they would repay him abundantly, either in corn or other articles; or, if preferred, they would send the payment to the Indians. He promised to come to Plymouth.

Just after sunset Aspinet appeared upon the shore, leading the boy, and accompanied by a train of nearly one hundred men. Fifty of these, unarmed, came wading through the water to the side of the shallop, bringing the boy with them. The other fifty remained at a little distance, armed with bows and arrows, ready to meet any hostile demonstration. In token of peace, and of his desire to cherish friendly relations with the English, Aspinet had decorated the boy with Indian ornaments. The Pilgrims here received also the rather alarming intelligence that Massasoit had been defeated in a battle with the Narragansets. Seven men only had been left for the protection of the colony. It was feared that the hostile Narragansets might make an attack upon them. It therefore appears that as soon as the tide came in, that very night, they spread their sails for home. They made Aspinet the present of a knife, and also gave a knife to the Indian who first found the boy and protected him.

The route which they had followed along the shore was so circuitous that they estimated that they had reached a point eighty miles from Plymouth. The wind was contrary and their progress was slow. When they reached Cummaquit they put in ashore for water Here they found Tyanough, who, having returned by land, had reached the place before them. The obliging chief took their water cask upon his own shoulders and led them a long distance through the dark to a spring of not very sweet water. The shallop was anchored near the shore. The Indian women, in manifestation of their good will, sang and danced upon the beach, clasping hands.

Again they set sail, still encountering contrary winds, but at length they reached their home in safety Soon after their return, they learned that the defeat of Massasoit was more disastrous than had at first been reported. It seems that a portion of the Indians were much opposed to any friendly relations with the white men, and wished for the extermination of the colony. An Indian by the name of Hobbomak, who was chief of one of the minor tribes, had now strongly allied himself to the English. Consequently he and Squantum were peculiarly obnoxious to those of the savages who remained unfriendly.

One of Massasoit's petty chieftains, named Corbitant, led the hostile party. He was an audacious, insolent fellow, residing in the present town of Middleborough, at a point on the Namasket River just above the bridge, which passes from the Green to the Four Corners, on the Plymouth road. This man endeavored to excite a revolt against Massasoit, assailing the Pilgrims with the most opprobrious language, and storming at the peace which had been made with them by Massasoit and the tribes on the Cape. It seemed also that he was entering into an alliance with the Narraganset Indians against Massasoit and the Pilgrims.

Hobbomak was a war captain among the Wampanoags, and was greatly beloved by Massasoit. With Squantum he set out on a journey to visit Massasoit, with inquiries and words of cheer from the Pilgrims They were intercepted on their way by Corbitant, and both captured. Hobbomak, being a very powerful man, broke away and escaped. The next day, breathless and terrified, he reached Plymouth, reporting what had happened. On their journey they had entered a wigwam at Namasket, when suddenly the hut was surrounded by a band of armed savages. Corbitant himself, brandishing a knife, approached Squantum to kill him, saying, "When Squantum is dead the English will have lost their tongue." Just then Hobbomak escaped, and, outrunning his pursuers, reached Plymouth, not knowing the fate of his companion.

These were sad tidings, indicating that a very perilous storm was gathering. Governor Bradford immediately assembled all the men of the colony to decide what was to be done. After earnest prayer and deliberation, they were united in the opinion that, should they suffer their friends and allies to be thus assailed with impunity, none of the Indians, however kindly disposed, would dare to enter into friendly relations with them. They therefore resolved to send ten men, one-half of their whole number, under Captain Standish, with Hobbomak as their guide, to seize Corbitant and avenge the outrage. Never did a heroic little band set out upon a more chivalric adventure.

The morning of the 14th of August was dark and stormy. Regardless of wind and rain Captain Standish led his valiant companions in single file through the narrow and dripping paths of the forest. It was late in the afternoon when they reached a secluded spot within four miles of Namasket. Here they concealed themselves that they might suddenly fall upon their foe in the darkness of night. Cautiously Captain Standish, who was alike prudent and intrepid, led his band. Every man received minute instructions as to the part he was to perform. The night was so dark, with clouds and driving rain, that they could hardly see a hand's breadth before them. They lost their way, and after groping for some time in the tangled thickets, happily again found their trail. It was after midnight when, wet and weary, they arrived within sight of the glimmering fires of Namasket. After silently refreshing themselves from their knapsacks they crept along to the large wigwam, where they supposed that Corbitant, surrounded by several of his warriors, was sleeping. The darkness of the night and the wailings of the storm caused even the wary Indians to be deaf to their approach.

"At a signal, two muskets were fired to terrify the savages, and Captain Standish, with three or four men, rushed into the hut. The ground floor, dimly lighted by some dying embers, was covered with sleeping Indians, men, women, and children. A scene of indescribable consternation and confusion ensued. Through Hobbomak, Captain Standish ordered every Indian to remain in the wigwam, assuring them that he had come for Corbitant, the murderer of Squantum, and that, if he were not there, no one else should be injured.

"But the savages, terrified by the midnight surprise, and by the report of the muskets, were bereft of reason. Many of them endeavored to escape, and were severely wounded by the Pilgrims in their attempts to stop them. The Indian boys, seeing that the Indian women were not molested, ran around, frantically exclaiming, 'I am a girl! I am a girl!'

"At last order was restored, and it was found that Corbitant was not there, but that he had gone off, with all his train, and that Squantum was not killed. A bright fire was now kindled, that the hut might be carefully searched. Its blaze illuminated one of the wildest of imaginable scenes. The wigwam, spacious and rudely constructed of boughs, mats and bark; the affrighted savages, men, women and children, in their picturesque dress and undress, a few with ghastly wounds, faint and bleeding; the bold colonists, in their European dress and armor, the fire blazing in the centre of the hut, all combined to present a scene such as few eyes have ever witnessed." *

By this time all the inmates of the adjoining wigwams were aroused. Hobbomak in the darkness, climbed to the top of the wigwam and shouted aloud for Squantum. In his response to his well-known voice, Squantum soon appeared. Captain Standish deprived all the Indian warriors of their bows and arrows, and having established a watch, sought such repose as they could find until morning.

Many of these Indians were friendly to the English, and they, with the earliest light of the morning, gathered around Captain Standish. The hostile Indians, who belonged to the faction of Corbitant, fled during the night. It seemed, however, that a majority were disposed to be friendly, for a large group gathered around Captain Standish, with pledges of their good will. He addressed them in words of conciliation, and yet of firmness, assuring them that, though Corbitant had for the present escaped, if he continued his hostility he could find no retreat from the avenging hand of the white man. He also assured them that if the Narragansets continued the as-

* Abbott's Life of King Philip.

saults upon Massasoit or upon any of his subjects, the white men would punish them by the utter overthrow of their tribe. He expressed much regret that any of the Indians had been wounded, but told them that it was their own fault, as he had assured them that they should not be harmed if they would remain in the hut. He also offered to take home with him any who were wounded, that they might be carefully nursed. Two of the wounded availed themselves of this offer. The surgeon of the Pilgrim company, Mr. Samuel Fuller, tenderly cared for them.

Captain Standish led his triumphant little band back, accompanied by Squantum, and many other friendly Indians. The heroic achievement taught the friendly Indians that they could rely upon the protection of the white men, and was a loud warning to those who were disposed to be hostile. The enterprise occupied but two days. As the result of this adventure, many Sachems sent in the expression of their desire to enter into a friendly alliance with the Pilgrims. Corbitant himself was frightened by such an exhibition of energy, and by his own narrow escape. He sought reconciliation through the intercession of Massasoit, and subsequently signed a treaty of submission and friendship. Even Canonicus, the hostile and warlike chief of the Narragansets, sent an embassy to Plymouth, not improbably as spies, but with the professed object of treating for peace. The friendship of Massasoit, and his influence over the chiefs of the smaller tribes, contributed much to this happy result.

The Blue Hills of Milton were then called Mount Massachusetts. Many rumors had reached the colonists that the tribes residing in that vicinity, about forty miles north from Plymouth, were very unfriendly, had uttered many threats, and were preparing for hostile measures. The Pilgrims decided to send an expedition to that region, to establish, if possible, friendly relations with the natives, and they also wished to examine the country.

Captain Miles Standish was, of course, the one to be entrusted with the command of the important enterprise. He took a party in the shallop, of nine of the colonists, and three Indians, as interpreters, one of whom was Squantum. They set sail at midnight, in consequence of the favoring tide. It was Tuesday morning, the 18th of September, O. S. A gentle southerly breeze pressed their sails, and they glided over a smooth sea until they reached a point which they estimated to be about sixty miles from the port which they had left. As they had been informed that the tribes were numerous and warlike, as well as **unfriendly**, and it was a mild autumnal night, Captain Standish did not deem it prudent to land, but **they all remained** until morning in the boat.

They had entered a bay, which was doubtless Boston harbor, and anchored but a short distance from a cliff, which some have supposed to have been Copp's Hill, at the north end of Boston. This cliff rose about fifty feet from the water, and presented a precipitous front on the seaward shore.

The next morning they put in for the shore and landed.* Here they found quite a quantity of lobsters which the savages had collected, but for some unknown reason had left. Captain Standish, with characteristic prudence, left three men to guard the shallop, and stationed two as sentinels, in a commanding position on the shore, to give warning of any appearance of danger. Then, with characteristic enterprise and courage, taking four men with him, and an Indian as guide and interpreter, he entered one of the well-trodden trails of the forest and pressed forward in search of the habitations of the Indians. It was a bold deed; for, though they had guns, a hundred Indian warriors, shooting their barbed arrows from behind trees, would soon lay them all weltering in blood.

They had not gone far before they met an Indian woman who it seems, owned some of the lobsters,

---

* Mr. Drake, in his History of Boston, supposes that the "cliff" alluded to must have been that pile of rocks now called "the chapel," in Quincy Bay.

and was going to the shore to get them. But the colonists had feasted upon the savory food. They paid the woman, however, abundantly, to her entire satisfaction. She informed them that the small tribe to which she belonged, and whose chieftain's name was Obbatinewat, resided in a village a little farther along the coast. They therefore sent Squantum forward to the Indian village to inform Obbatinewat that the Pilgrims were coming to make him a friendly visit. Captain Standish returned to the shallop to continue their voyage to the settlement.

It required but a short sail. The Indian chief and his people, being prepared for their coming, received them kindly. It is a remarkable fact that the chief of the Massachusett tribe, probably the most powerful tribe then in these borders, was a woman— a squaw. Upon the death of her husband, Nanepashemet, she had been recognized as his successor. She was known as the Squaw Sachem, and was at war with Obbatinewat. Captain Standish offered his services to promote reconciliation. This was certainly magnaminious, for according to the principles of selfish worldly policy, it would have seemed expedient to keep the tribes warring against each other, thus to prevent their combining against the Pilgrims, and thus enabling the Pilgrims to retain what is called the balance of power. But Miles Standish, a straight-

EXPLORING TOURS. 159

forward, honest man, scorned all such arts of expediency.

Obbatinewat resided near the bottom of the inner Massachusetts Bay. He was ever trembling in view of the incursions of a powerful tribe of Indians, who resided on the Kennebec, the Penobscot, and other rivers of Maine. They came in great numbers in time of harvest, robbing them of their corn and committing all manner of savage outrages.

Very gladly Obbatinewat, who seems to have been an amiable, peace-loving man, availed himself of the friendly offer of Captain Standish, and, with some of his people, accompanied him in the shallop across the harbor, it is supposed from Quincy to what is now Charlestown, to visit the squaw sachem. Mr. Winslow describes the visit in the following words:

"Again we crossed the bay, which is very large, and hath at least fifty islands in it; but the certain number is not known to the inhabitants. Night it was before we came to that side of the bay where this people were On shore the savages went, but found nobody. That night also we rode at anchor aboard the shallop.

"On the morrow we went ashore, all but two men, and marched, in arms, up in the country. Having gone three miles we came to a place where corn had been newly gathered, a house pulled down, and the people gone. A mile from hence Nanepashemet, their king, in his lifetime, had lived. His house was not like others: but a scaffold was largely built with poles and planks, some six feet from the ground and the house upon that, being situated on the top of a hill

"Not far from here, in a bottom, we came to a fort, built by their deceased king; the manner thus: There were poles, some thirty or forty feet long, stuck in the ground as thick as they could be set one by another. With these they enclosed a ring, some thirty or forty feet long. A trench, breast-high, was digged on each side. One way there was to go into it with a bridge. In the midst of this palisade stood the frame of a house, wherein, being dead, he lay buried.

About a mile from here we came to such another, but seated on the top of a hill. Here Nanepashemet was killed; none dwelling in it since the time of his death. At this place we staid, and sent for two savages to look for the inhabitants, and to inform them of our ends in coming, that they might not be fearful of us. Within a mile of this place they found the women of the place together, with their corn on heaps, whither we supposed them to have fled for fear of us; and the more, because in divers places they had newly pulled down their houses, and for haste, in one place, had left some of their corn, covered with a mat, and nobody with it.

"With much fear they entertained us, at first; but seeing our gentle carriage towards them, they took heart, and entertained us in the best manner they could, boiling cod and such other things as they had for us. At length, with much sending for, came one of their men, shaking and trembling for fear. But when he saw we intended them no hurt, but came to truck, he promised us his skins also. Of him we inquired for their queen. It seemed that she was far from thence. At least we could not see her.

"Here Squantum would have had us rifle the savage women, and take their skins and all such things as might be serviceable for us; for, said he, they are a bad people, and have often threatened you. But our answer was, 'Were they never so bad, we would not wrong them, or give them any just occasion against us. For their words we little weighed them; but if they once attempted any thing against us, then we would deal far worse than he desired.'"

Having passed the day thus pleasantly, they returned to the shallop. Nearly all the women accompanied them. The Indians had quite a quantity of beaver skins, from which very comfortable garments were made. The Pilgrims were eager to purchase these skins, and the Indian women were so eager to obtain, in exchange for them, such articles as the English had to dispose of, that we are told "they sold their coats from their backs, and tied boughs about them, but with great shamefacedness, for indeed they are more modest than some of our English women are."

The savages reported that there were two rivers emptying into the bay, the Mystic and the Charles. The Pilgrims, however, saw but one, and they had not time to explore even that. They saw evidences that most of the islands in the harbor had been inhabited, having been cleared, and prepared for corn from end to end. But they were now desolate, the plague having swept the whole of their populations into the grave. The food of the exploring party becoming scarce, and there being a bright moon and a fair wind, they set sail in the evening, and by noon of the next day, Saturday, September 22d, they reached home, having been absent four days. Mr. Winslow was one of the party, and it is supposed that he wrote the account from which we have quoted.

The adventurers brought back so glowing a report of the harbor, with its beautiful and fertile islands, the rivers and the rich soil, that the colonists quite regretted that they had not found that spot for their settlement. "The country of the Massachusetts," said they, "is the paradise of all those parts, for here are many isles, all planted with corn, groves, mulberries and savage gardens.

The summer had passed away with the Pilgrims very pleasantly and prosperously. Friendly relations had been established with the Indians, and a lucrative traffic opened in valuable furs. There had been no want of provisions. Fishing had been successful, furnishing them with an abundant supply of cod and bass. Water fowl, such as ducks and wild geese, abounded, and the forests were filled with deer and turkeys. In the autumn they gathered in a fine harvest of corn, and though they had no mills to grind it, by hand-pounding they converted it into meal, with which they made very palatable cakes. Thus amply supplied with food, they made their houses more tight and comfortable, and gathered their fuel for the winter fires. They wrote home such glowing letters of their prosperity, that very many others were inspired with the desire to join them. One of these letters, written by Edward Winslow, will be given in the next chapter

CHAPTER VII.

Manners of Boston and Tea.

Arrival at the Pastures.—Diary of a Trip to the East Indies.—Character of the New Zealanders.—A Voyage; Letters.—First Thanksgiving.—Letter to [illegible]—Thomas Anderson.—Meeting Jackson.—The Morningstar.—James Richardson's Trip—Mr. Beecher.—Forty-ninth Psalm.—The Meeting of Council at the Island.—The Letter.—The Meeting Dismissed.

Early in July of that year, which was Plymouth's [illegible] worth of our life, there came across the [illegible] a ship sailed from London on the [illegible]. There were [illegible]-five passengers on board, [illegible] of whom appear to have been [illegible] adventurers, [illegible]ing to the New World through recklessness [illegible] or love of gain. The rest of this party represented the serious Pilgrims who were still living in Plymouth. Their aim [illegible] was exhibited in the [illegible] given adversely to the religious element which had hitherto prevailed in [illegible] Mr. Robert Cushman: "Reasons & the Reasons for Emigrating from England to America," he wrote.

"After long waiting we finally gave for the conveniences of the baggage, we were [illegible] whether there be not some [illegible] [illegible] [illegible] for us to make to convert them; or whether prayer for them be only referred to God's extraordinary work from Heaven. Now it seemeth unto me that we ought also to endeavor and use the means to convert them. And the means cannot be used unless we go to them or they come to us. To us they cannot come. Our land is full. To them we may go. Their land is empty This then is sufficient reason to prove our going thither to live, lawful."

The reckless men on board the Fortune, supposing that they should find an ample supply of everything in the New World, took with them scarcely provisions enough to last during the voyage. Contrary winds so retarded their progress that they did not clear the English channel until the end of August. It was not until the 9th of November that, in almost a famishing condition, they cast anchor in the harbor at the extremity of Cape Cod. Mr. Cushman, who had been left behind by the abandonment of the Speedwell, was with this party. The Fortune entered Plymouth harbor on the 23d of November. The Pilgrims were, of course, very happy to welcome such a re-enforcement from home. They were not then aware of the uncongenial elements of which it was composed. Mr. Bradford, in his account of this event, writes:

"Most of them were lusty young men, and many

of them wild enough, who little considered whither or about what they went, till they came into the harbor at Cape Cod, and there saw nothing but a naked and barren place.

"They then began to think what would become of them if the people here were dead, or cut off by the Indians. They then began to consult upon some speeches that some of the seamen had cast out, to take the sails from the yards lest the ship should get away and leave them there. But the master, hearing of it, gave them good words, and told them that if anything but well should have befallen the people here, he hoped he had victuals enough to carry them to Virginia; and that while he had a bit they should have their parts; which gave them good satisfaction.'

These men were landed at Plymouth in a state of great destitution. Of the thirty-five thus added to the colony twenty-seven were men. The remainder were women and children. Some of these men constituted a valuable addition to the colony; but others of them were utterly worthless. They brought with tnem no food, no furniture, no domestic utensils, no extra clothing; and, worst of all, no habits of industry or established principles of industry.

The Fortune remained at Plymouth but about a fortnight, and on the 13th of December commenced her return voyage. She took back, as freight, various kinds of timber, sassafras, and beaver skins. The estimated value of her cargo was about two thousand five hundred dollars. We may mention, in passing, that England was then at war with France. The Fortune, when near the coast of England, was captured by a French cruiser, relieved of her cargo, and sent home.

It will be remembered that there were but seven families composing the colony at the time of the arrival of the Fortune. The Governor disposed of these destitute and half famished new-comers, in these families, as best he could. The Pilgrims had, before this arrival, an ample supply of food for the winter. But upon this unexpected doubling of their number of hungry mouths, it was found, upon careful examinatisn, that their food was quite inadequate to meet their wants until another harvest. The fishing season was over; the summer game was gone; the harvest was all gathered in. There could be no more addition to their supply of provisions for many months. There could be nothing obtained from the Indians. The thoughtless creatures would themselves be hungry before another summer should come. Under these circumstances the Pilgrims, quite to their dismay, found it necessary to put the colony upon half allowance of food.

Before the arrival of the Fortune they were rejoicing in abundance. Now they found themselves upon the verge of famine. Mr. Edward Winslow wrote a letter to Mr. George Morton, probably the " G. Mourt," author of the celebrated " Relation." This letter was sent to England by the Fortune, on her return voyage, and was dated the 21st of December, 1621. It was consequently written just a year after the arrival of the Pilgrims. It gives a very glowing account of the prosperity of the colony, for it was written before the facts were ascertained consequent upon the irruption of the destitute adventurers in the Fortune. Its statements can, of course, be relied upon, as coming from one of the most illustrious of the Pilgrims, and one who had taken a conspicuous part in the scenes which he describes. It was as follows :

"Loving and Old Friend :

" Although I received no letter from you by this ship * yet forasmuch as I know you expect the performance of my promise, which was to write you truthfully and faithfully of all things, I have therefore, at this time, sent unto you accordingly, referring you for further satisfaction, to our large " Relations."

" You shall understand that, in the little time that a few of us have been here, we have built seven †

---

* The Fortune.

† It will be remembered that, as half of their number had died, seven houses accommodated the survivors.

dwelling houses, and four for the use of the plantation, and have made preparation for divers others. We set, the last spring, some twenty acres of Indian corn, and sowed some six acres of barley and pease. And, according to the manner of the Indians, we manured our ground with herrings, or rather shads, which we have in great abundance, and take with with great ease at our doors. * Our corn did prove well; and, God be praised, we had a good increase of Indian corn, and our barley indifferent good; but our pease were not worth the gathering, for we feared they were too late sown. They came up very well and blossomed, but the sun parched them in the blossom.

"Our harvest being gotten in, our governor (Bradford) sent four men on fowling, that so we might, after a special manner, rejoice together after we had gathered the fruit of our labors. They four in one day killed as much fowl as, with a little help beside, served the company almost a week. At which time,

---

* Morton, in his New English Canaan, writes: "There is a fish, by some called shads, that at the spring of the year pass up the rivers to spawn in the ponds, and are taken in such multitudes in every river that hath a pond at the end, that the inhabitants dung their ground with them. You may see in one township a hundred acres together set with these fish, every acre taking a thousand of them. And an acre thus dressed will produce and yield so much corn as three acres without fish."

It was the rule of the Indians to plant their corn when the leaves of the white oak were as big as the ear of a mouse. They put two or three fishes in every cornhill.

among other recreations, we exercised our arms, many of the Indians coming amongst us, and, among the rest, their greatest king, Massasoit, with some ninety men, whom for three days we entertained and feasted and they went out and killed five deer, which they brought to the plantation, and bestowed on our Governor and the Captain, (Standish,) and others "

In reference to this festival, we read, in the Life of Elder Brewster: "The provisions for the little colony being secured for the ensuing winter, their Governor set apart a day for public thanksgiving. Accordingly, with the fruits of their labors, the thankful feast was prepared, that all might, in a special manner, rejoice together, under a grateful sense of these tokens of divine mercy. It was their first thanksgiving or harvest festival in the New World. And we may well conjecture what were the feelings and what the theme of the Elder (Brewster), as, assembled in their Common House, he led the devotions of these worshippers, and spoke to them words befitting the occasion."

"We have found the Indians," continues Mr. Winslow, "very faithful in their covenant of peace with us; very loving and ready to pleasure us. We often go to them and they come to us. Some of us have been fifty miles by land in the country with them; the occasions and Relations whereof you shall understand, by one general and more full declaration of such things as are worth the noting. Yea, it hath pleased God so to possess the Indians with a fear of us, and love unto us, that not only the greatest king among them, called Massasoit, but also all the princes and peoples round about us, have either made suit unto us, or been glad of any occasion to make peace with us; so that seven of them, at once, have sent their messengers to us to that end. Yea, an isle,* at sea, which we never saw, hath also, together with the former, yielded willingly to be under the protection, and subjects to our sovereign lord, King James; so that there is now great peace among the Indians themselves, which was not formerly, neither would have been but for us.

"We, for our parts, walk as peaceably and safely in the woods as in the highways of England. We entertain them familiarly in our houses, and they as friendly bestow their venison upon us. They are a people without any religion, or knowledge of any God,† yet very trusty, quick of apprehension, ripe witted, just. The men and women go naked, only a

---

* Probably Martha's Vineyard, then called Capawock.
† Subsequently Mr. Winslow wrote, correcting this statement· "Whereas, myself and others, in former letters, wrote that the Indians about us are a people without any religion or knowledge of any God, therein I erred, though we could then gather no better."—Winslow's Good News.

skin about their middles. For the temper of the air here, it agreeth well with that of England. And if there be any difference at all, this is somewhat hotter in summer. Some think it to be colder in winter; but I cannot, out of experience, so say. The air is very clear and not foggy, as hath been reported.

"I never in my life remember a more seasonable year than we have here enjoyed. And if we have once but kine horses and sheep, I make no question but men might live as contented here as in any part of the world. For fish and fowl we have great abundance. Fresh cod in summer is but coarse meat with us. Our bay is full of lobsters all the summer, and affordeth variety of other fish. In September we can take a hogshead of eels in a night, with small labor, and can dig them out of their beds all the winter. We have muscles and clams * at our doors. Oysters we have none near; but we can have them brought by the Indians when we will. All the spring time the earth sendeth forth naturally very good salid herbs.

Here are grapes, white and red, and very sweet and strong also; strawberries, gooseberries, raspberries, etc.; plums of three sorts, white, black and red, being almost as good as a damson; abundance of roses, white, red and damask, single, but very sweet indeed.

* There is some uncertainty about this word, but this is probably the true reading.

"The country wanteth only industrious men to employ; for it would grieve your hearts if, as I, you had seen so many miles together, by goodly rivers, uninhabited, and withall to consider those parts of the world wherein you live to be even greatly burdened with abundance of people. These things I thought good to let you understand, being the truth of things as near as I could experimentally take knowledge of, and that you might on our behalf give God thanks who hath dealt so favorably with us.

"Our supply of men from you came the 9th of November, 1621, putting in at Cape Cod, some eight or ten leagues from us. The Indians, who dwell thereabout, were they who were owners of the corn which we found in caves, for which we have given them full content, and are in great league with them. They sent us word there was a ship near unto them, but thought it to be a Frenchman; and, indeed, ourselves, we expected not a friend so soon.

"But when we perceived she made for our bay, the Governor commanded a great piece to be shot off, to call home such as were abroad at work. Where upon every man, yea boy, that could handle a gun was ready, with full resolution that, if she were an enemy, we would stand in our just defense, not fearing them. But God provided better for them than we had supposed. These came all in health, not any being sick by the way, otherwise than by sea sickness, and so continue, at this time, by the blessing of God.

"When it pleaseth God we are settled and fitted for the fishing business and other trading, I doubt not but, by the blessing of God, the grain will give content to all. In the mean time, that which we have gotten we send by this ship; and though it be not much, yet it will witness for us that we have not been idle, considering the smallness of our number, all this summer.

"Now, because I expect your coming unto us,[*] with other of our friends, whose company we much desire, I thought good to advise you of a few things needful. Be careful to have a very good bread-room to put your biscuits in. Let your cask for beer and water be iron-bound, for the first tire, if not more. Let not your meat be dry salted; none can better do it than the sailors. Let your meal be so hard trod in your cask that you shall need an adz or hatchet to work it out with. Trust not too much on us, for corn at this time, for by reason of this last company that came, depending wholly upon us, we shall have little enough till harvest.

[*] Mr. George Morton, to whom this letter was addressed, came out in the next ship, the Ann, which sailed from London about the last of April, 1622.

"Be careful to come by some of your meal to spend by the way. It will much refresh you. Build your cabins as open as you can, and bring good store of clothes and bedding with you. Bring every man a musket or fowling-piece. Let your piece be long in the barrel, and fear not the weight of it, for most of our shooting is from stands. Bring juice of lemon, and take it fasting; it is of good use. For hot waters, aniseed water is the best; but use it sparingly. If you bring anything for comfort in the country, butter or sallet oil, or both, is very good. Our Indian corn, even the coarsest, maketh as pleasant meat as rice; therefore spare that, unless to spend by the way. Bring paper and linseed oil for your windows, with cotton yarn for your lamps. Let your shot be most for big fowls, and bring store of powder and shot."

The Pilgrims, it seems, had only oiled paper to keep out the storms of a New England winter. Eight years after this, the arts had made such progress that Mr. Higginson in the year 1629, in a letter addressed from Salem to his friends in England writes, "Be sure to furnish yourselves with glass for windows." Indeed, glass windows were not introduced into England until the year 1180. Then they were so costly that none but the most wealthy could have them. Even in the time of Henry VIII. they were considered a luxury which the common people could not think of enjoying.

One of the passengers in the Fortune, Mr. William Hilton, in a letter addressed to his friends at home, immediately after his arrival, having written in glowing terms of the richness of the country and the prospects of the colony, adds :

"We are all freeholders. The rent day doth not trouble us ; and all those good blessings we have of which and what we list in their seasons for taking. Our company are, for the most part, very religious, honest people. The word of God is sincerely taught to us every Sabbath ; so that I know not anything a contented mind can here want. I desire your friendly care to send my wife and children to me, where I wish were all the friends I have in England."

Mr. Hilton's family came in the next ship. Not only had the Fortune brought no supply to the colonists, but they were compelled to take from their own rapidly diminishing stores to supply the ship's crew with provisions for her return voyage. Another winter came. In the absence of all domestic animals such as horses, mules, cows, oxen, sheep, there was but little of the usual winter work of farmers which remained for the Pilgrims to perform. Fishing, hunting and the collection of fuel, which they drew with their own hands to their doors, occupied the most of their time.

On Christmas day rather an amusing event occur

red, which has been recorded by Governor Bradford. In the papal church and with the common people in England, Christmas had become a day of revelry, carousing and drunkenness. Ostensibly set apart as a religious festival, the depravity of man had so perverted it that, of all the days in the year, Christmas was the one most utterly abandoned to wickedness. Under these circumstances the Puritans, perhaps unwisely, deemed it expedient to abolish the observance of the day altogether.

On the morning of Christmas day the Governor, as usual on other days, went out with the Pilgrims of the Mayflower to their usual occupation in the fields. But some of the new-comers, idle and frivolous, and accustomed to the Christmas games of England, excused themselves from going into the field, saying that their consciences would not allow them to do any work on Christmas day.

The Governor replied that if it were a matter of conscience they might certainly be excused,—that he did not wish that any persons in the colony should have violence done to their religious convictions. He therefore left these men at home, while he went, with the rest of the colonists, to their daily toil. But when they returned at noon, they found these scrupulous men, whose consciences would not allow them to perform any useful labor on Christmas day, out in the streets engaged in all manner of old country sports. They were pitching the bar, playing ball, and engaged in games of petty gambling. Governor Bradford went to them, and by virtue of his office, took away from them their implements of gaming, saying:

"It is against my conscience that you should play while others work. If your religious convictions constrain you to observe Christmas, you should keep the day religiously, at home or in the church. But there must be no gambling or revelry on that day."

This settled the question, and there were no more demands for an idle or riotous Christmas.

Soon after the departure of the Fortune, in the depth of winter, painful rumors came that the powerful Narragansets, under their redoubtable Chief, Canonicus, were assuming a threatening attitude. The English had now about fifty men capable of bearing arms, and not a large supply of ammunition. The Narragansets could bring against them five thousand warriors. They occupied the region extending from the western shores of Narraganset Bay to Pawcatuck River and the tribe was estimated to number about thirty thousand. The Pilgrims, all counted, men, women and children, were less than one hundred in number. This was a fearful cloud of war with which they thus found themselves menaced.

While such was the position of affairs, one day a

strange Indian entered the settlement. It soon appeared that he was a Narraganset. He seemed not a little embarrassed, and enquired for Squantum, the interpreter. It seemed some relief to him to learn that he was absent. He then left for him a bundle of arrows, wrapped up in the skin of a rattlesnake, and was hastily departing, when Governor Bradford, wishing to know the significance of this strange conduct, ordered Captain Standish to detain him. He was arrested and entrusted to the safe keeping of Mr. Winslow and Mr. Hopkins. Captain Standish gave orders that he should be treated with the utmost kindness, supplied with everything he needed, and while assured that he should not be harmed, Mr. Winslow and Mr. Hopkins should endeavor to obtain from him a full and minute account of the object of his strange mission.

At first he was so terrified that he could scarcely speak a word. But gradually regaining composure, he stated that the messenger who had been sent to the Pilgrims in the summer with terms of peace, had brought back such tidings of the weakness of the colony that Canonicus was encouraged to seek its destruction; that he was angry in consequence of the alliance of the colonists with his enemies, the Wampanoags; that he professed to despise the meanness of the presents sent to him by the Governor, and scorned to receive them; and that the arrows and the rattlesnake skin were to be understood as his declaration of war.

It is worthy of notice that this savage chieftain should have had such a sense of honor as to send this warning to his foes, instead of treacherously falling upon them when unprepared. And it is also remarkable that this challenge should have been so similar to that which, in ancient days, the Scythian prince sent to Darius, which consisted of five arrows.

When the Governor and Captain Standish were informed of the results of the interview, they justly regarded their captive as an innocent messenger, whom, in accordance with all the laws of war, they were to hold unharmed. They therefore, after offering him food, which he refused to eat, set him at liberty, directing him to say to Canonicus, that while they wished to live at peace with all men, and while they had done him no harm, they were indignant in view of his threatenings, had no fear of his power, and bade him defiance.

A violent storm was raging. But, notwithstanding the storm and the entreaties of the Pilgrims, that he would remain with them until it should abate, he refused to accept of their hospitality, and soon disappeared, travelling with all speed through one of the trails of the drenched and surging forest.

The Pilgrims held a council. It was deemed important that no timidity whatever should be manifested, but that they should present a bold front to their foes. In the mean time Squantum had returned to aid them with his counsel. After some deliberation, they sent a friendly Indian, as a messenger, to Canonicus, returning to him his rattlesnake skin, filled with powder and bullets. This was a defiance which would be understood. The superstitious savage chief was quite alarmed by this response. Squantum, who appears to have been quite a meddling, unscrupulous man, had declared to the Indians that the English had a box in which they kept the plague, and that if the Indians offended them they would let the awful scourge loose. They still retained a very vivid recollection of the horrors of the pestilence which had swept over them.

Canonicus feared that the snake-skin contained some secret and fatal charm for his destruction. He dared not touch it. He dared not attempt to destroy it. He dared not allow it to remain in his house or country. And thus it was conveyed from place to place until finally it was returned whole to the colony at Plymouth.

Notwithstanding the brave attitude the colonists had assumed, they had great cause for uneasiness. They promptly decided that it was necessary to sur round the whole of their little village with a palisade consisting of strong posts, ten or twelve feet high, planted in the ground in contact with each other This palisade also included a portion of the top of the hill, where their ordnance was planted, and at the bottom of which their village was built. There were three gates of entrance, which were locked every night, and carefully guarded every day. Captain Standish divided his whole force into four companies of about twelve men each, and appointed a captain over each band. A general muster was appointed, which was the first general muster in New England. At this gathering, Captain Standish reviewed his troops and gave minute directions to each company where to assemble and what to do in case of alarm. The months of January and February were devoted incessantly to fortifying their little village, the work being completed early in March.

Captain Standish, in his visit to the Massachusetts, had informed the natives that he would soon visit them again, to purchase such furs as they might have collected. It was deemed important now to fulfill this promise, one principal object being to impress the Indians with the conviction that the colonists had no fear of them. It was also rumored to them that the several tribes of Massachusetts Indians, and that even their friends the Wampanoags, under Massa soit, were entering into the confederacy of the Narraganset's against the white men. The friendly Indian, Hobbomak, who resided with the Pilgrims at Plymouth, seemed deeply impressed with the conviction that the Massachusetts Indians were hostile, and assured Captain Standish that should he attempt a journey to Massachusetts, he would be surely cut off by the savages. He gave many plausible reasons in support of the correctness of his views, and even declared that Squantum, in whom they reposed much confidence, was treacherously their foe, aiding the Indians; and that Squantum would endeavor to draw them as far as possible from their shallop, that the Indians might fall upon them and destroy them. He however did not believe that Massasoit meditated any treachery.

The Governor, Captain Standish, and few others of the most judicious men held a council together, and came to the following conclusion, which I give in the words of Edward Winslow, who was one of the council:

"That as hitherto, upon all occasions between the Indians and us, we had ever manifested undaunted love and resolution, so it would not now stand with our safety to mew ourselves up in our new-enclosed town; partly because our store was almost empty, and therefore we must seek out our daily food, without which we could not long subsist; but especially that thereby they would see us dismayed and be encouraged to prosecute their malicious purposes with more eagerness than ever they had intended.

"Whereas, on the contrary, by the blessing of God, our fearless carriage might be a means to discourage and to weaken their proceedings. And therefore we thought best to proceed in our trading voyage, making this use of what we had heard, to go the better provided, and use the more carefulness both at home and abroad, leaving the event to the disposing of the Almighty; whose providence, as it had hitherto been over us for good, so we had now no cause, save our sins, to despair of his mercy in our preservation and continuance, where we desired rather to be instruments of good to the heathen about us, than to give them the least measure of just offense."

In accordance with this resolve, early in April Captain Standish took ten men, with Squantum and Hobbomak as interpreters, and set out in the shallop for what is now Boston harbor. In Plymouth bay there is a remarkable promontory, connected with Marshfield by a beach, now called Salt-house beach, about six miles long. The extremity of this promontory was call Gurnet's Nose, from its resemblance to a similar point of land on the coast of England. The peninsula contains about twenty-seven acres of good land, and, upon its southern extremity, there have since been erected two light-houses.

Just as the shallop was doubling Gurnet's Nose, an Indian, who was one of the family of Squantum, came rushing in apparent terror, his face covered with blood, to some of the Pilgrims at work in the woods, looking behind him as if pursued, and calling upon them to hasten with all possible speed within the protection of the palisades. Breathlessly he told them that at Namasket, now Middleborough, within fifteen miles of Plymouth, a war party of Narragansets and Wampanoags, united under Massasoit, the professed friend, but treacherous foe, of the colonists, was marching to attack them. He said that he had been attacked and wounded for speaking friendly words in behalf of the colonists, and that by breaking away he had narrowly escaped death.

Upon receiving this startling intelligence, the Governor ordered the cannon upon the hill to be instantly discharged to recall the shallop. The day was calm, the boat had been retarded in its progress, and the report, booming over the still waters of the bay, reached the ears of the crew just as the shallop was disappearing around the point of Gurnet's Nose. Captain Standish immediately returned, the whole military force of the colony was at once called into requisition and measures were adopted for a vigorous defense.

Upon the return of the shallop, Hobbomak, who was with Captain Standish, declared, with great positiveness, that the rumor was false. He said that he was sure that Massasoit would prove faithful to his pledges; that it was impossible that he could undertake such an enterprise without communicating his intentions to his sub-chiefs, of whom Hobbomak himself was one of the principal. This tended rather to increase the suspicions of the colonists that Squantum might be playing a double part.

To ascertain the facts, the wife of Hobbomak, who seems to have been a very intelligent and reliable woman, was sent as a secret agent or spy to Pokanoket, the seat of Massasoit, to inform herself respecting the true posture of affairs, and to bring back a report. Her difficult and important mission she performed very creditably. Finding there everything quiet, and no indication whatever of any hostile movement, she frankly informed Massasoit of the rumors which had reached the ears of the Pilgrims. He was very indignant in being thus traduced, threw much blame upon Squantum, and expressed his gratitude that the Governor had not distrusted him. He requested the squaw to assure the Governor that he would prove faithful to his treaty obligations, and that should he see any indications of hostility in any quarter he would immediately give the Governor warning

CHAPTER IX.

The Weymouth Colonists.

The Double-Dealing of Squantum.—False Alarm.—Voyage to Massachusetts.—Massasoit Demands Squantum.—The Arrival of the Boat.—The Virginia Massacre.—Preparations for Defense.—Arrival of the Charity and the Swan.—Vile Character of the Weymouth Colonists.—Arrival of the Discovery.—Starvation at Weymouth.—Danger of the Plymouth Colony.—Expeditions for Food. Death of Squantum.—Voyage to Massachusetts and the Cape.

Speaking of the apprehended double-dealing of Squantum, Mr. Winslow writes:

"Thus, by degrees, we began to discover Squantum, whose ends were only to make himself great in the eyes of his countrymen, by means of his nearness and favor with us, not caring who fell so he stood. In the general, his course was to persuade them he could lead us to peace or war at his pleasure, and would oft threaten the Indians, sending them word in a private manner that we were intending shortly to kill them, that thereby he might get gifts to himself to work their peace; insomuch that they had him in greater esteem than many of their sachems. So that whereas divers were wont to rely on Massasoit for protection, and resort to his abode, now they began to leave him and seek after Squantum.

"Now, though he could not make good these, his large promises, especially because of the continued peace between Massasoit and us, he therefore raised this false alarm, hoping, while things were hot in the heat of blood, to provoke us to march into his country against him; whereby he hoped to kindle such a flame as would not easily be quenched; and hoping if that block were once removed, there were no other between him and honor, which he loved as his life, and better than peace."

The above is undoubtedly the true explanation of the strange conduct of Squantum. The Governor very severely reprimanded him for his trickery. Massasoit was so indignant that he sent a messenger to Plymouth, entreating that Squantum might be put to death. The Governor admitted that he deserved death, but he could not possibly be spared. As he alone understood both languages, without him there could scarcely be any intercourse between the Pilgrims and the Indians.

"It was, perhaps," writes Francis Baylies, "after all, but natural for Squantum, who does not appear to have possessed much influence with the natives, at the time of the arrival of the English, to endeavor to make the most of their favor. His knowledge of the English language gave him a decided advantage over all others. His own small tribe had been exterminated by the plague. He was a solitary man, unaided by the influence or favor of kindred, and he only used the means which fortune had placed in his hands to acquire wealth, consideration and influence. Another of his devices, to magnify the power of the English, and consequently his own, was to persuade the natives that the English had buried the plague in their store-house, and that they could loose it at will, and ravage the whole country. The apprehension of this kept the Indians in great fear." *

The alarm created by this false rumor having subsided, Captain Standish again set out with his party to visit Massachusetts. It is to be regretted that we have not a detailed account of the incidents which occurred upon this voyage. The only record we have is contained in the few following words, by Mr. Winslow:

"After this, we proceeded in our voyage to the Massachusetts, where we had good store of trade; and, blessed by God, returned in safety, though driven from before our town in great danger and extremity of weather." †

Upon their return in May, they found Massasoit still in a state of great excitement in reference to the

---

* Memoir of the Colony of Plymouth, by Francis Baylies. Part the First, page 91.
† Winslow in Young; p. 290.

conduct of Squantum. By the treaty, which the English had entered into with the Indian King, both parties were bound to surrender criminals. Squantum, as an adopted member of the Wampanoag tribe, was a subject of Massasoit. The Indian chief now sent an imposing delegation to Plymouth, formally demanding the surrender of Squantum, that, in accordance with Indian law, he might be put to death as a traitor. With the delegation, he sent executioners to cut off Squantum's head and hands, and to bring them to him. In token of his friendship for the English he sent to the Governor a rich present of beaver skins.

Governor Bradford was much embarrassed. He sent for Squantum. The culprit, though fully aware of the object of the Indian envoys, and even that Massasoit had sent his own knife, with which to cut off his head and hands, made no effort to escape. With true Indian stolidity he yielded himself to the Governor to be delivered to death, or not, as he might think best.

The terms of the treaty seemed clear. The Governor decided that he could not, without violating his solemn pledge, refuse to surrender Squantum to Massasoit. He was just about to make this surrender, which would have resulted in the immediate death of the Indian, and which, of course, created the most intense excitement in the little colony, when all were startled by the apparition of a shallop, under full sail, rounding Hither Monomet Point, which constituted the southern boundary of Plymouth Bay. A panic pervaded the colony. It was feared that it was a French boat, accompanying some French man-of-war, and that they were approaching in concert with the Indians for the destruction of the colony. Every man sprang to arms. Captain Standish mustered his whole force for defence. It might be that the hostile Indians would rush upon them in an hour. There was no doubt that Squantum, with all his great imperfections of character, was the friend of the English. His services as interpreter, under these circumstances, became more important than ever. Governor Bradford therefore informed the envoys that he could not deliver Squantum to their custody. This roused their indignation. "Being mad with rage," writes Mr. Winslow, "and impatient at delay, they departed in great heat."

It was soon ascertained, greatly to the relief of the colonists, that the shallop belonged to an English fishing vessel, called the Sparrow. The ship had been fitted out by Mr. Thomas Weston, a London merchant, and brought seven passengers to be landed at Plymouth. The vessel, engaged in fishing, had cast anchor at a place called Damari's Cove, near Monhegan, upon the coast of Maine, about one hundred and twenty miles northeast from Plymouth. This was famous fishing ground, and there were, at that time, thirty-five vessels riding at anchor there. The Sparrow, while most of her crew were engaged in fishing, had sent her shallop to convey the seven passengers to Plymouth.

The boat brought seven more mouths to be fed, and no provisions. It was the last of May, 1622 The colonial store of food was almost entirely consumed, and for a long time the colonists had been placed upon very short allowance. This boat brought a very friendly letter from the captain of the Swallow, John Huddston, communicating the startling intelligence that the Indians in Virginia had risen against the colony there on the 22d of March, and four hundred of the Indians had been massacred. There could be no doubt that this success of the Indians in Virginia would be speedily communicated to all the tribes; and that it would inspire the hostile Indians in New England with the desire to imitate their example.

The crew of the shallop had barely provision sufficient to serve them until their return to the ship. The destitution of food in the colony was so great that the colonists were threatened with absolute starvation. The Governor therefore sent Mr. Winslow in the shallop with a small crew, to the fishing vessels, to obtain from them, if possible, some supplies. The boat from the Swallow led the way. The fishermen were very generous. Though they had but a scant supply of provisions for themselves, yet with an abundant store of fish on board, they were in no danger of starving. They refused to take any pay for the contributions they furnished to meet the wants of the Pilgrims. Governor Bradford writes:

"What was got, and this small boat brought, being divided among so many, came but to a little. Yet by God's blessing it upheld them till harvest. It arose to but a quarter of a pound of bread a day to each person. The Governor caused it to be daily given them; otherwise, had it been in their own custody, they would have eaten it up and then starved. But thus, with what else they could get, they made pretty shift until corn was ripe." *

The question naturally arises, How was it possible that the colonists should find themselves in a state of such utter destitution, in a country so overflowing with abundance as Mr. Winslow's letter has described, where the forests were filled with game and the waters with fish. We will allow Mr. Winslow himself to reply to this question.

"I answer, everything must be expected in its proper season. No man, as one saith, will go into an orch

* History of Plymouth Plantation, by William Bradford, p. 127.

ard in the winter to gather cherries. So he that looks for fowl there, in the summer, will be disappointed. The time they continue plenty with us is from the beginning of October to the end of March. But these extremities befell us in May and June. I confess that as the fowl decrease, so fish increase. And, indeed, their increasing abundance was a great cause of increasing our wants. For, though our bays and creeks were full of bass and other fish, yet, for want of fit and strong seines, and other netting, they for the most part broke through, and carried all away before them. And, though the sea were full of cod, yet we had neither tackling nor hawsers for our shallops. And, indeed, had we not been in a place where divers sorts of shell fish are that may be taken with the hand, we must have perished, unless God had raised some unknown or extraordinary means for our preservation." *

Mr. Winslow, upon his return from the fishing fleet, found the colony in great weakness. The hostile Indians were not blind to this. The massacre in Virginia had roused their savage natures, and many insulting speeches, by them, were reported to the English. Even Massasoit was disposed to frown, being sorely displeased at their refusal to surrender Squantum, according to the terms of the treaty.

The menaces of war had become so serious that

* Young's Chronicles of the Pilgrims, p. 295.

Captain Standish deemed it necessary immediately to increase and strengthen their fortifications. They at once set to work to build a strong fort upon Burial Hill, within the limits of their palisades. It consisted of a large, square building, with a strong flat roof, made of thick planks, supported by oaken beams. Upon this roof they placed their cannon, commanding all the approaches. The large room below served them for a church. Their mode of assembling for public worship is described by Isaac de Rassieres, who visited Plymouth in 1627:

"They assemble," he writes, "by beat of drum, each with his musket or firelock, in front of Captain Standish's door. They have their cloaks on, and place themselves in order, three abreast, and are led by a sergeant without beat of drum. Behind comes the Governor, in a long robe. Beside him, on the right hand, comes the preacher, with his cloak on; and on the left hand the Captain, with his side arms and cloak on, and with a small cane in his hand. And so they march in good order, and each sets his arms down near him."

Early in July two trading ships from London, the Charity and the Swan, entered Plymouth harbor These ships brought fifty or sixty emigrants, who intended to settle in the country as the agents of a company in England. It was their object to establish a colony to trade with the Indians. The expedition was fitted out by Mr. Thomas Weston, a wealthy merchant in London, and hence the new-comers were generally called Weston's men. Many of them were utterly devoid of principle, profane and profligate Mr. Cushman wrote in reference to them :

"They are no men for us, and I fear that they will hardly deal so well with the savages as they should. I pray you, therefore, to signify to Squantum that they are a distinct body from us, and we have nothing to do with them, nor must be blamed for their faults, much less can warrant their fidelity."

Mr. John Pierce wrote respecting them : "As for Mr. Weston's company, they are so base in condition for the most part, as in all appearance not fit for an honest man's company. I wish they might prove otherwise."

At the time of the arrival of these rude and hungry adventurers, the Pilgrims had their gardens filled with growing vegetables, and they had sixty acres planted with corn, just then in the green ear At that time, when boiled or roasted, it made very palateable food. But it was wasteful to use it in that state unless there were great abundance. When ripened it contained much more nutriment, and would go much farther in feeding the hungry. But these wretched men, though received hospitably by the

Pilgrims, and treated with the utmost kindness, requited them by robbing their gardens and their cornfield. Their little growing harvest was thus most cruelly wasted. Indeed these godless wretches seemed wantonly to destroy the growing crop. Having no religion of their own, and only a God to swear by, they insulted, with oaths and ribald jests, those devout men, who daily looked in prayer to God for guidance, and whose voices were often blended in Christian hymns.

The Pilgrims seem to have been more grieved in view of the influence the conduct of these men would exert upon the savages, than by the outrages to which they themselves were exposed. Mr. Winslow wrote:

"Nevertheless, for their master's sake, who formerly had deserved well from us,* we continued to do them whatever good or furtherance we could, attributing these things to the want of confidence and discretion, expecting each day when God, in his providence, would disburden us of them, sorrowing that their overseers were not of more ability and fitness for their places, and much fearing what would be the issue of such raw and unconscionable beginnings." †

The Charity, which was the larger ship, having put these men ashore, continued her voyage to Vir-

---

* Mr. Weston had formerly befriended the plantation at Plymouth.
† Winslow in Your.g, p. 297.

ginia. The rabble crew remained, an almost intolerable burden upon the Pilgrims, during nearly all the summer. An expedition was fitted out to explore Massachusetts Bay, in search of a suitable location for Mr. Weston's colony. The expedition at length returned, recommending a place in Boston harbor, called by the Indians Wessagusset, but to which the name of Weymouth was subsequently given.

Inexpressible was the satisfaction of the Pilgrims when they saw these miscreants take their departure. They however left behind them quite a number of sick persons, whom the Pilgrims nursed with true Christian benevolence, placing them under the care of their own skilful physician, Dr. Fuller, and, as they recovered, sending them, without any charge, to their own distant colony.

But immediately after these men landed at Weymouth, complaints came to the ears of the Pilgrims of innumerable acts of violence and injustice which they were perpetrating. They stole the corn of the Indians, insulted their females in the grossest manner, and in all things seemed to regard the Indians as not entitled to any rights which white men were bound to respect. The Pilgrims were the more annoyed by these atrocities, since the Indians disposed to be friendly, had entreated Captain Standish to establish a colony of white men in their country, who could teach them many arts, and to whom they could sell their corn and furs. Their outrages, reported from tribe to tribe, tended also to exasperate everywhere the undiscriminating Indians against the English. But the Pilgrims had no power to redress these abuses. They remonstrated earnestly; but their remonstrances were in vain. The outrages were continued unabated.

The Weston men had brought scarcely any supplies with them. Before a month had passed they were actually in a starving condition. They had no harvest to gather in; winter was coming upon them, and death by famine stared them in the face. To add to their misery, anarchy reigned there, and the colony consisted of a rabble of profane, ungovernable men, in constant quarrels among themselves. These men had also so wasted and consumed the supplies upon which the industrious Pilgrims had been relying for the winter, that the Plymouth colony was also in great danger of perishing from want.

When in this alarming condition, and when the minds of the Pilgrims were agitated with great anxiety in view of the future, two ships, at the end of August, came into Plymouth harbor. One of them, the Discovery, was commanded by Captain Jones, formerly of the Mayflower. The other was one of Mr. Weston's small fishing vessels, the Swan, which had returned from a fishing expedition, and was bound for Virginia Providentially, Captain Jones had quite a large supply of provisions. He had never been in cordial sympathy with the Pilgrims, and now he very ungenerously took advantage of their great necessities Though the Pilgrims were consequently compelled to pay an exorbitant price for everything they obtained of him, still they were enabled to purchase such supplies as would save them from actual starvation. Mr. Winslow writes:

"And had not the Almighty, in His all-ordering providence, directed him to us, it would have gone worse with us than ever it had been, or after was. For as we had now but small store of corn for the year following, so, for want of supply, we were worn out of all manner of trucking stuff, not having any means to help us by trade. But, through God's good mercy towards us, he had wherewith, and did supply our wants, on that kind, competently." *

In consequence of the destitution of Mr. Weston's colony at Weymouth, the Swan was sent there, with a considerable supply of provisions, and with articles to trade with the Indians in exchange for corn The Swan was also left with the colony, to be used for coasting purposes. But not a month had passed before these reckless spendthrifts had squandered all

* Young's Chronicles; p. 299.

their provisions, and were again starving. And they were in such poor repute with the Indians that none dared venture into the colony with corn to sell, lest they should be robbed.

A man by the name of John Sanders was the leading man, a sort of governor over the Weymouth colony. He wrote to Governor Bradford, wishing to unite with him in an excursion along the eastern and southern coast of Cape Cod, to purchase corn of the Indians. He would furnish the vessel for the voyage, the Swan, but the colony at Plymouth must furnish the men to trade with the Indians and the articles for traffic. The corn was to be equally divided between them. He promised to repay the Pilgrims for such trading commodities as they should contribute, when the next supplies came from Mr. Weston.

The promises of such a man were of but little value. The Weymouth colony was already in a hopelessly ruinous condition. But the Pilgrims were well aware that they were daily in danger of an irruption of the whole vagabond gang to eat out their substance, and to fill their peaceful village with clamor and violence. They had far more to fear from these wretched colonists than from the savages. Policy therefore, as well as humanity, urged it upon them to do everything in their power to supply the wants of Weston's men, and thus keep them at a distance

Captain Standish, with a small crew, took command of the Swan for this trading expedition along the outer coast of Cape Cod. Squantum accompanied them as interpreter and pilot. They had succeeded in reconciling Massasoit to him. They set sail the latter part of September. But so violent a gale arose that they were compelled to put back, having suffered considerable harm. It took some time to repair damages, when again they weighed anchor. Squantum proved a very poor pilot. They were entangled among the shoals, and retarded by contrary winds ; and, to add to their calamities, Captain Standish was seized with a violent fever. Thus they were compelled a second time to put back, not having accomplished anything.

These delays brought them to the month of November. The captain continuing quite sick, Governor Bradford himself took command of the vessel. The Governor had but little confidence in Squantum's knowledge of the coast. Still he had to look to him alone, for no one else knew anything of the region. At last, much bewildered and in peril, they ran into an harbor with which Squantum was familiar, at a place called, by the Indians, Manamocki, now Chatham.

The Governor, accompanied by a small party, with Squantum for interpreter, went on shore that night.

THE WEYMOUTH COLONISTS.

But no Englshmen had visited the region before, and the natives, terrified by the sight of the vessel, had fled. Through Squantum, the Governor gradually succeeded in making his friendly intentions known, and cautiously they gathered around him. They brought venison and corn in considerable abundance, and seemed very glad to exchange them for the valuable articles which Governor Bradford offered in return. Still they manifested much fear of their visitors, and were very unwilling to let them know where their dwellings were. And when they found that the Governor intended to remain on shore all night, they suddenly disappeared, running to their wigwams, and carrying all their valuables away with them.

Again, through the intervention of Squantum, confidence was partially restored. The Governor was so successful in his trade that he purchased of them, though but a few and scattered people, eight hogsheads of corn and beans. Such facts seemed to indicate that all of the Indians did not depend so much upon the chase for sustenance as has generally been supposed. While thus engaged Squantum was taken sick of a fever, and, after a few day's illness, died. He was heard to pray, and he asked Governor Bradford to pray that God would take him to the heaven of the Englishmen. All his valuables he bequeathed to his English friends, as remembrances of his love. His death was considered a great loss to the colony Judge Davis, commenting upon it, writes:

"Governor Bradford's pen was worthily employed in the tender notice of the death of this child of nature. With some aberrations his conduct was generally irreproachable; and his useful services to the infant settlement entitle him to grateful remembrance."

The death of Squantum left the Governor without either pilot or interpreter. He did not venture, therefore, to go any further south, where he would encounter innumerable shoals, and where he would find himself among strange Indians. These considerations induced him to turn to the north. He was acquainted with the waters of Massachusetts Bay, and the Indians residing on those shores were in friendly relations with the Pilgrims. Indeed, they had been induced to plant more corn than usual, that they might have the means to purchase the valuable articles which the Pilgrims could offer them in exchange.

With a fair wind they soon entered Boston harbor. Here they found, to their grief, a fearful pestilence raging among the Indians, and many of them were dying. Bitter complaints were also brought to the Governor respecting the Weymouth colonists. The Massachusetts Indians were so exasperated by the infamous conduct of these men, that they were plotting for their utter extermination, many intending to follow up the massacre of the Weymouth colonists by the destruction of the Plymouth colony also. They were in no mood for peaceful traffic.

The Governor, therefore, speedily weighed anchor and spread his sails for Nauset, on the inner shore of Cape Cod. It will be remembered that the Pilgrims had formerly found some corn stored there, which, in their great need they took, but for which they afterwards fully paid the Indians. Captain Standish had also visited the region in search of the lost boy. Aspinet, the chief of the tribe, residing there, was very friendly. They landed in a small bay, between Barnstable and Yarmouth harbors. They had hardly made their port when a terrible storm arose. The gale was so furious that, notwithstanding their shelter, they came very near shipwreck. The shallop, attached to the Swan, was torn from them and driven they knew not where. This was a great calamity. The shoal water rendered it necessary to cast anchor at some distance from the shore, according to their estimate nearly six miles, and they had now no means of bringing on board such provisions as they might purchase. They had indeed one small boat, but it was so small and leaky that they scarcely ventured to go ashore in it, even in the most pleasant weather, for wood and water.

The Governor, however, opened a very successful trade with the Indians. He seems to have had much confidence in their honesty, for, having purchased a large quantity of corn, he stored it away, simply covering it with mats, and hired a neighboring Indian to watch and protect it from vermin till he could return and fetch it. In the meantime Aspinet had sent his men to traverse the shore in search of the shallop, which the storm had wrenched from them. It was found at the distance of several miles, much broken, and half buried in the sand at high water mark. It was entirely unserviceable until it should be repaired by a ship carpenter, and there was no carpenter on board the Swan.

The Governor, for some unexplained reason, decided to return to Plymouth by land, a distance of fifty miles. He took with him a single Indian guide, and traversing the wilderness on foot through the Indian trails, reached Plymouth in safety, weary and footsore. The Indians on the way treated him with great respect and hospitality. Three days after his arrival the Swan entered the harbor, and the portion of corn she had brought, which, by the division, belonged to the Weymouth colony, was immediately sent in the vessel to them.

Captain Standish having now recovered his health, took another shallop and a ship carpenter, and sailed in the Swan, which came back to Plymouth from Weymouth, across the bay to Nauset, to fetch the corn which they had stored there, and to repair and bring home the wrecked shallop. He found all safe. While the carpenter was repairing the shallop, he was busy with the other boat, transporting the corn out to the vessel, which, as we have mentioned, it was necessary to anchor at quite a distance from the shore.

It was the month of January, cold and stormy. The exposure and the labor were painful, for often the sea was very rough. The coast of Eastham, off which the Swan lay, abounds with creeks. Into one of these the shallop ran to take in its load. While in the creek one day, an Indian stole some beads, scissors, and other trifles from the boat. Captain Standish took one or two of his men with him, and going to the sachem, demanded the restitution of the articles, or he should take the law into his own hands and obtain redress. With this menace he left the chief, refusing to receive any hospitality from him. It so happened that the thief was known, and the sachem could, without difficulty, restore the stolen articles, were he disposed to do so.

The next morning Aspinet came to Captain Standish with a very imposing retinue. Both he and his men sa'uted the Captain, in the style of Indian homage, kissing his hand, indeed licking it, and bowing the knee very humbly before him. He then delivered up all the articles which had been taken, expressed his deep regret at the occurrence, and assured Captain Standish that the thief had been severely beaten for his crime. In token of his regret and friendship, the Indian women were ordered to bring to the Captain quite a supply of freshly-baked corn bread.

The Swan returned to Plymouth with about twenty-eight hogsheads of corn and beans, which were equally divided between the two colonies, as before. In the two colonies there were now about one hundred and fifty hungry mouths to be fed. Of course such a supply would soon disappear. It became immediately necessary to fit out new expeditions in search of food.

CHAPTER X.

The Sickness of Massasoit and End of the Weymouth Colony.

Search for Corn.—Trip to Buzzard's Bay.—Interesting Incident.—Energy and Sagacity of Captain Standish.—Hostile Indications. Insolence of Witeewamat.—The Plot Defeated.—Sickness of Massasoit.—The Visit.—Gratitude of the Chief.—Visit to Corbitant.—Condition of the Weymouth Colony.—The Widespread Coalition.—Military Expedition of Captain Standish.—His Heroic Adventures.—End of the Weymouth Colony.

The Governor soon took one or two men and went to Middleborough, the Namasket of the Indians, to purchase corn. It all had to be brought home in sacks upon the back. The Indian women aided in transporting it. The Pilgrims were astonished to see what burdens they would bear. "It is almost incredible," writes Roger Williams, "what burdens the poor women carry of corn, of fish, of beans, of mats, and a child besides." An Indian woman, of small stature, would take a hundred weight of corn upon her shoulders and trudge through the wilderness for miles without resting. But a small supply of corn could be obtained at Namasket.

The Governor then took an inland trip of sixty miles to an Indian settlement called Manomet, at the head of Buzzard's Bay. The distance across the cape here to Massachusetts Bay is but six miles. They could, after that short land carriage, by an easy voyage in the boats, transport their corn to Plymouth Here the Governor purchased quite a supply, which he left in the custody of the sachem, Canacum, until the boats could be sent to fetch it. While here, an incident occurred which is worthy of record, as illustrative of Indian customs :

It was the month of February. The night was bitterly cold, a fierce storm raging. The Governor was in the snug wigwam of the sachem, sitting by the bright fire blazing in the centre of the hut. Two stranger Indians entered. Without speaking a word they laid aside their bows and arrows, sat down upon the mats by the fire, took out their pipes and began to smoke. Having finished their pipes, one of them made a short address of greeting to the chief, and presented him with a basket containing tobacco and some beads. The chief received the gift graciously. The Indian then, in quite a long speech, delivered his message, which was interpreted to the Governor by Hobbomak. It was as follows :

Two Indians of the tribe to which the messengers belonged, while gambling, quarrelled, and one killed the other. The murderer was a man of special note, and one who could not be well spared. His chief

SICKNESS OF MASSASOIT.

was unwilling to order his execution. But the sachem of another powerful tribe had declared that unless he put the offender to death he would wage war against him with all his force. The chief therefore desired the advice of his powerful friend, Canacum, as to the course it was proper for him to pursue.

There was then, for some time, silence. At length Canacum asked the opinion of all who were present. When Hobbomak was questioned, he said: "I am a stranger; but it seems to me better that one should die than many, especially since that one deserves death, and the many are innocent." Canacum then directed the messengers to inform their sachem that in his opinion the murderer should be put to death.

The Governor returned to Plymouth, intending to send Captain Standish in the shallop, to fetch the corn which he had purchased. Just after his arrival, a messenger came from John Sanders, in Weymouth, stating that the colonists there were actually in a starving condition; that they could obtain no corn from the Indians, as the Indians would not lend it to them, and that they had no means of buying. Under these circumstances he said that he should be under the necessity of taking it from them by force. Weak as the colonists were, by the aid of powder and bullets, they could, without difficulty, rob the comparatively defenceless Indians. The Governor remonstrated in the strongest terms against this plan of robbery. He assured Sanders that such an act would inevitably combine all the tribes in a coalition against both colonies and might lead to the utter extirpation of the English from this continent. From his own scanty store of corn he sent to Weymouth a small supply, entreating them to make shift to live, as they did at Plymouth, upon ground-nuts, clams, and muscles.

In the mean time, Captain Standish took the shallop and sailed to Sandwich harbor, to get the corn which the Governor had purchased and ordered to be stored there. It was in the severest of winter weather. Icy gales swept the ocean, and dashed the surge upon the snow-drifted beach. They succeeded in entering the harbor, but the first night they were frozen up there. The outrageous conduct of the Weymouth colonists, and the threats which they had openly uttered of their intention to rob the Indians, had spread far and wide, producing great exasperation; and the natives who were adverse to the colonists were taking advantage of it to form a general coalition against them.

Captain Standish, upon landing, perceived at once that there was a change coming over the minds of the Indians. The friendliness they affected appeared to him constrained and insincere. He was frozen in and large numbers of Indians began to gather around him, some manifestly unfriendly; and there were not a few indications that a conspiracy was being formed for his destruction. The weather was so cold that the Pilgrims could not sleep in the shallop, but were constrained to accept the shelter and the fires found in the Indian wigwams.

The captain was not a man to be taken by guile. Avoiding all display of his suspicions, he gave strict charge that a part of the company should always watch by night while the rest slept. Some of the Indians stole several articles from the boat. Captain Standish immediately marched his whole force of six men, and surrounded the wigwam of the sachem, where many of the most prominent of the Indians were assembled. He then sent in word to the sachem that as he would not allow himself, or any of his men, to be guilty of the slightest injustice towards the Indians, neither would he submit to any injustice from them; that he held the sachem responsible for the stolen goods, and that unless they were immediately restored he should obtain redress by force of arms.

The crafty sachem sent agents who, without difficulty, obtained the goods and secretly conveyed them to the shallop. He then told Captain Standish that probably he had overlooked them, and he thought that if he should look more carefully he would find that they were all there. The captain, understanding this, sent to the shallop, and there the stolen goods were, lying openly upon the boat's cuddy. The sachem however was much alarmed by this decision and boldness manifested by the captain. In endeavors to win back his favor he brought to him quite an additional quantity of corn to sell. The captain loaded down his shallop with the treasure; and, a southerly wind freeing the harbor of ice, he returned in safety to Plymouth.

A portion of this supply was forwarded to Weymouth. It soon, however, was consumed, and, impelled by want, in March, Captain Standish again took the shallop and returned to Manomet, hoping to get an additional supply of food. He met with a chilling reception, and with increasing evidence that the Indians were plotting against the colonists. He soon found the explanation of this. Leaving three men in charge of the shallop, he took three with him, and went to the wigwam of Canacum, the sachem. While there, two Massachusett Indians came in. They were from the immediate vicinity of Weymouth, violent and hostile men, and had come to Canucum to engage him and his warriors in a coalition against the English.

"The chief of them," writes Mr. Winslow, "was called Wituwamat, a notable insulting villain, one who had formerly imbued his hands in the blood of English and French, and had often boasted of his own valor, and derided their weakness, especially because, as he said, they died crying, making sour faces, more like children than men."

This boastful fellow, in the presence of Captain Standish, presented Canacum with a dagger, which he had obtained from the Weymouth men. He then addressed him in a long speech, in a language which he knew that the Captain could not understand, but in a tone and with gestures which could not but be considered insulting. The purport of this address, as afterwards interpreted, was as follows:

We have decided to exterminate the weak and starving colony at Weymouth. We are strong enough to do it any day. But we fear that the colony at Plymouth will avenge the death of their countrymen. It is therefore necessary to destroy both colonies. To do this we must unite our tribes against them We now come to solicit your aid. The redoubtable Captain of the Plymouth colony is now with you, with six of his men. They can all easily be killed. This will make our work easy.*

Canacum was evidently impressed by this speech. He neglected Captain Standish, and treated his Indian guest with marked distinction. A plot was

---

* Young's Chronicles, p. 310.

formed for the assassination of the whole boat's crew
The Indians stood in deadly fear of the muskets of
the English, and did not dare approach the shallop
with hostile intent. The Captain did not allow any
armed men to draw near them. The Indians tried to
lure them all on shore, saying that it was too cold for
them to sleep in the shallop. They hoped to fall
upon them, in sudden massacre, while asleep in the
huts. With this purpose in their hearts they feigned
great friendship, made presents to Captain Standish,
and with alacrity aided in carrying corn to the shallop. The Captain evaded all their wiles, and a fair
wind soon bore him back again to his friends.

While he was absent, word came to Plymouth that
Massasoit was very dangerously sick, and that his
death was daily expected; and also that a Dutch ship
had been driven ashore almost opposite his dwelling.
It was a custom with the Indians that when any chief
was sick, all his friends should hasten to visit him.
In observance of this custom, and also to obtain some
intercourse with the Dutch, and hoping also to secure
the friendship of the neighboring sachems, it was decided that Mr. Winslow and Mr. Hampden, with
Hobbomak as a guide, should visit the dying chief at
his home in Paomet.

It was a perilous journey in the then unsettled
state of affairs. It was not known who of the Indians

were friendly, and who were hostile. The death of Massasoit might bring the hostile party into power, and then there would be hardly a possibility that the two envoys could escape with their lives. Hobbomak, who had embraced Christianity, and was apparently a consistent Christian, seemed to be deeply grieved in view of the death of his chief. He said to Mr. Winslow,

"I shall never see his like again. He was no liar; he was not bloody and cruel, like other Indians. In anger and passion he was soon reclaimed. He was easy to be reconciled to those who had offended him. Ruled by reason, he scorned the advice of mean men, and governed his people better with few strokes than others did with many. When he is gone the English will not have a true and faithful friend left among the Indians."

Massasoit had two sons, Wamsutta and Pometacom. According to Indian usage, upon the death of the father, the eldest son inherited the chieftainship. But it was feared that Corbitant, who had already manifested hostility, and in whose assumed reconciliation but little reliance could be placed, would by violence grasp the power, and bring the whole weight of the tribe against the colonists.

The deputation traveled the first day as far as the little Indian hamlet of Namasket, which, it will be remembered, occupied the present site of Middlebor ough. They passed the night in the wigwam of an Indian. The next day they continued their journey to Mattapoisit, in the present town of Swanzey. Here Corbitant resided. The rumor had already reached them that Massasoit was dead. There were indications that Corbitant had already taken steps as an usurper, and there were serious apprehensions that the two defenceless Englishmen would immediately fall victims to his hostile policy.

The two envoys, however, to avoid all appearance of suspicion, went directly to Corbitant's house. The sachem was not at home, but his wife received them kindly. They sent forward an Indian runner to Paomet, to bring them back tidings respecting the condition of Massasoit. He returned with the tidings that the chief was still living when he left, but was expected every moment to die. They hurried on, and reached Paomet late at night. In the following terms Mr. Winslow describes his visit to the dying chief:

"When we came thither we found the house so full of men as we could scarce get in, though they used their best diligence to make way for us. There were they in the midst of their charms for him, making such a hellish noise as it distempered us that were well, and therefore unlike to ease him that was sick. About him were six or eight women, who chafed his arms, legs and thighs, to keep heat in him. When they had made an end of their charming, one told him that his friends, the English, were come to see him. Having understanding left, but his sight being wholly gone, he asked who was come. They told him *Winsnow*, for they cannot pronounce the letter *l*, but ordinarily *n* in the place thereof. He desired to speak with me. When I came to him, and they told him of it, he put forth his hand to me, which I took. Then he said twice, though very inwardly, *Keen Winsnow*, which is to say, Art thou Winslow? I answered, *Ah he*, that is, Yes. Then he doubled these words, *Matta neen wonckanet namen, Winsnow!* that is to say, O Winslow, I shall never see thee again." *

Mr. Winslow then informed the dying chief, through Habbomak, that the Governor was sorry to hear of his sickness, and would have visited him in person had not important business prevented; that he had consequently sent Mr. Winslow and Mr. Hampden in his stead, with such medicines as the English used in case of sickness. Mr. Winslow administered these medicines, which proved so wonderfully efficacious that soon his patient quite revived, his sight was restored, and he was able to take some refreshing broth. All the Indians were surprised and del'ghted by the change. Two Indians were sent to Plymouth for more medicine, and for two

* Young's Chronicles, p. 318.

chickens for broth. They were dispatched at two o'clock in the morning, bearing letters informing the Governor of the success of their mission. Mr. Winslow gives the following account of his medical practice on this important occasion:

"He requested me that, the day following, I would take my piece and kill him some fowl, and make him some English pottage, such as he had eaten at Plymouth. After, his stomach coming, I must needs make him some without fowl, before I went abroad. This somewhat troubled me, being unacquainted and unaccustomed in such business, especially having nothing to make it comfortable, my consort being as ignorant as myself. But being we must do somewhat, I caused a woman to bruise some corn and take the flour from it, and set over the broken corn in a pipkin, for they have earthen pots of all sizes.

"When the day broke we went out, it being now March, to seek herbs, but could not find any but strawberry leaves, of which I gathered a handful and put into the same. And because I had nothing to relish it, I went forth again and pulled up a sassafras root, and sliced a piece thereof and boiled it till it had a good relish, and then took it out again. The broth being boiled, I strained it through my handkerchief, and gave him at least a pint, which he liked very well After this his sight mended more and more; and he took some rest, insomuch that we with admiration blessed God for giving his blessing to such raw and ignorant means; making no doubt of his recovery, himself and all of them acknowledging us the instruments of his preservation." *

The grateful chief requested Mr. Winslow to visit all the sick in his village, and to administer to them the same remedies which had been so available in his case. With true Christian philanthropy Mr. Winslow undertook this task, finding it needful to perform many revolting offices, from which he did not shrink. With the utmost tenderness he watched the fluctuations of the disease of the king, and administered remedies apparently with much intuitive skill. Having succeeded in shooting a duck, just before the men returned with the pigeons, Massasoit decided to preserve them alive for breed. His recovery excited so much astonishment that many persons came a hundred miles to see him. Great efforts had been made by the hostile Indians to prejudice him against the English, and to induce him to join their coalition.

"Now I see," he said, "that the English are my friends, and love me. And whilst I live I will never forget this kindness they have showed me. They have been more kind to me than any others have been."

* Young's Chronicles, p 320.

As Mr. Winslow was leaving, Massasoit called Hobbemak privately to him, one or two of his warriors only being present, and informed him in full of the plot of the Massachusetts Indians to destroy the Weston colony, and then to attack that at Plymouth. He mentioned seven tribes who were united with them in the coalition, among others mentioning some who were making loud professions of friendship. He said that he had been earnestly solicited to join them, but that he would not do so, neither would he allow any of the tribes under his sway to make any hostile movement.

Massasoit advised the pilgrims, through Hobbomak, that if they would save the lives of their countrymen, they should immediately put to death the leading men of the Massachusetts tribes who were organizing this formidable conspiracy. "Say to them," said he, "that they often say that they will never strike the first blow. But if they wait until their countrymen at Weymouth are killed, who are entirely unable to defend themselves, it will then be too late for them to protect their own lives. I therefore advise them, without any delay, to put the leaders of this plot to death. Communicate what I say to you to Mr. Winslow, on your way home, that he may relate the same to Governor Bradford."

Very affectionately the two parties took leave of

each other. The envoys were disappointed in not meeting the Dutch; but the day before their arrival, a high tide enabled them to move the ship from the shoals, upon which it had been stranded, and they had proceeded on their voyage. The Pilgrims called upon Corbitant on their return, and passed the night with him. He received them with great apparent cordiality. Mr. Winslow gives the following pleasing account of the visit.

"I had much confidence with him; he being a notable politician, yet full of merry jests and quibs, and never better pleased than when the like are returned upon him. Among other things he asked me, if in case he were thus dangerously sick, as Massasoit had been, and should send word thereof to Plymouth for medicine, whether the Governor would send it; and if he would, whether I would come therewith to him. To both which I answered, yea; whereat he gave me joyful thanks.

"After that, he demanded further how we durst, being but two, come so far into the country. I answered, where was true love there was no fear; and my heart was so upright towards them that, for my own part, I was fearless to come amongst them.

"'But,' said he, 'if your love be such, and it bring forth such fruits, how cometh it to pass that when we come to Plymouth, you stand upon your guard, with the mouths of your pieces presented towards us.'

"Whereupon I answered it was the most honorable and respective entertainment we could give them, it being an order amongst us so to receive our best respected friends. And as it was used on the land, so the ships also observed it at sea, which Hobbomak knew and had seen observed. But, shaking his head, he answered that he liked not such salutations."

Noticing that Mr. Winslow asked a blessing upon his food, and returned thanks after partaking of it, he asked him the meaning of the custom. He listened very attentively to Mr. Winslow's account of the ten commandments and of the Christian religion, and expressed his cordial approval of nearly all. The next day the Pilgrims continued their journey, and lodged that night at Middleborough. The next day, when they had reached about half way home, they met two Indians, who informed them that Captain Standish had that morning set sail for Massachusetts, but that contrary winds had driven him back. Upon their arrival, they found Captain Standish waiting for a fair wind to resume his voyage.

It was the latter part of February. The news from the Weston colony was continually becoming more disastrous. These wretched adventurers were sinking into degradation almost beneath that of the savages. John Sanders had taken the Swan, and, with a small crew, had sailed for the coast of Maine, hoping to obtain some food from the fishermen there. The religionless rabble, left behind, sold their clothes and bed coverings for food. They became servants to the insolent Indians, cutting wood and bringing water to them for a cup full of corn. They stole, night and day, from the Indians. Several died from cold and hunger. One man was digging clams. He got stuck in the mud, and was so weak that he could not extricate himself, and miserably perished. They scattered, wandering about in search of ground nuts and shell-fish, and became utterly despicable, even in the eyes of the savages.

"They became contemned and scorned by the Indians," writes Governor Bradford, "and they began greatly to insult over them in the most insolent manner; insomuch, many times, as they lay thus scattered abroad, and had set on a pot with ground nuts or shell-fish, when it was ready, the Indians would come and eat it up. And when night came, whereas some of them had a sorry blanket or such like to lap themselves in, the Indians would take it, and let the others lie all night in the cold; so as their condition was very lamentable. Yea, in the end they were fain to hang one of their men, whom they could not reclaim from stealing, to give the Indians content."*

A waggish report was circulated, with which Hudibras makes himself merry, that, the thief being a man of some importance, who could not well be spared, a poor decrepit old man, who was utterly unserviceable, was hung in his stead. There was no truth in this report. And it was still more atrocious, as a calumny, when attributed to the Pilgrims. It cannot be denied, however, that the deed would have been in character with the conduct of the Weymouth miscreants. They were not Puritans. There is no evidence that they had any church, any divine worship, or any religion.

The state of the Weston colony caused much anxiety at Plymouth. The savages were learning to despise the English. It was necessary to take some very decisive action, and yet it was difficult to determine what that action should be. Captain Standish's voyage was delayed, to wait for further developments, and many consultations were held. At length, on the 23d of March, the Governor assembled the whole company of the Pilgrims in general council, and, expressing the deepest regret that it seemed to be necessary to resort to warlike measure against those whose good only they sought to promote, proposed that Captain Standish should take so many

* Bradford's Plymouth Plantation; p. 130.

well-armed men as he judged to be necessary, and, assailing the Indians with the same weapons of guile which they were persistently using, should go to Massachusetts as if for trade with the Indians. On the way he was to visit Weymouth and inform the people there of the plot which was formed against them, and of the object of his coming, and to invite them to embark on board the Swan, and come to Plymouth for protection. He was then to visit the Indians, carefully scrutinize their conduct, and adopt such measures to thwart their plans and punish their ringleaders as in his judgment might seem expedient. He was particularly requested to bring back with him, as a warning to all the savages, the head of that bold and bloody villain Wituwamat, of whom we have before spoken, who was loud and boastful in his threats, and undisguised in his measures to array all the Indians against the English.

Captain Standish took eight men only, selecting those in whose courage and discretion he could repose perfect reliance. The day before he was to sail, a man by the name of Phineas Pratt came from Weymouth, through the woods, with his pack upon his back. He brought a deplorable report of the degradation and helplessness of the colonists. They were dispersed in three companies in search of food, and were almost destitute of powder and shot. He had fled from the impending ruin, and begged permission to remain at Plymouth.

The next day the wind was fair, and Captain Standish set sail on his difficult and perilous expedition. They entered the harbor at Weymouth, and proceeded first to the Swan, which was at anchor there, " but neither man, or so much as a dog therein." The discharge of a musket attracted the attention of the master of the vessel, who was on shore, with some of the colonists, searching for ground nuts. Upon Captain Standish reproaching them with their carelessness in leaving a vessel so important to their safety thus exposed, they replied, like men bereft of reason, that they had no fear of the Indians. The Captain gathered around him as many of the colonists as he could, and informed them of the plot then ripe for their massacre. He then gave them the invitation, on the part of the Governor and all the colonists, to repair to Plymouth, where they would share their scanty food with them until some better plan for their welfare could be devised. A more heroic act of hospitality than this the world has seldom witnessed. He also added that if there were any other plan which they preferred to adopt, he would do everything in his power to aid them in it.

These wretched men gladly accepted the generous offer which rescued them from the tomahawk of the savage, and decided at once to abandon the colony. Captain Standish then enjoined upon them the most entire secrecy in respect to their contemplated movement. The stragglers were all to be immediately called in, and ordered not to leave the town under penalty of death. A pint of corn was allotted to them each day, though this had to be taken from the store which the Pilgrims had reserved for planting.

The weather was cold, wet and stormy, and thus Captain Standish was much delayed in his operations. The Indians, hearing of the arrival of the shallop from Plymouth, sent a spy to Weymouth, ostensibly to sell some furs. Though the Captain treated him with the customary courtesy, the sagacious savage returned with the report that "he saw, by his eyes, that he was angry in his heart." But the Indians had become so emboldened that they hesitated not to use any language of insolence and menace. One of the vilest of them, a fellow of gigantic stature, by the name of Pecksuot, with Wituwamat and his brother, came swaggering into the little village. "Tell your Captain," said he, "that we know that he has come to kill us. But we do not fear him. Let him begin as soon as he dares. We are ready for him."

These three men, with another Indian, followed by quite a mob of the savages, entered one of the houses, where Captain Standish was with four of the

Pilgrims. The object, evidently, was to provoke a quarrel, and murder the Englishman. Captain Standish was a slender man, of small stature. Pecksuot was almost a giant. The savage approached him, whetting his knife, and boasting of his power to lay the ' little man " low. The other Indians were equally insuing and threatening, with both word and gesture. The Captain, perfectly preserving his calmness and self-possession, ordered the door to be shut and fastened, that no other Indians could come in. Then, giving the signal to the others of his men, he sprang, with the wonderful strength and agility for which he was celebrated, upon the burly savage, wrenched the knife, which was sharp as a needle at the point, from his hand, and after a desperate conflict, in which he inflicted many wounds, succeeded in plunging it to the hilt in the bosom of his foe. In like manner Wituwamat and the other Indian, after the fiercest struggle, during which not a word was uttered, were killed. Wituwamat's brother, a boastful, blood-thirsty villain of eighteen, was taken and hanged, for conspiring for the massacre of the English.

The Indians around the house, appalled by so unexpected an exhibition of courage and power, fled into the wilderness. Captain Standish marshalled his whole force to pursue. The Indians rallied in an advantageous position, and made a brief stand. But, three of their number falling before the bullets of the Englishmen, they again turned, and on swift foot disappeared.

The Weymouth men, aware of their danger of suffering from hunger in Plymouth, decided to embark in the Swan for the fishing fleet on the coast, hoping there to obtain provisions to enable them to return to England. It was probably an acceptable decision to the Captain. Retaining simply corn enough for his homeward trip, he gave all the rest he had with him to them. A few decided to go to Plymouth, whom the Captain took with him. Having seen the Swan set sail, and fairly clear of Massachusetts Bay, the conquering hero spread his sail, and was soon greeted by his friends for his success in his chivalric adventure. Thus the godless colory at Weymouth came to an ignoble end.

CHAPTER XI.

Domestic and Foreign Policy.

Letter from Rev. Mr. Robinson.—Defense of Captain Standish.—New Policy Introduced.—Great Destitution.—Day of Fasting and Prayer.—Answer to Prayer.—The First Thanksgiving.—The Colony at Weymouth.—Worthless Character of the Colonists.—Neat Cattle from England.—Captain Standish Sent to England.—Captain Wollaston and His Colony.—Heroism of Captain Standish.—Morton Vanquished.—Difficulty at Cape Ann.—Increasing Emigration.—The Division of Property.

When the Rev. Mr. Robinson, the Pilgrims' former pastor in Holland, heard of these sanguinary scenes, he was greatly afflicted. Captain Standish was not a church member, and Mr. Robinson feared that he had acted with the impetuosity of the soldier, and not with the forbearance of the Christian. He wrote to the Pilgrims:

"It is necessary to bear in mind the disposition of your captain, whom I love, who is of a warm temper. I had hoped that the Lord had sent him among you for good, if you used him right. He is a man humble and meek among you, and towards all in ordinary course. But I doubt whether there is not wanting that tenderness of the life of man, made after God's image, which is meet. O how happy a thing had it been that you had converted some before you had killed any."

To this it was replied that two of the Indians, Squantum and Hobbomak, it was hoped, had already become Christians; that Captain Standish was the military commander of the colony, and in a sense responsible for its safety; that the measures he adopted were purely in self-defense, and that in no other way could he possibly have saved the colonies from massacre. Captain Standish took back with him the head of Wituwamat, which was placed upon the fort as a warning to all hostile Indians. This measure has been severely censured. But it is replied that the savages, whose bloodthirsty desires were fully roused, could be influenced by deeds only, and not by words; that no people should be blamed for not being in advance of the age in which they lived, and that more than a century after this, in the year 1747, in refined and Christian England, the heads of the lords, who were implicated in the Scots rebellion, were exposed upon Temple Bar, the most frequented avenue between London and Westminster. Judge Davis, in his New England's Memorial, commenting upon Mr. Robinson's letter, writes:

"These sentiments are honorable to Mr. Robinson. They indicate a generous philanthropy, which must always gain our affection, and should ever be cherished. Still the transactions, to which the strictures relate, are defensible. As to Standish, Belknap places his defense on the rules of duty imposed by his character as the military servant of the colony. The government, it is presumed, will be considered as acting under severe necessity, and will require no apology if the reality of the conspiracy be admitted, of which there can be but little doubt. It is certain that they were fully persuaded of its existence; and with the terrible example of the Virginia massacre in fresh remembrance, they had solemn duties to discharge. The existence of the whole settlement was at hazard.

As we have mentioned, the unintelligent Indians often behaved like children. This energetic action seemed to overwhelm all those tribes with terror, who were contemplating a coalition with the Massachusetts Indians against the English. They acted as if bereft of reason, forsaking their houses, fleeing to the swamps, and running to and fro in the most distracted manner. Many consequently perished of hunger, and of the diseases which exposure brought on. The planting season had just come. In their fright they neglected to plant; and thus, in the autumn, from want of their customary harvest of corn, many more perished.

Tyanough, who, the reader will recollect, was sachem of the tribe at Mattakiest, the country between Barnstable and Yarmouth harbors, had been drawn into the conspiracy. He sent four men, in a boat, to the Governor, at Plymouth, with a present, hoping to appease his anger. The boat was cast away. Three were drowned. The one survivor went back, no' daring to show himself at Plymouth. The Indians regarded the disaster as evidence of the anger of the Englishman's God.

The month of April 1623 had arrived. It was necessary immediately to prepare the ground for planting. The Pilgrims had but a scanty supply of corn reserved for seed. Scarcely a kernel could be spared for food. Until now necessity had compelled the Pilgrims to act in partnership, having a common store of corn to be equally distributed, the fields being cultivated in common. It was now deemed best that each man should have his own lot, to possess whatever amount his industry might raise. As the wants of the Colony rendered it necessary that some should devote all their time to fishing, and there were certain other public employments which would engross the time of individuals, a small tax, in corn, was imposed, to defray these public expenses.

About the middle of April they began to plant, the weather being very favorable. Each man took about an acre of land. Without ploughs, or the aid of cattle, this was all one man could cultivate. Immediately the advantages of individual property, instead of having a community of interest, was manifest. All the boys and youth were ranged under some family. This created a new scene of active industry. Much more corn was planted, it is said, than would have been otherwise. Even the women went willingly into the field to aid in planting, taking their little ones with them. The situation of the colonists, at this time, seems to have been deplorable. Governor Bradford writes:

"By the time our corn is planted our victuals are spent; not knowing, at night, where to have a bit in the morning, and have neither bread nor corn for three or four months together, yet bear our wants with cheerfulness. Having but one boat left, we divide the men into several companies, six or seven in each, who take their turns to go out with a net and fish, and return not till they get some, though they be five or six days out, knowing there is nothing at home, and to return empty would be a great discouragement. When they stay long, or get but little, the rest go a digging shell fish. And thus we live in the summer, only sending one or two to range the woods for deer. They now and then get one, which we divide among the company. In the winter we are helped with fowl and ground nuts." *

* Bradford in Prince, p. 216.

The friends in England sent a supply ship, the Paragon, to the suffering colony. Three months passed, and no tidings were received of her. But fragments of wreck were picked up, which indicated her fate. It afterwards appeared that, having reached six hundred miles from land, she encountered a terrible gale, by which she was so much disabled as to be compelled to put back. Again she set sail, and again put back, with all her upper works carried by the board. A disastrous drouth, of six weeks continuance also ensued, which threatened the utter destruction of their corn crop. Inevitable starvation seemed to stare them in the face. Mr. Winslow writes:

"The most courageous were now discouraged, because God, who had hitherto been our only shield and supporter, now seemed, in his anger, to arm himself against us. And who can withstand the fierceness of his wrath?" *

In this extremity a day of fasting and prayer was appointed. It was the middle of July. The morning was cloudless, without a sign of rain. The sky was as brass, scarce a green herb was to be seen, and the earth was as ashes. The exercises of devotion continued for eight hours. All felt alike that there was no help but in God. Elder Brewster,

* Young's Chronicles p. 349.

an Israelite indeed, in whom there was no guile preached. Mr. Winslow writes:

"The exercises, on this special occasion, as of life and death, being continued eight hours or more, ere their close the clouds gathered, the heavens were overcast, and before the next morning passed, gentle showers were distilling upon the earth, and so it continued some fourteen days, with seasonable weather intervening. It were hard to say whether our withered corn or drooping affections were most quickened and revived, such was the bounty and goodness of our God."

Unexpectedly the withered corn thrust out green leaves and gave promise of a joyful harvest. Even the Indians were impressed with this evidence of divine interposition. Hobbomak said feelingly:

"Now I see that the Englishman's God is a good God, for he hath heard you and sent you rain, and without storms, tempest or thunder beating down your corn. Surely your God is a good God."

In the mean time, Captain Standish was sent out, with the shallop, and a few men, to explore the coast and purchase all the corn he could of the Indians. Valiant as he was in fight, he was, in ordinary life, a mild and gentle man, and eminently just in all his dealings. Much as the Indians dreaded his avenging arm, they seemed to be fully conscious that he would do them no wrong. Early in August he returned from this trading-voyage, with his shallop well loaded down with corn, which proved invaluable to the Pilgrims until their own harvest should come in.

He brought back with him Mr. David Thompson, a Scotchman, who, with a small party of emigrants, had commenced a plantation at the mouth of the Piscataqua, where Portsmouth now stands. For these many tokens of the divine goodness, Governor Bradford appointed another day of thanksgiving. It may be instructive here to insert Governor Bradford's testimony respecting the effect of a community of goods, which experiment was so fairly tried, and under such favorable circumstances, at Plymouth:

"The experience which was had in this common course and condition," he writes, " tried sundry years, and that amongst godly and sober men, may well evince the vanity of that conceit of Plato and other ancients, and applauded by some of later times,—that the taking away of property, and bringing a community into a commonwealth would make them happy and flourishing; as if they were wiser than God. For this community, so far as it was such, was found to breed much confusion and discontent, and to retard much employment which would have been to their benefit and comfort. For the young men, who were the most able and fit for labor and service, did repine that they should spend their time and strength to work for other men's wives and children, without any recompense.

"The strong, or man of parts, had no more in the livision of victuals and clothes, than he that was weak and not able to do a quarter the other could. This was thought injustice. The aged and graver men to be ranked and equalized in labors, victuals, clothes, etc., with the meaner and younger sort, thought it some indignity and disrespect unto them. As for men's wives to be commanded to do service for other men, as dressing their meat, washing their clothes, etc., they deemed it a kind of slavery, neither could many husbands well brook it. Let none object, this is men's corruption, and nothing against the course itself. I answer, seeing all men have this corruption in them, God, in his wisdom, saw another course fitter for them." *

Early in August two ships arrived, the Anne and the Little James. The latter was a small vessel of about forty-four tons, which was built for the company and was to remain at Plymouth. The two vessels brought sixty passengers. Some of them were very worthy people and constituted a valuable addition to the colony. Others were such sad miscreants that the Pilgrims instructed by the disasters which the

* Bradford's Plymouth Plantation, p. 135.

Weymouth colonists had caused, refused to receive them into their colony. The thriftless creatures, unable to establish a settlement of their own, were compelled to return to England.

The corn harvest was not yet ripe, and the new comers were greatly surprised at the destitution in which they found the colonists. "The best dish," writes Bradford, "they could present them with, was a lobster or a piece of fish, without bread or anything else but a cup of fair spring water." The new-comers were afraid that the hungry colonists would eat up all the provisions they had brought with them. On the other hand the colonists were fearful that the newcomers would devour their harvest of corn, which was scarcely sufficient for so large an addition to their numbers. They therefore decided that each of the parties should rely upon its own resources.

On the 10th of September the Anne returned to England, laden with clapboards and furs. Mr. Winslow also sailed in her, on business for the colony. The harvest was now in, and there was comparative plenty. Many had raised more corn than their own families would consume, and thus they had a supply to sell to others. About the middle of this month Captain Robert Georges arrived in Massachusetts Bay with a number of families, to commence a new plantation there. His grant of land was very indefinite. It embraced all the land lying on the northeast side of Massachusetts Bay, together with all the shores and coasts, for ten English miles, in a straight line towards the northeast, and thirty miles into the main land. He selected for his settlement, the spot at Weymouth which had been abandoned by the Weston Colony. Governor Georges visited Governor Bradford, where he met with a very kind reception.

Some of the seamen, carousing in one of the houses, built a great fire on a cold and windy night, which was communicated to the thatch, and four houses were burnt down. The storehouse was greatly endangered. Its loss would have been irreparable. The Little James went on a cruise to the coast of Maine, and there, in a violent storm, was wrecked. Mid-winter now frowned around the Pilgrims as they entered upon a new year, the year 1624.

Mr. Winslow returned from England, bringing with him two heifers and a bull, an invaluable acquisition to the colonists, being the first cattle that were brought over. As they had no money, corn had become the circulating medium. With the opening spring all hands set to work to raise as much corn as possible. This led to a petition to the Governor to have a portion of land assigned, in perpetuity, to each individual. When assigned yearly, by lot, that field which one man, by skill and industry, had brought into a good state of cultivation, was often taken from him, and he received, perhaps, instead, a field neglected and overrun with weeds. The request was manifestly so reasonable, than one acre was given to every man, as near the village as might be, to be held seven years. It was deemed necessary, for safety against the Indians, to keep as close together as possible.

With some internal disorders, the affairs of the colony went on prosperously during the year, nothing occurring to call the energies of Captain Standish into requisition. The colony numbered one hundred and eighty souls. They had some cattle and goats, quite a number of swine, and numerous poultry. Thirty-two dwelling houses were now occupied. The palisades which surrounded the village were half a mile in extent. A well-built fort stood upon Burial Hill.

Mr. Winslow made a trading-voyage eastward one hundred and fifty miles, in an open boat, " up a river called the Kennebec." He brought home seven hundred pounds of beaver and other furs, having exchanged corn for them. It was mid-winter, and they encountered much tempestuous weather. The boat was built by their ship carpenter, and had a small deck over her midships to keep the corn dry. But the men were exposed, unsheltered to winter on the coast of Maine. These furs were purchased of the natives, at a small price, and were sold in London at a great profit.

The Pilgrims wished to hire money with which to purchase in England the commodities which the Indians greatly prized, and which they could exchange with them for furs. Captain Standish was sent to England to adjust certain difficulties which had arisen between the colonists and their partners in London, and also to hire money with which to purchase goods to trade with the Indians. But the Captain arrived in London at a very unfortunate hour. The city was then desolated by that awful plague which was sweeping thousands into the grave. It would also appear that the credit of the colony was far from good. With great difficulty Captain Standish succeeded in raising seven hundred and fifty dollars, for which he paid the enormous interest of fifty per cent. The risk to the lender was indeed great. The only chance the colonists had to pay the debt, was mainly in sending home furs. But the ships thus laden had to run the gauntlet of the hostile fleets of France and Turkey, with both of which powers England was then at war.

Captain Standish expended the small sum he had raised, in trading commodities. He also brought back the mournful intelligence of the death of the

Reverend Mr. Robinson, who died at Leyden the 1st of March, 1625. There were so many vessels sent from England to the coast of Maine, engaged in the fishing business, that the colonists, in consequence of the competition, relinquished the fisheries, and engaged in trading and planting, both of which had now become profitable. Immense numbers of fishes were, however, taken at their very door, which were used to enrich the fields.

The rapid brook of fresh water, which ran at the south side of the town, took its rise in several lakes in the land above. Early in May vast shoals of herring darkened the waters as they ascended the brook from the sea to deposit their spawn in the lakes. The colonists constructed, at the mouth of this brook, a sort of net, made of planks and trellis work, so that at one tide they would often take twelve thousand fishes. Three or four were deposited in each hill of corn, which promoted a luxuriant growth. This corn was eagerly purchased by the Indians, they paying one pound of beaver skin for one bushel of corn. Fishing vessels occasionally called and purchased their corn at six shillings a bushel. Several other colonies were also established, which needed supplies. Thus days of prosperity dawned upon the colony, which had so long struggled with adversity. But little occurred during the year 1626 worthy of especial notice. The coasting-trade was becoming increasingly important. Governor Bradford writes:

"Finding they ran a great hazard to go so long voyages in a small, open boat, especially in the winter season, they began to think how they might get a small pinnace. They had no ship carpenter among them, neither knew how to get one at present. But they having an ingenious man, who was a house carpenter, who had also wrought with the ship carpenter that was dead, when he built their boats, at their request, he put forth himself to make a trial that way, of his skill, and took one of the biggest of the shallops and sawed her in the middle, and so lengthened her some five or six feet, and strengthened her with timbers, and so built her up and laid a deck on her, and so made her a convenient and wholesome vessel, very fit and comfortable for their use, which did them service seven years. And thus passed the affairs of this year." *

The prospects of the colony had so far brightened that Mr. Allerton, who had been sent to England this year, succeeded in raising one thousand dollars at thirty per cent interest. During the year 1625 Captain Wollaston, with thirty emigrants, commenced a settlement at a place they named Mount Wollaston, in the northerly part of Braintree, now Quincy, in

* Bradford's Plymouth Plantation, p. 211.

Massachusetts. Most of these emigrants were men of low condition, the hired laborers of Wollaston. He soon became discontented, and took a large portion of his servants to Virginia, where he disposed of their labor as best he could. He left a man by the name of Fitcher to guide the labor of those who remained until his return. In the mean time one Thomas Morton, "a pettifogging attorney of Furnival's Inn, a man of low habits," succeeded in persuading those who were left to renounce the authority of Fitcher, and to live on terms of perfect equality and freedom, without any laws whatever. He arranged a great feast, and induced the men, in the frenzy of intoxication, to drive Fitcher from the settlement They then entered upon an astonishing course of rioting and drunkenness. They prosecuted vigorously a trade with the natives, which was forbidden by royal charter, of muskets, powder and bullets. This trade was very profitable. The Indians, eager to obtain muskets, would pay almost any sum for them. Morton taught them how to use the guns, and employed them to hunt, purchasing their furs.

Thus they rioted in abundance, and disgraced themselves with the most shameless indulgence in profanity and profligacy. They erected a May-pole, and danced around it with the Indian women. In accordance with these scenes of revelry, they changed the name of the place to Merry Mount. Morton was an Atheist: teaching that this was the only life; that there was no responsibility to God, and that it was the part of wisdom to indulge freely in all one's desires.

This state of things created great alarm, in all the various settlements, which had by this time been established. The Indians, if once supplied with European weapons of war, could easily, by combining, destroy all the colonies. Governor Bradford complains very bitterly of the peril. The Indians had muskets in abundance; they were taught how to repair their muskets when injured; they were furnished with moulds for running bullets of various sizes.

"Yea," writes Governor Bradford, "some have seen them have their screw-plates to make screwpins themselves, when they want them, with sundry other implements, wherewith they are ordinarily better fitted and furnished than the English themselves. It is well known that they will have powder and shot when the English want it, and cannot get it; and yet in a time of war or danger, as experience hath manifested, when lead hath been scarce, and men for their their own defense would gladly have given four pence a pound, which is dear enough, yet hath it been bought up and sent to other places, and sold to such as trade it with the Indians at twelve pence a pound

And it is likely the Indians give three or four shillings the pound, for they will have it at any rate.

"And these things have been done in the same times when some of their neighbors and friends are daily killed by the Indians, or are in danger thereof, and live but at the Indians' mercy. Yea, some have told them how gunpowder is made, and all the materials in it, and that they are to be had in their own land; and I am confident that could they attain to make saltpetre they would teach them to make powder. Oh the horribleness of this villainy! How many, both Dutch and English, have been lately slain by those Indians thus furnished! And no remedy provided, nay the evil more increased, and the blood of their brethren sold for gain; and in what danger all these colonies are is too well known.

"Oh! that princes and parliaments would take some timely order to prevent this mischief and, at length to suppress it, by some exemplary punishment upon some of those gain-thirsty murderers, for they deserve no better title, before their colonies in these parts be overthrown by these barbarous savages, thus armed with their own weapons, by these evil instruments and traitors to their neighbors and country.

"But I have forgotten myself, and have been too long in this digression; but now to return. This Morton having thus taught them the use of muskets he sold them all he could spare; and he and his consorts determined to send for many out of England, and had, by some of the ships, sent for above a score. The which being known, and his neighbors meeting the Indians in the woods, armed with guns in this sort, it was a terror unto them who lived strugglingly and were of no strength in any place. And other places, though more remote, saw that this mischief would quickly spread over all if not prevented. Besides, they saw they should keep no servants, for Morton would entertain any, how vile soever, and all the scum of the country, or any discontents would flock to him from all places, if this nest was not broken; and they would stand in more fear of their lives and goods, in a short time, from this wicked and debauched crew, than from the savages themselves.

The leading men of several settlements met together to deliberate upon what measures to adopt in this emergence. The Plymouth colony was stronger than all the rest united.

The delegates came from Plymouth, from the trading-house at the Kennebec, from the small settlement at Salem, from Weymouth, and from several other places where infant settlements had been commenced. They decided to write a joint and friendly letter to Morton, informing him of the danger to which **he was** exposing all the English, and entreating **him,** out of regard to the common safety, to change his course. A messenger was sent with this letter, and to bring back an answer. Morton replied insultingly and defiantly, saying that they were meddling with that which they had no concern; that he should continue trade with the Indians just as he pleased, selling them muskets, powder and shot, without asking any one's advice. The answer throughout was couched in the most insulting terms.

Again, with the most singular moderation, a messenger was sent to him with another friendly letter, saying that they were consulting, not for selfish interests, but for the good of all alike; that the lives of all were endangered, and that the King's proclamation had forbidden the sale of fire-arms to the savages. Another insolent answer was returned. He assured them that he cared neither for the King's proclamation nor for them; and that if they thought they could coerce him, they might come on as soon as they pleased; he was ready for them.

It was now manifestly time to summon the energies of Captain Standish to the rescue. He was exactly the man for the occasion. With a small body of armed men, eight in number, as valiant as himself, Captain Standish set out for Merry Mount. In some way, Morton had heard of his approach. With his desperate men he had barricaded himself in a strong log house, with an ample supply of powder and balls They well knew the reputation of the foe they were to encounter, and in order to stimulate their waning courage, had all become drunk. From their fortress, which they deemed impregnable, they shouted their scurrilous defiance to the Captain and his little band There are men with whom apparently the most reckless bravery is combined with prudence and sound judgment; who seem to be endowed with a sort of instinct which teaches them when an act of seeming desperation may be demanded by wisdom. Captain Standish was such a man.

He was making arrangements to carry the house, perhaps by approaching it from some unguarded point, and setting it on fire, when Morton, drunk as he was, saw his danger. Selecting a few of his men, he emerged from his fortress, with the intention of making a sudden and simultaneous rush upon Captain Standish, and shooting him. Morton himself was so intoxicated that, as afterwards found, his carbine was overloaded, being nearly half filled with powder and shot.

The captain, though of short stature, possessed dignity of character and authority of bearing which often overawed his foes. Without a moment's hesitation, he advanced with stately tread upon Morton, totally regardless of his weapon, seized him by the collar, wrenched the gun from his hands, and delivered him over to his men, a humiliated and helpless captive. The rest of the drunken crew, deprived of their leader, were deemed powerless. The culprit was taken to Plymouth, and was sent to England by the first vessel that sailed, there to be tried for his crimes.

The Pilgrims, at Plymouth, had for some time been in the habit of sending yearly to the fishing-grounds off Cape Ann for a supply of cod. They had erected quite a commodious stage upon the cape, where they dressed and dried their fish. Some London adventurers fitted out a fishing vessel for the cape, and arriving there before the Plymouth people, took possession of their stage, which they refused to surrender when the Pilgrims came and demanded their own.

The code militaire was, at this time, the rule of life with Captain Standish. He would do no wrong; and he would submit to no wrong. He was immediately sent to Cape Ann to adjust the difficulty. There was no room for question about the right and wrong in the case. The new-comers had stolen the property of the Pilgrims. Captain Standish peremptorily demanded its restoration. The thieves barricaded themselves on the stage. Captain Standish prepared for battle, and would doubtless have recovered the stage by force. "But Mr. Conant," writes Baylies, "who dwelt there, and who was a man of a mild and conciliatory disposition, and Captain Pierce, a fast friend of the Plymouth people, also happening to be there with his ship, interposing their good offices, the dispute was compromised, the ship's crew having promised to build another stage." *

Emigration to the New World was now rapidly increasing. Many new settlements sprang up and many worthless characters came over, lured by the love of adventure. Not a few of these came to the flourishing Plymouth colony. This led to a new organization of the colony, the details of which it is not necessary to enter into here. The company in London, who had obtained the charter from the King and held the territory, sold out their whole property to the colonists, for nine thousand dollars, to be paid in nine annual instalments of one thousand dollars. The general features of this important change is thus given by Baylies.

" Every head of a family, and every prudent young man who was of age, both of the first and later comers, were admitted into a general partnership; and all agreed that the trade should be managed as usual, devoting all its profits to the payment of the debt; that every single freeman should have a single share, and that every father of a family should have leave

* Baylies' Memoir of Plymouth Colony, p. 140.

to purchase a share for himself, another for his wife, and one for each of his children who lived with him, and that every one should pay his share of the debts, according to his number of shares. One cow and two goats were divided by lot to every six shares, and the swine in proportion. And to every share, in addition to the acre lots, which they already held, and the gardens and homestead of which they were possessed, twenty acres of tillage land was assigned by lot, which were to be five acres broad on the water and four acres deep."

The meadow lands, for mowing, being quite small in extent, were held in common, mowing places being assigned, as the seasons came around, to all the families, according to their number of cattle. As the Pilgrims were living in constant apprehension of a combination of the Indians against them, it was deemed important that they should not be widely scattered in their fields of labor. A sudden attack might expose them to destruction, unless they could be speedily rallied. Twenty acres of land was much more than any one man could cultivate with the agri-cultural facilities then at their control. It was therefore agreed, before any lots were cast, that those whose lots should fall next to the town, should take a neighbor or two, whom they best liked, to plant corn with them for four years. By that time it was supposed the colony would be out of danger from any hostile attack. This arrangement gave general satisfaction and inspired the colonists with new energies

CHAPTER XII.

Increase and Growth of the Settlements.

The Virginia Emigrants.—Humanity and Enterprise of the Governor.—Envoy Sent to England.—Trading Posts on the Kennebec and Penobscot Rivers.—Capture by the French.—The Massachusetts Colony.—Its Numbers and Distinguished Characters.—Trade with the Indians.—Wampum the New Currency.—Trading Post at Sandwich.—Sir Christopher Gardener.—Captain Standish Moves to Duxbury.—Lament of Governor Bradford.

An incident occurred at this time, quite interesting, as illustrative of the adventurous life upon which these men had entered, in the wilderness of this New World; a life of excitement and heroic achievements, with its full share of earthly joys as well as griefs.

A ship, laden with passengers and goods, left England for Virginia. The captain was taken sick, so that he could not leave his cabin. The inefficient mate became bewildered. After six weeks at sea their provisions were exhausted. Starvation stared them in the face. Knowing not where they were, in the night, and in a gale of wind, they were almost miraculously swept over the shoals of Cape Cod, and striking a sand bar, were driven over it into a little bay, then called Manamoyake, now Chatham. The vessel leaking badly, with many of her planks sprung was forced high upon the beach, so that, with the receding tide, not only the crew safely landed, and the cargo, though much damaged with salt water, was aken on shore.

The shipwrecked people, rejoicing to have escaped with their lives, reared their huts upon the shore, not knowing where they were or what would become of them. While in this state of suspense and sadness, they were alarmed one morning in seeing several birch canoes coming around a headland filled with Indians. They seized their guns and stood upon defense. But the Indians paddled rapidly along as if apprehending no harm, and addressing them in English, inquired if they were the Governor of Plymouth's people, or his friends. The Indians told them where they were, offered to conduct them to Plymouth, or to take letters for them. The Englishmen were greatly comforted by this intelligence. They gave the Indians several valuable presents from their shipwrecked stores, and despatched, under their guidance, two men, with a letter to Governor Bradford, entreating him to send a boat to them with spikes, oakum, pitch and sundry other materials, with which they hoped to repair their vessel, and again to get her afloat from her soft bed in the sand.

The Governor immediately loaded a large boat

with the needful articles, including a generous supply of corn, and taking also trading commodities with which to buy additional supplies of the Indians, went himself to the aid of his unfortunate countrymen. It was winter, when the chill sea was swept by angry storms. It was not safe, at that season, in the boat, to attempt to sail around the head of the cape, and to brave the storms of the Atlantic on the eastern shore. He therefore sailed across the bay in a southeasterly direction, and entering Barnstable Bay, ascended a little creek called Namskeket, which ran inland nearly a mile. From the head of this creek it was but two miles across the cape to Manamoyake Bay, where the vessel was stranded.

The Indians, accustomed to portages, were readily hired to transport the articles across the land. The shoulders of the Indian women would bear very heavy burdens. The arrival of the Governor with the abundant supplies caused great rejoicing. He spent a few days with them, and then, returning to his boat, sailed along the inner coast till he had purchased of the natives a full cargo of corn, with which he replenished the granaries at Plymouth.

The stranded vessel was repaired and floated, when another fierce tempest arose, and she was driven, a hopeless wreck, upon the shore. The beach in Chatham, where she was stranded, is still called the "Old Ship." Remains of the wreck were visible within the present century.

Some of these shipwrecked emigrants were men of wealth, bringing with them many servants to cultivate large estates in Virginia. But the majority were men in the humble walks of life. Application was immediately made to Governor Bradford that they all might be permitted to repair to Plymouth, and to remain there until they should have the means to convey themselves to Virginia. The humane Pilgrims, ever ready to do a kind deed, without hesitancy acceded to their request. Boats were sent up the Namskeket Creek, and with great labor the shipwrecked emigrants and their goods were transported to the Christian colony.

"After they were hither come," writes the Governor, "and something settled, the masters desired some ground to employ their servants upon, seeing it was like to be the latter end of the year before they could have passage for Virginia, and they had now the winter before them; they might clear some ground and plant a crop, to help bear their charge, and keep their servants in employment. And if they had opportunities to depart before the same was ripe, they would sell it on the ground. So they had ground appointed them in convenient places."

Among these emigrants there were many irrelig

ious and disorderly men. Some were men of high character, who were highly appreciated by the Pilgrims. But there was general rejoicing in the little colony at the end of the summer, when two vessels arrived from England, and conveyed them to their original destination in Virginia.

It was now decided to build a pinnace, on the southern coast of the Cape, so that they could easily run along the shore there, in both directions, engaging in trade with the Indians. About twenty miles south of Plymouth, upon the shore of Buzzard's Bay, in the present town of Sandwich, there was a small harbor called Manomet, which the Pilgrims had not unfrequently visited. Sailing down from Plymouth on the north side, they could approach this spot within about four or five miles. Thus all the furs and corn which they could purchase on the south and eastern shores of the cape, could be sent across this "carrying place," and thence could be conveyed to Plymouth, avoiding the dangerous navigation around the cape. A boat-house was built here, and also a dwelling-house, where a few agents were stationed, to navigate the boat and to engage in agriculture. The enterprise proved eminently successful.

Again the company sent Mr. Allerton to England with a cargo of furs, to meet their engagements there, and to obtain authority to establish a trading-post on the Kennebec River. The Dutch were establishing trading-posts and agricultural colonies near the mouth of the Hudson, and many friendly messages and courteous acts were interchanged between these two parties. There were many English refugees in Leyden who, upon the death of their pastor, Mr. Robinson, were anxious to join their friends in America. They had expressed this desire very earnestly; but they were poor. They were unable to provide themselves with an outfit, or even to pay for their passage across the Atlantic. In order to aid these exiled and impoverished brethren, Governor Bradford, Captain Standish, and several others, formed a company and purchased of the Plymouth colony all their right to trade with the Indians for six years. For this they paid twelve thousand dollars. The main object of the purchasers seemed to be to raise money enough to bring over their friends from Holland. There were eight of the Pilgrim fathers united with four gentlemen in London who assumed these responsibilities. Very truly Mr. Baylies writes:

"The generosity of the chiefs of the colony to their Leyden brethren is unparalleled. They almost deprived themselves of the common necessaries of life to get them over, and to support them until they were able to support themselves; laboring at the same time under heavy debts, for which they paid exorbitant interest. But their necessities seemed only to stimulate them to greater exertions." *

This new company, having obtained a patent for a trading-post on the Kennebec River, erected a house in a place called Cushenoe, now the city of Augusta. Here they collected, for purposes of trade, a large supply of coats, shirts, rags, blankets, biscuit, pease, etc. In the month of August, 1629, thirty-five families arrived at Plymouth from Leyden. Nine months after, in May, 1630, another ship arrived, bringing several more families. The new company, of which the Governor and the captain were the principal men, paid all their expenses, though they amounted to two thousand seven hundred dollars. Houses were assigned to them; grounds were purchased for them, and they were fed from the public stores for more than a year. When we remember that there was no blood relationship between these parties, no partnership, no bond of union excepting Christian charity; that the benefactors were poor, struggling for their own support, and that many of those whom they were thus aiding they had never seen before, we must regard this act as one of extraordinary generosity.

A trading-post had been established on the Penobscot River, at a point called Bagaduce, now Cas-

* Blake's Plymouth Colony, p. 153.

tine. Here a very lucrative trade was transacted with the Indians, mainly in furs. The French claimed this post as within their domain. A small French vessel entered the bay, and finding the post defenceless, rifled it of all its contents, and carried off three hundred pounds of beaver skins and other property to the value of over two thousand dollars. Governor Bradford, in his description of this annoying event, writes:

"It was in this manner: The master of the house, and part of the company with him, were come with their vessel to the westward to fetch a supply of goods which was brought over for them. In the mean time comes a small French ship into the harbor; and amongst the company was a false Scot. They pretended that they were newly come from the sea, and knew not where they were, and that their vessel was very leaky, and desired that they might haul her ashore and stop her leaks. And many French compliments they used and conges they made. And in the end, seeing but three or four simple men, that were servants, and by this Scotchman understanding that the master and the rest of the company were gone from home, they fell of commending their guns and muskets that lay upon racks by the wall-side. They took them down to look on them, asking if they were charged. And when they were possessed of them, one presents a piece, ready charged, against the servants, and another a pistol, and bid them not stir, but quietly deliver up their goods. They carried some of the men aboard, and made the others help to carry away the goods. And when they had taken what they pleased, they set them at liberty and went their way with this mockery, bidding them tell their master when he came, that some of the Isle of Rye gentlemen had been there."

The emigration from England rapidly increased and, ere long, the colony numbered fifteen hundred souls. In the year 1628, John Endicot, with a party of emigrants, established rather a feeble settlement at Salem, then called Naumkeag. On the 30th of May, 1630, another party commenced a colony at Dorchester, then called Mattapan. In the months of June and July of the same year, a fleet of eleven vessels arrived from England, bringing over a large number of passengers, and, after some deliberation, they selected what is now Charlestown for their principal settlement. A part of the company went to Watertown. About fifteen hundred came over during the year.

The Puritans in England were now gaining the ascendency. Men of influence and rank were joining them. They were not at all disposed to bow the knee to those who had heretofore been their persecutors. The eminent John Winthrop came as Governor of the powerful Massachusetts colony, which colony was stronger in numbers, and far stronger in wealth and influence, when it first landed, than was the Plymouth Colony after long years of struggle with the hardships of the wilderness. Governor Winthrop was a gentleman of culture, position and wealth. Two of the emigrants, Humphry and Johnson, had married sisters of the Earl of Lincoln. Sir Richard Saltonstall, who was one of their number, was son of the Lord Mayor of London. There were many others, men of family and fortune, who, having lived in the enjoyments of large estates, were accustomed to all the refinements of polished society. Others, such as Hampden, Cromwell and Pym, who subsequently became conspicuous in the overthrow of the tyrannic throne of Charles I, wished to join them, but were prevented by a royal edict.

As early as 1623 there were as many as fifty vessels engaged in fishing on the New England coast. Several of these were owned by parties in Dorchester, England. They sent a party of fourteen persons to a spot near Cape Ann, where Gloucester now stands, to commence a small settlement. It was their main object to provide a home upon the land, to which the sailors might resort for refreshment and rest, and where they might be brought under religious influences. The site was purchased of the Plymouth colony. They carried out live stock, and erected a house, with a stage to dry fish, and with vats for the manufacture of salt. The experiment proved an utter failure, from the incompetence of the colonists.

The New World, as affording facilities for promising homes, was attracting ever increasing attention This led to the organization of a powerful company, who obtained a grant of lands extending from the Atlantic to the Western Ocean, and in width, running from three miles north of the Merrimac river to a line three miles south of the Charles. The company invested with this immense territory consisted of a number of private individuals, who, by their charter, became invested with almost imperial powers. The Plymouth colonists recognized the superior numbers, opulence and rank of their Massachusetts brethren, and were ever ready to render to them the precedence. And though the Massachusetts colonists were occasionally somewhat arrogant, as if fully conscious of their superiority, they were generally just, and at times even generous, to those brethren who were in entire accord with them in religious faith, and whose virtues they could not but revere.

The advent of these colonists was a great blessing to the Indians. The men of Plymouth and of Massachusetts, alike recognizing tnat universal brotherhood which Christianity so prominently enforces, were disposed to treat the Indians with the utmost kindness, and to do everything in their power to elevate and bless them. They purchased their lands, their corn and their furs, and paid fair prices for them, thus introducing into their wigwams comforts of which they previously had no conception. The Indians were thus stimulated to industry, and these friendly relations would have continued, to the inestimable benefit of both parties, but for the outrages inflicted upon the savages by such godless wretches as the infamous Captain Hunt, the low and thieving gang of Weymouth adventurers, and drunken sailors and reckless vagabonds, who, fleeing from crimes in their own country, gave loose to unrestrained passions in this New World.

The Pilgrims had no power to prevent these atrocities. The poor savages, ignorant and degraded, knew not how to discriminate. If drunken white men, vagabond sailors from some English vessel, pilfered their wigwams, insulting their wives and daughters, there was no law to which they could appeal, and, in their benighted state, the only redress before them was to violate, with still more terrible atrocities, with torture and flame and blood, the inmates of some white man's log house, the home, perhaps, of piety and prayer, where the Indian, if hungry, would be fed, if sick, would be nursed with true brotherly and sisterly tenderness. Thus, in God's mysterious government of this world, the consequences of the crimes of the vilest men fell with awful desolation upon the heads of the best of men.

The Indians had no circulating medium. Indeed they had no trade among themselves. In illustration of the benefits which the coming of the Pilgrim Fathers conferred upon them, let us again refer to the trading-post established, about twenty miles south from Plymouth, at Manomet, now Sandwich. Here, upon a small but navigable stream, a dwelling and storehouses were erected, where canoes and coasting vessels from all along the shore, as far as New Amsterdam, at the mouth of the Hudson, could meet in the exchange of their articles of value. A land carriage of but about six miles, over the neck of the Cape, the Suez of America, as it was then called, brought them to the waters of Massachusetts Bay, and to intercourse with all the settlements and Indian villages scattered along its shores. Indian runners could easily transport the light articles of traffic, and thus the dangerous passage around the vast peninsula of Cape Cod was avoided. Some circulating medium seemed essential in the trade thus commenced and rapidly extending.

The Narragansets and Pequots, residing upon

Narraganset and Buzzard's Bays, made from the small shells of a species of clam, a very beautiful ornamental belt, called wampum. The shells, graceful in form, beautifully colored and highly polished, were strung like beads, by a hole drilled through the centre, or were woven into rich embroidery. Three purple shells or six white ones were considered equivalent to an English penny. A string, two yards in length, was valued at five shillings. The Dutch, from New Amsterdam, sent cargoes to this trading-post. Thus sugar, cloths of various texture, cutlery and garden tools were obtained by the Indians. Friendly relations existed, and the happiness thus fostered might have continued uninterrupted but for the wickedness of men who were strangers to the principles which animated the Pilgrims.

A powerful Indian chief had his seat upon an adjoining hill, at the foot of which a busy Indian village was nestled. When the Dutch, at the mouth of the Hudson, first heard of this post, they sent a small trading-vessel to it, with very friendly letters to Governor Bradford. They landed and marched up to the trading-house, accompanied by a band of music. The trumpet notes, reverberating through those wilds, must have emptied the Indian village to gaze upon the unwonted scene. The Dutch commander sent an Indian runner to Governor Bradford, requesting

INCREASE OF THE SETTLEMENTS. 271

him to send a boat for him to the other side of the bay, as he could not travel so far on foot through the Indian trails. A boat was at once despatched to what is now called Scussett, and the chief men of the Dutch party were conveyed to Plymouth, where they were received with the highest honors. They remained several days with the Pilgrims, enjoying their profuse hospitality, and were then sent back in the boat. The friendly intercourse thus commenced, was continued for several years uninterrupted. Governor Bradford, speaking of the trade thus introduced, and of its great advantage to the Indians, writes :

"But that which turned most to their profit, in time, was an entrance into the trade of wampum. Strange it was to see the great alteration it made in a few years among the Indians themselves. For all the Indians of these parts and the Massachusetts had none or very little of it, excepting the chief and some special persons, who wore a little of it for ornament. It being only made and kept by the Pequots and Narragansets, who grew rich and potent by it; whereas, the rest, who use it not, are poor and beggarly.

"Neither did the English of this plantation, or any other in the land, till now, that they had knowledge of it from the Dutch, so much as know what it was, much less that it was a commodity of that worth and value. But after it grew thus to be a commodity in these parts, these Indians fell into it also, and to learn how to make it. It hath now continued a current commodity about this twenty years, and it may prove a drug in time. In the mean time it makes the Indians of these parts rich and powerful."

Such were the humble beginnings of the commerce of New England. The very spot upon which this trading-house stood can now be pointed out. " On it may the traveller pause and reflect how things then were! how they now are! Now, on what sea, to what coast of the habitable globe have not their descendants carried the products of their soil and industry, outstripping all other nations, with only England as a rival." *

In the year 1630 the first public execution took place. It will be remembered that one John Billington, a man of worthless character, had, in some way, smuggled himself into the company of the Pilgrims. He had two boys, who seem to have been as worthless as he himself. Governor Bradford had written of him, " He is a knave, and so will live and die." He had already, in 1621, for vile abuse of Captain Standish, been condemned to have his neck and heels tied together. For some alleged injury or insult, he waylaid and shot a young man by the name of John Newcomen. The murderer had adopted the opinion

* Life of Elder William Brewster, p 335.

that the colonists had no power granted them to inflict capital punishment. He had a fair trial before a jury of twelve men. There was no doubt whatever respecting his guilt. The court had some doubt as to its authority to inflict the penalty of death, since the Council, from whom its authority was derived, had no such power. The advice of Governor Winthrop was sought, and that of the ablest men of the Massachusetts colony. They advised, with perfect unanimity, "that the murderer ought to die, and the land be purged from blood." He was accordingly executed in October, 1630.

In the year 1631, a singular event occurred. A very eccentric man, calling himself Sir Christopher Gardner, visited Massachusetts. He was descended, it is said, from the illustrious house of the Bishop of Winchester, and in his extended travels had visited nearly all quarters of the globe. At Jerusalem, he had been made knight of the Holy Sepulchre. Weary, as he said, of the world, and desiring to do penance, by bodily mortification, for his sins, he came to the Pilgrims, offering to perform the most menial services for his living. Still he brought over with him two servants, and a very fine-looking woman whom he called his cousin. He endeavored to join the church, but they would not receive him. Being guilty of conduct for which he was about to be arrested and brought to trial, he fled into the wilderness, and took refuge with the Indians. The Massachusetts authorities offered a reward for his capture and return to them

Some of the Namasket Indians came to Governor Bradford, from the vicinity of Middleborough, and told him where Sir Christopher was, and that they could easily kill him, but could not easily take him alive; that he was a desperate man, and had a gun and sword, and that he would certainly kill some of them should they attempt to take him. The Governor told them by no means to kill him, but to watch their opportunity and to capture him. They did so, and catching him one day by the side of a river, endeavored to surround him. In his attempts to escape, by getting into a canoe to cross the stream, as he presented his musket to his pursuers, to keep them off the frail structure of bark, swept by the current against a rock, turned under him, and he was thrown, with his musket, into the water. Dripping, he reached the shore, his musket no longer of any use, and his only resource the rapier. He brandished that so fiercely that the Indians did not dare close in upon him. They, however, got some long poles, and with blows such as savages would be likely to strike, beat the sword out of his hands, fearfully bruising and mangling them.

He being thus disarmed and rendered **helpless,**

they seized him and conveyed him to Governor Bradford. As the Governor looked upon the poor man, with his arms and hands terribly inflamed and swollen, the Indians said: "We did not hurt him; we only whipped him a little with our sticks." The Governor censured the Indians for beating him so cruelly, and had his wounds tenderly nursed. Some papers upon his person showed that he was a concealed papist, and one who had enjoyed the highest advantages of university education. Governor Winthrop, being informed of his apprehension, caused him to be brought to Massachusetts, and then sent him immediately to England.

This man sent in a petition, which two others signed, to the British Government, condemning severely both the colonies of Plymouth and Massachusetts, stating that they intended rebellion; "that they meant to be wholly separate from the church and laws of England, and that their ministers and people did continually rail against the state, the church and the bishops."

Sir Richard Saltonstall, and two other prominent members of the Massachusetts colony, were then in England. They were called before the Council to answer the accusation. They did it in writing, and so satisfactorily, as to draw from the Council a vote of approbation instead of condemnation. They were also informed that, as freedom of religious worship was one of the principal reasons of emigration to New England, and that, as it was important to the government to strengthen New England, it was not the intention of his Majesty to impose the ceremonies of the Church of England upon the colonists.

The first party of colonists for Massachusetts embarked in six vessels. It consisted of three hundred men, eighty women, married and single, and twenty-six children, with an abundant outfit of food, clothing, tools, and military weapons, and "a plentiful provision of godly ministers." Mr. Francis Higginson, one of the most prominent of these emigrants, soon after his arrival wrote home saying:

"When we first came to Naumkeag, we found about half a score of houses, and a fair house newly built for the Governor. We found also abundance of corn planted by them, very good and well liking. And we brought with us about two hundred passengers and planters more, which, by common consent of the old planters, were all combined together in one body politic, under the same Governor. There are in all of us, both old and new planters, about three hundred, whereof two hundred of them are settled at Naumkeag, now called Salem, and the rest have planted themselves at Massachusetts Bay, beginning to build a town there which we do call Charlestown

"But that which is our greatest comfort and means of defense above all others is, that we have here the true religion and holy ordinances of Almighty God taught among us. Thanks be to God we have here plenty of preaching and catechizing, with strict and careful exercise and good and commendable orders to bring our people into a christian conversation, with whom we have to do withal. And thus we doubt not that God will be with us; and if God be with us, who can be against us?"[*]

About that time an Episcopal clergyman, by the name of William Blackstone, was the sole occupant and proprietor of the peninsula of Boston, then called Shawmut. The water at Charlestown was not good. But there was a very fine supply of crystal water gushing abundantly from a spring in Shawmut. Rev. Mr. Blackstone, had left England because "he disliked the power of the Lords-Bishops." By his invitation many were led to transfer their habitations across the water, to the forest-covered peninsula, and thus were laid the foundations of the renowned capital of New England.

In the year 1632 Plymouth colony was in a state of greater prosperity than ever before. Increasing troubles in England and encouraging reports from America gave new impetus to the spirit of emigra

[*] Higginson's New England Plantation, p 123.

tion. The products of agriculture were in greater demand. Cattle of all kinds had much increased and brought high prices. More land was required for cultivation. All the land in Plymouth was occupied, and still new settlers were coming. Fears of any attack on the part of the Indians had greatly subsided. Enterprising men began to push into the surrounding region, seeking choice localities and larger farms.

Just across the bay of Plymouth, on the north, there was a reach of land commanding a fine view of the little settlement at Plymouth and of the adjacent waters. Captain Standish selected for himself a very attractive location there, including what is still called " Captain's Hill." Here the descendants of an ancestor so illustrious are now rearing a monument to his memory.

The town was named Duxbury, in honor of the captain, as that was the name of the seat which his family occupied in England. Elder Brewster took a farm by his side. Here both of these distinguished men, warm friends, could often be seen in their solitary fields, clearing away the forests, where no sound of the axe had ever before been heard since the creation of the world. These lands were deemed among the best in the colony. Governor Bradford

INCREASE OF THE SETTLEMENTS.

seems to have deplored the gradual dispersion of the colonists. He wrote in terms of lamentation:

"Now as their stocks increased and their increase was vendible, there was no longer holding them together. They could not otherwise keep their cattle; and having oxen grown they must have land for ploughing and tillage. And no man now thought he could live, except he had cattle and a great deal of ground to keep them; all striving to increase their stocks. By which means they were scattered all over the bay, and the town, in which they lived compactly till now, was left very thin, and, in a short time, almost desolate. And if this had been all, it had been less, though too much; but the church must also be divided.

"Those that lived on their lots, on the other side of the bay, called Duxbury, could not long bring their wives and children to public worship and church meetings here; but they sued to be dismissed and to become a body of themselves. So they were dismissed, though very unwillingly. To prevent any further scattering from this place, it was thought best to give out some good farms to special persons who would promise to live at Plymouth, and who would be likely to be helpful to the church or commonwealth, and so to tie the lands to Plymouth as farms for the same. There they might keep their cattle, and till the land by some servants, and retain their dwellings here.

"And so some special lands were granted at a place general, called Green's Harbor, (Marshfield) where no allotments had been in the former division; a place very well meadowed and fit to keep and rear cattle, in good store. But alas! this remedy proved worse tnan the disease. For within a few years those that had thus got footing tore themselves away, partly by force, and partly by wearing out the rest with importunity and pleas of necessity, so that they must either suffer them to go, or live in continual opposition and contention. This I fear will be the ruin of New England, at least of the churches of God there." *

* Bradford's Plymouth Plantation.

CHAPTER XIII.

The Courtship of Miles Standish.

Removal to Duxbury.—Intercourse with the Dutch.—Trading Posts on the Connecticut.—Legend of the courtship of Miles Standish.—Personal Appearance of the Captain.—Proposition to John Alden.—His Anguish and Fidelity.—Interview with Priscilla.—The Indian Alarm.—Departure of Captain Standish.—Report of his Death.—The Wedding.

Notwithstanding the removal of Captain Standish across the bay, to his beautiful and fertile farm there, he still took a very lively interest in everything relating to the welfare of the colony, and of the little village which he had been so instrumental in founding. Mr. Bradford had for twelve successive years been chosen Governor. He was anxious to be released from the cares of office. In the annual election of 1633, he importuned for release so earnestly that the people yielded to his request, and chose Edward Winslow as his successor. At the same time seven assistants were chosen, of whom Captain Miles Standish was the first.

The Dutch, from the mouth of the Hudson, had explored the Connecticut river. The natives were anxious to have a trading post established on that beautiful stream, which was lined with Indian tribes They sent a delegation to Plymouth with this request. The Pilgrims were not prepared to commence a settlement there, but they sent a small vessel up the river, and had great success in their traffic. The Indians then applied to the Governor of the Massachusetts colony. But he was not inclined to embark in an enterprise so difficult, where the post could only be reached by a long and perilous voyage around Cape Cod, or by a journey of many days through a pathless forest.

Some however of the private members of both of these colonies foreseeing the danger that the Dutch might anticipate them there, held a conference at Boston with some of the prominent men of Plymouth, and tried to form a partnership to engage in the undertaking. They were however discouraged by the representations which were made to them. It was urged that the Indians were very numerous, that they could bring many thousand warriors into the field, that many of them were hostile, that the river was difficult of access in consequence of a bar, and that during seven months in the year it was closed by ice. Thus influenced, they abandoned the enterprise.

In the mean time, the Earl of Warwick had obtained a patent of all the land, extending west, one hundred and twenty miles from Narraganset Bay, to the Dutch settlements at the mouth of the Hudson. This included the whole of the present State of Connecticut. The Dutch heard of this, and prepared to anticipate the English, by making an immediate settlement on the Connecticut River. This roused Governor Winslow and ex-Governor Bradford, and they determined immediately to commence a settlement in that region. At the same time, they sent a courteous message to Governor Winthrop, expressing the hope that their brethren of Massachusetts would not be displeased with their adventure, since the Massachusetts colony had declined embarking in the enterprise.

In the mean time, the Dutch had dispatched an expedition, accompanied by quite an armed force, which ascended the river and, disembarking where Hartford now stands, erected a fort and commenced a settlement. Two pieces of ordnance were placed in position to sweep the river; and they loudly proclaimed that they should not allow any of the English to pass by.

The Plymouth colonists took a small vessel, which could easily cross the bar at the mouth of the river, and placed on board of it the frame of a house, with all the materials for putting it together. The expedition was commanded by Lieutenant Holmes. When they arrived opposite Hartford, the Dutch, standing by their guns with lighted matches, ordered them to stop, threatening to shoot if they did not immediately comply with the demand. But Holmes pushed boldly by, and the Dutch commander did not venture to proceed to those measures of violence, which would surely have brought down upon the Dutch colonies the vengeance of the British navy.

Lieutenant Holmes proceeded a short distance farther up the river, to a place called Nattawanute now Windsor, where, near the mouth of a little stream, he put up his house, which was both fort and dwelling, surrounded it with palisades, and, unfurling the British flag, was ready to bid defiance to all foes, whether Dutch or Indians.

The Dutch commander at Hartford sent word to the authorities at the mouth of the Hudson of what had been done. Governor Van Twiller dispatched an armed band of seventy men, with orders to tear down the house at Windsor and drive away the occupants. He supposed that this could easily be done without any bloodshed, and thus without necessarily introducing war. But the intrepid Holmes was ready for battle against any odds. The leader of the Dutch party saw that a fierce conflict must take place, and one uncertain in its results. He therefore came to a parley and finally retired. An immense quantity of furs, beaver and otter skins, was this year sent to

England, which enabled the company to meet all its obligations.

It would be hardly warrantable, in a Life of Captain Miles Standish, to omit reference to a remarkable legend with which his name has ever been associated, though some have expressed the opinion that it was not very clearly verified by authentic documents. A literary gentleman who has investigated the subject more thoroughly probably than any other person, writes in reference to these doubts: "The anecdote is in all the histories. Why should it not be true? I am inclined to think it is; and am willing to back it against most historic facts that are two hundred years old." The story, as it has drifted down to our times is in brief as follows. We give it as presented by Mr. Longfellow, in his exquisite poem entitled "The Courtship of Miles Standish." It is very evident that Mr. Longfellow had minutely studied our early colonial history, as the reader will perceive that he is very accurate in his historical allusions. The poem opens with a description of Captain Standish, in his lonely and humble log hut. His beautiful wife, Rose, was one of the first who had died, and the place of her burial, like that of others, was carefully concealed, that the Indians might not perceive how the colony had become weakened:

" In the old colonial days, in Plymouth, the land of the Pilgrims,
To and fro in a room of his simple and primitive dwelling,
Clad in doublet and hose and boots of Cordovan leather,
Strode with a martial air Miles Standish, the Puritan Captain.
Buried in thought he seemed, with his hands behind him, and pausing
Ever and anon to behold his glittering weapons of warfare,
Cutlass and corslet of steel, and his trusty sword of Damascus,
Curved at the point and inscribed with its mystical Arabic sentence,
While underneath in a corner were fowling piece, musket and matchlock.
Short of stature he was, but strongly built and athletic,
Broad in the shoulders, deep chested, with muscles and sinews of iron,
Brown as a nut was his face, but his russet beard was already
Flaked with patches of snow, as hedges sometimes in November."

A very handsome young man, by the name of John Alden, shared with Captain Standish the comforts and discomforts of the widower's home. He had fair hair, azure eyes and a Saxon complexion, and was sufficiently unlike the Captain for them to be very warm friends. There could be no rivalry between the gentle young man of books and romance, and the stern veteran of facts and the sword. John Alden was deeply in love with Priscilla, the most beautiful maiden in Plymouth. Death had robbed her of both father and mother, and she was equally in love with John. But the bashful student had not yet summoned courage to declare his love. But it so happened that Captain Standish, without any knowledge of his friend's state of mind, had also turned his eyes to Priscilla, as the successor of Rose. Conscious of his own imperfections as a lady's man, and fearful that he could not woo the beautiful maiden in fitting phrase, he applied to his scholarly friend to speak in his behalf. In the following melodious strains the poet gives utterance to the Captain's speech:

" 'Tis not good for man to be alone, say the scriptures,
This I have said before, and again and again I repeat it,
Every hour in the day I think it, and feel it, and say it.
Since Rose Standish died, my life has been weary and dreary,
Sick at heart have I been, beyond the healing of friendship.
Oft, in my lonely hours, have I thought of the maiden Priscilla;
She is alone in the world; her father and mother and brother
Died in the winter together. I saw her going and coming,
Now to the grave of the dead, now to the bed of the dying,
Patient, courageous and strong, and said to myself, that if ever
There were angels on earth, as there are angels in heaven,
Two have I seen and known; and the angel, whose name is Priscilla,
Holds in my desolate life the place which the other abandoned.
Long have I cherished the thought, but never have dared to reveal it,
Being a coward in this, but valiant enough for the most part.
Go to the damsel Priscilla, the loveliest maiden of Plymouth,
Say that a blunt old captain, a man not of words but of actions,
Offers his hand and his heart, the hand and heart of a soldier;
Not in these words, you know, but this in short is my meaning.
I am a maker of war, and not a maker of phrases;
You, who are bred as a scholar, can say it in elegant language,
Such as you read in your books of the pleadings and wooings of lovers,
Such as you think best adapted to win the heart of a maiden.

Poor John Alden, the fair-haired, timid youth, was aghast, overwhelmed with anguish. He tried to smile, but the nerves of his face twitched with painful convulsions. He endeavored to excuse himself, but his impetuous friend, whose commanding mind overawed him, would listen to no excuse. To all John's remonstrances he replied:

"I was never a maker of phrases.
I can march up to a fortress, and summon the place to sur. ender
But march up to a woman, with such a proposal, I dare not.
I am not afraid of bullets, nor shot from the mouth of a cannon,
But cf a thundering 'no!' point blank from the mouth of a woman
That I confess I'm afraid of, nor am I ashamed to confess it."

John Alden, anguish-stricken as he was, could not refuse. The strong mind dominated over the weaker one. Agitated, almost convulsed with contending emotions, he entered the paths of the forest, crossed the brook which ran south of the village, and gathering a handful of wild flowers, almost in delirium, approached the lonely dwelling of Priscilla. As he drew near, he heard her sweet voice singing a hymn as she walked to and fro beside the spinning-wheel. Priscilla met him on the threshold, with a cordial greeting, hoping that he had come to declare his love. He was greatly embarrassed, and after a long parley, very awkwardly blurted out the words, that he had come with an offer of marriage from Captain Miles Standish. Priscilla was amazed, grieved, wounded. With eyes dilated with sadness and wonder, she looked into John's face and said, after a few moments of ominous silence:

"If the great Captain of Plymouth is so eager to wed me,
Why does he not come himself and take the trouble to woo me?
If I am not worth the wooing, I surely am not worth the winning."

John, exceedingly embarrassed, said, in unfortutunate phrase, that the captain was very busy, and had no time for such things. The offended maiden replied :

"Has he no time for *such things*, as you call it, before he is married
Would he be likely to find it, or make it, after the wedding?"

Quite forgetting himself, John launched forth eloquently in the praise of his military friend,

"Spoke of his courage and skill, and all his battles in Flanders,
How with the people of God he had chosen to suffer affliction.
How, in return for his zeal, they had made him Captain of Plymouth.
He was a gentleman born, could trace his pedigree plainly
Back to Hugh Standish, of Duxbury Hall, in Lancashire, England,
Who was the son of Ralph, and the grandson of Thurston de Standish;
Heir unto vast estates, of which he was basely defrauded,
Still bore the family arms, and had for his crest a cock argent
Combed and wattled gules, and all the rest of the blazon.
He was a man of honor, of noble and generous nature;
Though he was rough, he was kindly; she knew how, during the winter,
He had attended the sick, with a hand as gentle as woman's.
Somewhat hasty and hot, he could not deny it, and headstrong,
Stern as a soldier might be, but hearty and placable always;
Not to be laughed at and scorned, because he was little of stature,
For he was great of heart, magnanimous, courtly, courageous;
Any woman in Plymouth, nay, any woman in England,
Might be happy and proud to be called the wife of Miles Standish."

As Priscilla listened to this glowing and eloquent eulogy, it only increased her admiration for the young and beautiful John Alden. She had long loved him. Maidenly instinct taught her that she also was beloved by him. Though this love had never been communicated to her in words, it had again and again been expressed in loud-speaking glances of the eye and in actions. With tremulous voice she ventured to reply, "Why don't you speak for yourself, John?"

The tone, the look which accompanied the words, revealed at once, to the bashful youth, the love of Priscilla. A tempest of conflicting emotions rushed into his soul. How could the magnanimous youth plead his own cause, and thus apparently betray his friend. Perplexed, bewildered, he burst from the house, like an insane man; hurried to the sea shore, wandered along the sands, where the surf was breaking with loud roar; bared his head to the ocean breeze, and endeavored in vain to cool the fever, which seemed to burn in both body and soul. His tender conscience condemned him as being unfaithful to his friend.

He could not, without a sense of guilt, suppplant his friend ; and he could not live in Plymouth and refuse the hand of Priscilla, so delicately and yet so decidedly proffered. Heroically he resolved to return to England.

There was a vessel in the harbor which was to sail on the morrow. The poet speaks of it as the returning Mayflower. Chronology will hardly permit us to accept that representation. Rose Standish died on the 8th of February, N. S. The Mayflower sailed, on her return voyage, the 5th of April, but two months after the death of the wife Captain Standish so tenderly loved. As the frenzied youth gazed upon the vessel riding at anchor, and rising and falling upon the ocean swell, he exclaimed :

"Back will I go o'er the ocean, this dreary land will abandon,
Her whom I may not love, and him whom my heart has offended.
Better to be in my grave, in the green old churchyard in England,
Close by my mother's side, and among the dust of my kindred;
Better be dead and forgotten, than living in shame and dishonor
Sacred and safe and unseen, in the dark of the narrow chamber
With me my secret shall lie, like a buried jewel that glimmers
Bright on the hand that is dust, in the chambers of silence and darkness,
Yes, as the marriage ring of the great espousal hereafter.

Thus resolving he hurried, in the gathering twilight, through the glooms of the forest to the "seven houses" of Plymouth. He entered the door of his home and found the Captain anxiously awaiting his return. He had been gone long and was rather severely reproached for his tardiness. He then gave a minute account of the interview. But when he came to her declaration, " Why don't you speak for yourself, John ?" the Captain rose from his seat in a towering passion. As he was vehemently uttering his reproaches a messenger came, with the information that hostile Indians were approaching. Instantly the bold warrior forgot Priscilla, and all his displeasure at John

Alden, in contemplation of his immense responsibilities as military protector of the colony. Hastily he girded on his armor and left the house. He found the leading men already assembled in the council room. Upon the table lay the skin of the rattlesnake, to which we have before alluded, filled with arrows, with the Indian who brought it, by its side. Captain Standish at once understood the significance of the mysterious gift. He said,

" ' Leave this matter to me, for to me by right it pertaineth.
War is a terrible trade ; but in the cause that is righteous
Sweet is the smell of powder ; and thus I answer the challenge.'
Then, from the rattlesnake's skin. with a sudden contemptuous gesture
Jerking the Indian arrows, he filled it with powder and bullets,
Full to the very jaws and handed it back to the savage,
Saying in thundering tones, ' Here, take it ! this is your answer.'
Silently out of the room then glided the glistening savage,
Bearing the serpent's skin, and seeming himself like a serpent,
Winding his sinuous way in the dark to the depths of the forest."

Early the next morning Captain Standish took eight men, well armed, and marched, under the guidance of Hobomak, to the point where he supposed the hostile Indians were gathering. The vessel was about to sail. The signal gun was fired. All the inhabitants of the little village flocked to the beach The ship's boat was at Plymouth rock, waiting to convey the captain of the vessel, who was on shore, to the ship. He was bidding his friends adieu and cramming the capacious pockets of his storm coat w'th let ters and packages. John Alden, with others, was seen hurrying down to the sea shore. The captain stood with one foot on the rock and the other on the gunwale of the boat, speaking his last words and just ready to push off. Alden, in his despair, was about to enter the boat, without any words of adieu to his friends, thinking in absence and distance to find relief to his tortured feelings, when he saw Priscilla looking sadly upon him.

" But as he gazed on the crowd, he beheld the form of Priscilla
Standing dejected among them, unconscious of all that passing.
Fixed were her eyes upon his, as if she divined his intention,
Fixed with a look so sad, so reproachful, imploring and patient,
That, with a suden revulsion, his heart recoiled from its purpose
As from the verge of a crag, where one step more is destruction."

Thus influenced, he abandoned his intention of returning to England more suddenly than he had formed it. As he stepped back he said, with a true lover's fervor,

" There is no land so sacred, no air so pure and so wholesome
As is the air she breathes, and the soil that is pressed by her footsteps.
Here for her sake will I stay, and like an invisible presence
Hover around her forever, protecting, supporting her weakness.
Yes! as my foot was the first that stepped on this rock at the landing.
So, with the blessing of God, shall it be the last at the leaving."

The captain of the ship sprang into the boat, waved an adieu to the lonely band of exiles, numbering but about fifty men, women and children, who were gathered upon the shore, and the boat, driven by the sturdy arms of the rowers, soon reached the ship. The anchor was raised, the sails unfurled, and the only link which seemed to connect them with the home of their fathers was sundered. Long the saddened Pilgrims stood gazing upon the vessel as it receded from their view, and then returned to their lowly cabins, their homely fare, and to the toils and perils of their life of exile.

"So they returned to their homes; but Alden lingered a little,
Musing alone on the shore and watching the wash of the billows."

As he thus stood, lost in painful thought and almost distracted by the perplexities in which he found himself involved, he perceived Priscilla standing beside him. They had a long conversation together, which the poet manages with admirable skill. The artless, frank, affectionate Priscilla was unwittingly every moment exciting deeper emotions of tenderness and admiration in the heart of her lover. And yet, in the most painful embarrassment from respect to his friend Miles Standish, he refrained from offering her, as he longed to do, his hand and heart.

In the mean time Captain Standish, at the head of his brave little band, was tramping through the trails of the forest, through thickets and morasses, over hills and across streamlets,

"All day long, with hardly a halt, the fire of his anger,
Burning and crackling within, and the sulphurous odor of powder,

Seeming more sweet to his nostrils than all the scents of the forest.
Silent and moody he went, and much he revolved his discomfort."

After a march of three days, he is represented as coming to an Indian encampment. The little cluster of huts was upon a meadow, with the gloomy forest on one side, and the ocean surf breaking upon the other. A few women were scattered around among the wigwams. A formidable band of warriors, evidently on the war path, plumed and painted, and thoroughly armed, were gathered around their council fires. As soon as they saw the bright armor of the Pilgrims, as the brave little band emerged from the forest, two of the chiefs, men of gigantic stature, came forward to meet them. With much historic accuracy of detail the poet describes the scene which ensued—a scene which has been presented to the reader in the preceding narrative.

One of these was Pecksuot, the other Wattawamat. These burly savages, huge as Goliath of Gath, met Captain Standish, at first with deceitful words, hoping to disarm his suspicions. Through Hobbomak, the interpreter, who had accompanied the Captain, they proposed to barter their furs for blankets and muskets. But they soon saw, in the flashing eyes of Captain Standish, that he was not to be thus beguiled. The poet, giving utterance to authentic history in glowing verse, and making use of almost the very expressions uttered by the savages writes :

"Suddenly changing their tone, they began to boast and to bluster.
Then Wattawamat advanced with a stride in front of the other,
And with a lofty demeanor, thus vauntingly spake to the Captain:
' Now Wattawamat can see, by the fiery eyes of the Captain,
Angry is he in his heart; but the heart of the brave Wattawamat
Is not afraid at the sight. He was not born of a woman,
But on the mountain, at night, from an oak tree riven by lightning.'
Forth he sprang at a bound, with all his weapons about him,
Shouting, ' Who is there here to fight with the brave Wattawamat '
Then he unsheathed his knife, and, whetting the blade on his left hand,
Held it aloft and displayed a woman's face on the handle,
Saying, with bitter expression and look of sinister meaning,
' I have another at home, with the face of a man on the handle;
By and by they shall marry; and there will be plenty of children.' "

Pecksuot also indulged in similar language and gesture of insult and menace, brandishing his gleaming knife, boasting that it could eat, though it could not speak, and telling the Captain that he was so small in stature that he ought to go and live with the women. Meanwhile many Indians were seen stealthily creeping around, from bush to bush in the forest with the evident design of making a simultaneous attack upon the little band of white men. Some of these Indians were armed with muskets, others with arrows set on their bow strings. Nearer and nearer they were approaching, to enclose him in the net of an ambush from which there could be no escape As Captain Standish watched with his eagle eye these proofs of treachery, and listened to the insults and threats of the herculean chiefs, who, he knew, were only waiting for the fit moment to leap upon him,

> All the hot blood of his race, of Sir Hugh and of Thurston de Standish,
> Boiled and beat in his heart, and swelled in the veins of his temples
> Headlong he leaped on the boaster, and snatching his knife from its scabbard,
> Plunged it into his heart; and, reeling backward, the savage
> Fell with his face to the sky, and a fiend-like fierceness upon it.
> Straight there arose from the forest the awful sound of the war-whoop,
> And, like a flurry of snow, on the whistling wind of December,
> Swift and sudden and keen came a flight of feathery arrows."

This was followed by a discharge of musketry from the Pilgrims. A bullet pierced the brain of Pecksuot, and he fell dead. The savages, having lost both of their chiefs, fled like deer. As the head of Wattawamat, the gory trophy of war, was sent to Plymouth, and was exposed on the roof of the fort, Priscilla averted her face with terror and, shuddering, thanked God she had not married such a man of war as Captain Standish.

Month after month passed away, while the captain is represented as scouring the land with his forces, watching the movements of the hostile Indians, and thwarting their intrigues. Though Priscilla had refused his hand, the bashful John Alden did not feel that he could, in honor, take advantage of the absence of his friend, the Captain, and seek her for his bride. So assuming simply the attitude of friendship, the two lovers lived, with some degree of tranquility and in constant intimacy, side by side.

"Meanwhile, Alden at home had built him a new habitation, Solid, substantial, of timber, rough-hewn from the firs of the forest. Wooden-barred was the door, and the roof was covered with rushes, Latticed the windows were, and the window-panes were of paper, Oiled to admit the light, while wind and rain were excluded."

The description which the poet gives of the intercourse between these simple children of the wilderness, whose hearts glowed with purity and love, is beautiful in its pastoral simplicity. At length the tidings, very appalling to the Pilgrims, reached the little settlement, that their redoubtable Captain had been slain in a battle with the Indians—shot down by a poisoned arrow. It was said that he had been led into an ambush, and, with his whole band, had perished. John and Priscilla were together when an Indian brought this intelligence to Plymouth. Both joy and grief flashed through the soul of John Alden. His friend was dead. The bonds which had held John captive were forever sundered. Scarcely knowing what he did, he threw his arms around Priscilla, pressed her to his bosom, and devoutly exclaimed, "Those whom the Lord hath united, let no man put them asunder."

The wedding day soon came. The simple ceremony was performed by Elder Brewster. All the Pilgrims were present.

Lo! when the service was ended, a form appeared on the threshold,
Clad in armor of steel, a sombre and sorrowful figure.
Why does the bridegroom start and stare at the strange apparition?
Why does the bride turn pale and hide her face on his shoulder?
Is it a phantom of air,—a bodiless, spectral illusion?"

It was Captain Miles. The report of his death was unfounded. He had arrived unexpectedly in the village (for there were no mails in those days), just in time to be present at the close of the wedding. With characteristic magnanimity he advanced to the bridegroom, cordially shook his hand and wished him joy.

"'Forgive me,' he said,
I have been angry and hurt—too long have I cherished the feeling;
I have been cruel and hard, but now, thank God, it is ended.
Mine is the same hot blood that leaped in the veins of Hugh Standish;
Sensitive, swift to resent, but as swift in atoning for error.
Never so much as now was Miles Standish the friend of John Alden.'"

In a similar strain he addressed the bride. The Pilgrims were amazed and overjoyed to see their heroic Captain returned to them. Tumultuously they gathered around him. Bride and bridegroom were forgotten in the greeting which was extended to the Captain.

Some cattle had, by this time, been brought to the colony, and a snow-white bull had fallen to the lot of John Alden. The animal was covered with a crimson cloth upon which was bound a cushion. Priscilla mounted this strange palfrey, which her husband led by a cord tied to an iron ring in its nostrils. Her friends followed, and thus she was led to her home.

'Onward the bridal procession now moved to their new habitation,
Happy husband and wife and friends conversing together.
Pleasantly murmured the brook, as they crossed the ford in the forest,
Pleased with the image, that passed like a dream of love through its bosom,
Tremulous, floating in air, o'er the depth of the azure abysses,
Down through the golden leaves the sun was pouring his splendors,
Gleaming on purple grapes that, from branches above them suspended,
Mingled their odorous breath with the balm of the pine and the fir-tree,
Wild and sweet as the clusters that grew in the valley of Eschol;
Like a picture it seemed of the primitive pastoral ages,
Fresh with the youth of the world, and recalling Rebecca and Isaac,
Old, and yet ever new, and simple and beautiful always,
Love immortal and young in the endless succession of lovers,
So, through the Plymouth woods, passed onward the bridal procession."

Such is the poetic version of the legend of the Courtship of Miles Standish. Nearly every event which the poet has woven into his harmonious lines, is accurate even in its most minute details. We have given but a meagre view of the beauties of this Idyl and commend the same, in full, to the perusal of the reader.

CHAPTER XIV

The Trading-Posts Menaced.

Menace of the Narragansets.—Roger Williams.—Difficulty on the Kennebec.—Bradford's Narrative.—Captain Standish as Mediator.—The French on the Penobscot.—Endeavors to Regain the Lost Port.—Settlements on the Connecticut River.—Mortality among the Indians.—Hostility of the Pequots.—Efforts to Avert War. — The Pequot Forts. — Death of Elder Brewster. — His Character.

In the spring of the year 1632 an Indian runner came, in breathless haste, into the village of Plymouth, with the intelligence that the Narragansets, under Canonicus, were marching against Mount Hope, and that Massassoit implored the aid of the Pilgrims. The chief of the Wampanoags had fled, with a party of his warriors, to Sowams, in the present town of Warren, R. I., where the Pilgrims had a trading-post. It used to be said, in the French army, during the wars of Napoleon I., that the presence of the Emperor, on the field of an approaching battle, was equivalent to a re-enforcement of one hundred thousand men. It seems to have been the impression, with both colonists and Indians, that Captain Standish, in himself alone, was a resistless force. He was immediately despatched to Sowams, *with three men*, to repel an army of nobody knew how many hundreds of savage warriors.

Upon his arrival at Sowams, the captain soon learned that the Wampanoags were indeed in serious peril. The Narragansets were advancing in much strength. Captain Standish sent promptly a messenger to Plymouth to forward a re-enforcement to him immediately, with powder and muskets. As there was but little ammunition at that time in Plymouth, application was made to Governor Winthrop, of Massachusetts, for a supply. There were but few horses then in either of the colonies, and the messenger returned on foot through the woods with twenty-seven pounds of powder upon his back, which Governor Winthrop had contributed from his own stores. Fortunately the Pequots, taking advantage of the absence of the Narraganset warriors, made an inroad upon their territory, which caused Canonicus to abandon his march upon Sowams and to make a precipitate retreat to defend his own realms.

Mr. Roger Williams, whose name is one of the most illustrious in the early annals of New England, had a little before this time come over to Massachusetts. Being displeased with some things there, he left that colony and came to Plymouth.

"Here," writes Governor Bradford, "he was friendly entertained, according to their poor ability, and exercised his gifts among them, and after some time was admitted a member of the church. And his teaching was well approved, for the benefit whereof I still bless God, and am thankful to him, even for his sharpest admonitions and reproofs. He this year began to fall into some strange opinions, and from opinion to practice; which caused some controversy between the church and him, and, in the end, some discontent on his part, by occasion whereof he left them somewhat abruptly."

In the year 1634 a serious difficulty occurred upon the Kennebec River. The Plymouth colony claimed this river, and fifteen miles on each side of it, by special patent. They thus were enabled to monopolize the very important trade with the Indians. A man by the name of Hocking, from the settlement at Piscataqua, with a boat load of goods, entered the river, and ascending above the trading coast of the Plymouth colony, commenced purchasing furs of the Indians. Mr. John Howland was in command of the post at that time. He forbade the trade; but Hocking, with insulting language, bade him defiance. Howland took a boat and some armed men, and ascended the river to the spot where the heavily laden boat of Hocking was riding at anchor, and earnestly expostulated with him against his illegal procedings.

The result we will give in the words of Governor Bradford :

"But all in vain. He could get nothing of him but ill words. So he considered that now was the season for trade to come down, and that if he should suffer him to take it from them, all their former charge would be lost, and they had better throw all up. So consulting with his men, who were willing thereto, he resolved to put him from his anchors, and let him drift down the river with the stream ; but commanded the men that none should shoot a shot upon any occasion, except he commanded them.

"He spoke to him again, but all in vain. Then he sent a couple in a canoe to cut his cable, the which one of them performs. But Hocking takes up a piece, which he had laid ready, and, as the bark sheared by the canoe, he shot him, close under her side, in the head, so that he fell down dead instantly.* One of his fellows, who loved him well, could not hold, but with a musket shot Hocking, who fell down dead, and never spake word. This was the truth of the thing."

Mr. John Alden, probably the husband of Priscilla, was one of the men in the bark with the Pilgrims. They returned to the trading post, much afflicted by the untoward adventure. Not long after this Mr. Alden, visiting Boston, was arrested for the deed

* The name of the man thus shot was John Talbot.

upon the complaint of a kinsman of Hocking, and held to bail. The Massachusetts government had no right of jurisdiction in the affair. But Governor Winthrop was quite embarrassed to know what was best to be done in a case thus far without any precedent. He wrote very courteously to Governor Winslow, then Chief Magistrate of Plymouth, informing him of what had been done, and enquiring if the Plymouth people would take action in a case which seemed rather to belong to their jurisdiction.

"This we did, writes Governor Winthrop, "that notice might be taken that we did disavow the said action, which was much condemned of all men, and which, it was feared, would give occasion to the king to send a general governor over. And besides, it had brought us all, and the gospel, under a common reproach, of cutting one another's throats for beaver."

Governor Bradford was also greatly troubled, being apprehensive respecting the influence it might exert upon the home government. He speaks of the occurrence as "one of the saddest things that befel them since they came." There was embarrassment all around. It was hardly consistent with the dignity of Plymouth to surrender the case to the Massachusetts court. Mr. Alden, who had been arrested, was no actor in the business. He simply happened to be in the boat, having gone to the Kennebec with supplies.

Under these difficult circumstances Captain Standish was sent to Massachusetts to consult with the authorities there upon the best course to be pursued; to make explanations, and to endeavor to obtain the release of John Alden. Great wisdom was requisite in discharging the duties of this mission, combining conciliation with firmness. The Captain was equal to the occasion. He represented that the Plymouth people exceedingly regretted what had happened, but they felt that they were not the aggressors, but had acted in self defense. It was admitted that one of their servants had shot Hocking, but that he had first shot Talbot, and would have killed others had he not himself been killed. It was urged that the Massachusetts colony had no jurisdiction in the case, and that it had done unjustly in imprisoning, and arraigning before its court, one of the Plymouth men. The spirit of conciliation manifested by both parties was admirable, as is manifest in the following admission made to the Massachusetts court, as recorded by Governor Bradford:

"But yet, being assured of their Christian love, and persuaded that what was done was out of godly zeal, that religion might not suffer, or sin be in any way covered, especially the guilt of blood, of which all should be very conscientious, they did endeavor to appease and satisfy them the best they could; first by informing them of the truth in all circumstances about the matter; and secondly, in being willing to refer the case to any indifferent and equal hearing and judgment of the thing here, and to answer it elsewhere when they should be duly called thereto. And further, they craved Mr. Winthrop's, and others of the revered magistrates there, their advice and direction therein. This did mollify their minds, and bring things to a good and comfortable issue in the end." *

In accordance with Governor Winthrop's advice, a general conference of prominent men, both ministers and laymen, was held in Boston. After seeking divine guidance in prayer, the matter was very thoroughly discussed. Then the opinion of each one was taken, both magistrates and ministers. With entire unanimity they came to the conclusion that, "Though they all could have wished that these things had never been, yet they could not but lay the blame and guilt on Hocking's own head. And thus," writes Governor Bradford, "was this matter ended, and love and concord renewed."

In the struggle between the Dutch and the English, for the possession of the Connecticut River and its lucrative trade, a party of Dutch ascended the

* Bradford's Plymouth Plantation, p. 321.

river far above their trading house, at the present site of Hartford. Here there was a powerful tribe of Indians. Being, as usual with the Indians, at war with their neighbors, about one thousand of them had built a fort, which they had strongly palisadoed. Some Dutch traders went up to pass the winter with them, and to purchase their furs. A terrible plague came upon the Indians, and nine hundred and fifty died in the course of a few weeks. The living could not bury the dead. Their bodies were left to decay in the open air. The Dutch, with difficulty, amidst the snows of winter, made their escape from this horrible pestilence, and succeeded, when almost dead with hunger and cold, in reaching their friends in Hartford.

The account of the ravages of the small pox among the Indians, around the English settlements, is too revolting to be transferred to these pages. The suffering was awful. Though the English ministered to them with the greatest humanity, yet not one of them was attacked by the disease. The judgment of God seemed to have fallen upon the Indians, and they were everywhere perishing.

The Plymouth colony had a very flourishing trading-house on the Penobscot River. In the year 1635, a French frigate appeared in the harbor, and took possession of the post, in the name of the king of France. The captain, Monsieur d' Aulney, made an inventory of their goods, took a bill of sale at his own price, promised to pay when convenient, put the men on board their shallop, supplied them amply with provisions, and, with many bows and compliments, sent them home to Plymouth. Once before this post had been thus captured. The Plymouth people were greatly disturbed by the loss. The French commander threatened to come again the next year, with eight ships, and to seize all the plantations in that section of the country which was claimed by the king of France.

Plymouth applied to Massachusetts to co-operate in the endeavor to recapture the post, and to drive out the French. The Governor of Plymouth and Captain Standish were sent to meet the Massachusetts commissioners. They urged that both colonies were equally interested in the dislodgement of the French, and that the expense should be equally borne. But the Massachusetts commissioners insisted that as the post belonged to Plymouth alone, that colony ought to defray all the expenses of the expedition Thus the negotiation terminated.

Plymouth, thus left to its own resources, hired a vessel, the Great Hope, of about three hundred tons, well fitted with ordnance. It was agreed with its commander that he should recapture the post, and surrender it, with all the trading commodities which were there, to the agents, who were to accompany him from Plymouth. As his recompense, he was to receive seven hundred pounds of beaver skins, to be delivered as soon as he should have accomplished his task. If he failed, he was to receive nothing.

Thomas Prince was then Governor of Plymouth He sent Captain Miles Standish, in their own bark with about twenty men, to aid, should it be needful, in the recovery of the post, and to take the command there, should the post be regained. Captain Standish's bark led the way, and piloted the Great Hope into the harbor, on the Penobscot. He had in his vessel the seven hundred pounds of beaver, with which to pay for the expedition. But Golding proved a totally incompetent man, displaying folly almost amounting to insanity. He would take no advice from Captain Standish. He would not even allow Captain Standish to summon the post to surrender. Had this been done, the French would at once have yielded, for they were entirely unprepared to resist the force sent against them. Neither would he bring his ship near enough to the post to do any execution, as without any summons and at a great distance, he opened a random and harmless fire.

Captain Standish earnestly remonstrated, assuring Golding that he could lay his ship within pistol shot of the house. As the stupid creature burned his powder and threw away his shot, the French, behind an earth-work out of all harm's reach, made themselves merry over the futile bombardment. At length Golding became convinced of his folly, and placed his vessel upon the spot which Captain Standish had pointed out. Then he ascertained, to the excessive chagrin of Captain Standish and his party, that he had expended all his ammunition. The wretch then designed to seize upon the bark and the beaver skins. But Captain Standish, learning of this, spread his sails and returned in safety to Plymouth.

The Governor and his assistants in Massachusetts Bay, hearing of this utter failure of the expedition, became alarmed in reference to their own safety. They wrote very earnestly to Plymouth, saying:

"We desire that you would, with all convenient speed, send some man of trust, furnished with instructions from yourselves, to make such agreement with us about this business, as may be useful for you and equal for us."

Captain Standish, with Mr. Prince, was immediately sent to Massachusetts with full powers to act in accordance with instructions given them. The negotiations, however, failed; as the Massachusetts colonists were still not prepared to pay their share of the expense. The French remained undisturbed on the Penobscot. They carried on a vigorous trade with the Indians, supplying them abundantly with muskets and ammunition.

The terrible mortality, which had swept away so many thousand Indians from the Connecticut, turned the attention of the Massachusetts colonists again to that beautiful and fertile region. The Dutch claimed the country. The Plymouth colony claimed it. And now the Massachusetts colonists were putting in their claim. Jonathan Brewster, the oldest son of Elder Brewster, was at the head of the little Plymouth settlement at Windsor. The following extracts from one of his letters addressed to the authorities at Plymouth, give a very clear idea of the state of the question at that time. The letter is dated Matianuck (Windsor), July 6, 1835.

"The Massachusetts men are coming almost daily, some by water and some by land, who are not yet determined where to settle, though some have a great mind to the place we are upon, and which was last bought. Many of them look for that which this river will not afford, except it be at this place, to be a great town and have commodious dwellings for many together. I shall do what I can to withstand them. I hope that they will hear reason; as that we were here first, and entered with much difficulty and danger, both in regard of the Dutch and Indians, and bought the land and have since held here a chargea ble possession, and kept the Dutch from further encroaching, who would else, long ere this, have possessed all, and kept out all others.

"It was your will that we should use their persons and messengers kindly; and so we have done, and do daily to your great charge. For the first company had well nigh starved had it not been for this house; I being forced to supply twelve men for nine days together. And those who came last I helped the best we could, helping them both with canoes and guides. They got me to go with them to the Dutch, to see if I could procure some of them to have quiet settling near them; but they did peremptorily withstand them. Also I gave their goods houseroom, according to their earnest request. What trouble and charge I shall be further at I know not; for they are coming daily, and I expect those back again from below, whither they are gone to view the country. All which trouble and charge we undergo for their occasion, may give us just cause, in the judgment of all wise and understanding men, to hold and keep that we are settled upon." *

The question was finally settled by treaty, and the Massachusetts colonists soon planted settlements at Wethersfield, Hartford, and some other places on the river. There were three dominant nations, if we may

* Bradford's Plymouth Plantation, p. 339.

so call them, at this time, in southern New England. The chiefs of these nations exercised a sort of feudal domination over many petty tribes. The Wampanoags, under Massasoit, held the present region of Massachusetts generally. The Narragansets, under Canonicus, occupied Rhode Island The Pequots, under Sassacus, extended their dominion over nearly the whole of Connecticut. These tribes, powerful and jealous, were almost invariably engaged in hostilities. Roger Williams estimated the number of Pequots at thirty thousand souls. They could bring four thousand warriors into the field. The seat of their chief was at Groton, near New London. Twenty-six smaller tribes were held in subjection by him. The Pequots were deemed the most fierce and cruel race of all the tribes who dwelt in New England.

The Narragansets were a nobler race of men. They somewhat surpassed the Pequots in numbers, and manifested traits of character far more generous and magnanimous. They could bring five thousand warriors into the field. The seat of Canonicus, their chief, was not far from the present town of Newport.

The Wampanoags had suffered terribly from the pestilence which ravaged New England just before the arrival of the Pilgrims. The number of their warriors had been reduced from over three thousand to about five hundred. Early in the year 1637 the

Pequots began to manifest decided hostility against the English. There was a small settlement at Saybrook, near the mouth of the Connecticut river. As the colonists were at work in the fields, unsuspicious of danger, a band of Indians fell upon them and killed several men and women. The Indians retired with loud boastings and threats. Soon after they came in larger numbers and attacked a fort. Though they were repelled, their attack was so bold and spirited as to astonish the English and cause them great alarm.

The Peqots endeavored to make peace with the Narragansets, that they might enter into an alliance with them against the English. Not a little ability was displayed in the plan of operations which they suggested. "We have no occasion to fear," they said, "the strength of the English. We need not come to open battle with them. We can set fire to their houses, shoot their cattle, lie in ambush for them whenever they go abroad. Thus we can utterly destroy them without any danger to ourselves. The English will be either starved to death, or will be compelled to leave the country."

For a time the Narragansets listened to these re presentations, being quite inclined to accept them The anxiety of the English was very great. They desired only peace, with the prosperity it would bring. War and its ruin they greatly deplored.

The Pilgrims did everything which could be done to avoid the Pequot war; but it was forced upon them. Sassacus was a very shrewd man, and laid very broad plans for his military operations. He could summon thousands of warriors who would fall furiously upon all the scattered settlements, lay them in ashes, and massacre the inhabitants.

In the year 1634, just after a very flourishing trading post had been established on the Connecticut river at Windsor, two English traders, Captains Norton and Stone, ascended the river in a boat, laden with valuables for the Indian trade, which they intended to exchange for furs. These traders had eight white boatmen in their employ. The Indians were peaceful, and they had no apprehensions of danger One night, as the boat was moored by the side of the stream, a band of Indians, with hideous yells, rushed from an ambush upon them, put every man to death and, having plundered the boat of all its contents sunk it in the stream.

These traders were from Massachusetts. This powerful colony demanded of Sassacus that the murderers should be surrendered to them, and that payment should be made for the plundered goods. The bloody deed had been performed at midnight in the glooms of the forest. There was no survivor to tell the story. Sassacus fabricated one, very ingeniously to palm off upon the English. No one could deny the villany of Captain Hunt, who, some years before, had kidnapped several Indians and sold them into slavery. Sassacus declared that Captains Norton and Stone, without any provocation, had seized two Indians, bound them hand and foot in their boat, and were about to carry them off, no one knew where.

The friends of these captives crept cautiously along the shore watching for an opportunity to rescue them. The white men were all thoroughly armed with swords and muskets, rendering any attempt to rescue the captives extremely perilous. The right of self-defense rendered it necessary, in the conflict which would ensue, to kill. In the darkness of the night they rushed upon the boat which was drawn up to the shore, killed the white men and released the captives. He also stated that all the Indians engaged in the affray, excepting two, had since died of the small-pox.

This plausible story could not be disproved. The magistrates of Massachusetts, high-minded and honorable men, wished to treat the Indians not merely with justice, but with humanity. It could not be denied that, admitting the facts to be as stated by Sassacus, the Indians had performed a heroic act-- one for which they deserved praise rather than censure The Governor of Massachusetts therefore accepted this explanation, and resumed his friendly alliance with the treacherous Pequots.

Roger Williams, who had taken up his residence in Rhode Island, had secured the confidence of the Indians to a wonderful degree. He exposed himself apparently, to the greatest perils, without any sense of danger. He had acquired wonderful facility in speaking the language of the Narragansets, in the midst of whom he dwelt. There were still so many indications that the Pequots were plotting hostilities, that the Governor and Council of Massachusetts wrote to Mr. Williams, urging him to go to the seat of Canonicus, and dissuade him from entering into any coalition with the Pequots, should such be in process of formation. This truly good man immediately left his home and embarked alone, in a canoe, to skirt the coast of Narraganset Bay, upon his errand of mercy. It is probable that he made this journey in a birch canoe, paddling his way over the smooth waters of the sheltered bays. He encountered many hardships, and many great perils, as occasional storms arose, dashing the surf upon the shore. After several days of such lonely voyaging, he reached the royal residence of Canonicus. The barbarian chieftain was at home, and it so happened that when Mr. Williams arrived at his wigwam, he found several Pequot warriors there, who had come on an embassage from Sassacus to engage the Narragansets in the war.

For three days this bold man remained alone among these savages, endeavoring, in every way, to thwart the endeavors of the Pequot warriors. These agents of Sassacus were enraged at Mr. Williams' influence in circumventing their plans. They plotted his massacre, and every night Mr. Williams had occasion to fear that he would not behold the light of another morning. But Canonicus, unlettered savage as he was, had sufficient intelligence to appreciate the fearlessness and true grandeur of character of Mr. Williams. He dismissed the discomfited Pequots, refusing to enter into any alliance with them. He renewed his treaty of friendship with the English, and engaged to send a large party of his warriors to coöperate with them in repelling the threatened assault of the Pequots.

The benefits thus conferred upon the English by the efforts of Mr. Roger Williams were incalculable. Many distant tribes, who were on the eve of joining Sassacus, alarmed by the defection of the Narragansets, also withdrew; and thus the Pequots were compelled to enter upon the war with forces considerably weaker than they had originally intended. Still they were foes greatly to be dreaded. The English settlements were now widely scattered, and each was in itself feeble. The Pequots could marshal four thou sand of as fierce warriors as earth has ever see. A small bag of pounded corn would furnish each warrior with food for many days. They could traverse the forest trails with almost the velocity of the wind Rushing upon some unprotected hamlet at midnight, with torch and tomahawk, they could, in one awful hour, leave behind them but smouldering ashes and gory corpses. Disappearing, like wolves, in the impenetrable forest, they could again rush upon any lonely farm-house, leagues away, and thus, with but little danger to themselves, spread ruin far and wide. No man in the scattered settlements could fall asleep at night without the fear that the hideous war-whoop of the Indian would rouse him and his family to a cruel death before morning.

The Pequots were continually perpetrating new acts of violence, while the English, with great forbearance, were doing everything in their power to avert the open breaking out of hostilities. To add to the embarrassment of the English they received conclusive evidence that Captains Norton and Stone, with their boats' crew, were wantonly murdered by the Indians, and that the statement of extenuating circumstances, made by Sassacus, was an entire abrication. The forbearance of the English only stimulated the insolence of the Pequots.

In July 1635, John Oldham ventured on a trading expedition to the Pequot country. He went as an agent of the Massachusetts colony, one object being to ascertain the disposition of the savages. The Indians captured his boat, killed Captain Oldham, horribly mutilating his body, and the rest of the crew, two or three in number, were carried off as captives. The time for attempts at conciliation was at an end. It was resolved to prosecute the war with all vigor, and so to punish the Pequots as to give them a new idea of the power of the English, and to present a warning to all the other savages against the repetition of such outrages.

Plymouth colony furnished fifty soldiers, commanded by Captain Miles Standish. Massachusetts raised two hundred men. The settlements on the Connecticut furnished ninety men. The Mohegans and Narragansets sent to the English camp of rendezvous about two hundred warriors, promising many more. It was decided to strike the Pequots a sudden and heavy blow. We cannot here enter into the details of the fierce and decisive war which ensued.

These military bands rendezvoused on the shores of Narraganset bay, and commenced a rapid march through the forest. The Narragansets were exceedingly jubilant in the prospect of inflicting vengeance upon a foe who had often compelled them to bite the

Just As they hurried along through the narrow trails towards the Pequot territory, volunteer Narragansets joined them until five hundred feathered warriors were in their train.

The Indian guides led them to a strong fort, on the banks of the river Mystic. A large number of Pequot warriors were assembled here, quite unapprehensive of the attack which was about to fall terribly upon them Silently, in the night, the English and the Indians surrounded them, that there might be no escape.

"And so," writes Governor Bradford, "assaulted them with great courage, shooting amongst them, and entering the fort with all speed. Those that first entered found sharp resistance from the enemy, who both shot at and grappled with them. Others ran into their houses, and brought out fire and set them on fire, which soon took in their mats, and, standing close together, with the wind, all was quickly in a flame. Thereby more were burned to death than were otherwise slain. It burned their bow-strings, and rendered them unserviceable. Those that escaped the fire were slain with the sword. Some were hewed to pieces, others were run through with their rapiers, so that they were quickly dispatched, and very few escaped. It was conceived that they thus destroyed about four hundred at this time.

"It was a fearful sight to see them thus frying in the fire, the streams of blood quenching the same, and horrible was the scent thereof. But the victory seemed a sweet sacrifice, and they gave the praise thereof to God, who had wrought so wonderfully for them, thus to give them so speedy a victory over so proud and insulting an enemy." *

"The Narraganset Indians all this while stood round about, but aloof from all danger, and left the whole execution to the English, except it were the stopping of any that broke away; insulting over their enemies in this their ruin and misery, when they were writhing in the flames. After this service was thus happily accomplished, they marched to the water side, where they met with some of their vessels, by which they had refreshing with victuals and other necessaries."

The war was continued with vigor, and the Pequot warriors became nearly exterminated. Sassacus fled to the Mohawks, in New York. They cut off his head. Thus the war ended. The Pequots were no longer to be feared. Driven from their homes, they took refuge, in their dispersion, in different tribes, and this formidable barbaric nation became extinct.

War is always demoralizing. Many, rioting in its scenes of carnage and of crime, lose all sense of humanity, and become desperadoes. After the close of

* Bradford's Plymouth Plantation, p. 363.

the Pequot war, a young fellow, lusty and desperate, by the name of Arthur Peach, who had done valiant service in cutting down the Indians, felt a strong disinclination to return to the monotony of peaceful life He became thoroughly dissolute, a wild adventurer, ripe for any crime. To escape the consequences of some of his misdeeds, he undertook, with three boon companions, as bad as himself, to escape to the Dutch colony at the mouth of the Hudson. As they were travelling through the woods they stopped to rest, and, kindling a fire, sat down to smoke their pipes. An Indian came along, who had a quantity of wampum, which had become valuable as currency, recognized by all the tribes. They invited him to sit down and smoke with them. As they were thus smoking together, Peach said to his companions that he meant to kill the Indian, "for the rascal," said he, "has undoubtedly killed many white men." The Indian, who did not understand English, was unsuspicious of danger. Peach, watching his opportunity, thrust his sword through his body once or twice, and taking from him his wampum and some other valuables, he and his companions hurried on their way, leaving him as they supposed, dead.

Though mortally wounded, the Indian so far revived as to reach some of his friends, when, having communicated to them the facts of the murder, he died. The men were all arrested. The proof was so positive that they made no denial of their guilt. They were all condemned, and three were executed, one having made his escape. Francis Baylies, commenting upon this occurrence, writes:

"This execution is an undeniable proof of that stern sense of duty which was cherished by the Pilgrims. To put three Englishmen to death for the murder of one Indian, without compulsion, or without any apprehension of consequences, for it does not appear that any application was made on the part of the Indians, for the punishment of the murderers, and they might have been pacified by the death of one, and probably even without that, denotes a degree of moral culture unknown in new settlements. It stands in our annals without a parallel instance. The truth of the fact is avouched by all our early historians, and it stands an eternal and imperishable monument of stern, unsparing, inflexible justice. And, in all probability it was not without its earthly reward, for the Indians, convinced of the justice of the English, abstained from all attempts to avenge their wrongs, by their own acts, for many years." *

The Plymouth colonists were still much embarrassed in consequence of their relations with their partners in England, to whom they were still consid-

* Memoir of Plymouth Colony, by Francis Baylies, p. 249.

erably indebted. The agent of the company there wrote that he could not make up his accounts, unless some one from the colony should come over to England to aid him; and he urged that Mr. Winslow should be sent. But Mr. Winslow was afraid to go. Neither was he willing that any of his partners should go. The angry tone of letters from England led him to apprehend serious danger. "For he was persuaded," writes Governor Bradford, "that if any of them went they would be arrested, and an action of such a sum laid upon them as they should not procure bail, but must lie in prison; and then they would bring them to what they list."

Still it was very important that some one should go. Captain Standish was applied to. He seems to have had as little fear of an English prison as of the tomahawks and arrows of the Indians. Without any hesitancy he was ready to embark in the perilous enterprise. But upon mature deliberation his more cautious friends decided it not to be prudent to expose him to such peril. But the spirit of justice, which inspired them in all their transactions, is again conspicuous. They offered to submit the matter to any gentlemen and merchants of the Massachusetts colony, whom the company in England themselves might choose. Before these commissioners both sides should have a hear'ng. "We will be bound," they added, "to stand by their decision, and make good their award, though it should cost us all we have in the world."

The company in England declined this magnanimous offer. In the year 1645 Elder Brewster died, at the advanced age of eighty-four years. He was in Duxbury the next neighbor and the ever warm friend of Miles Standish. Among the remarkable men who composed the Plymouth colony, he was one of the most remarkable. By birth, education and wealth he occupied a high position in English society. In his earlier days he was the companion of ministers of state. He was familiar with the magnificence of courts, having represented his sovereign in foreign embassage. His ample fortune had accustomed him to the refinements and elegances of life. He might doubtless have spent his days in ease, honor and opulence. But, true to his religious convictions, all these he cast aside to share the lot of the humble and persecuted Puritans. He deemed conformity to the mode of worship adopted by the Parliament as sinful. And " he chose rather to suffer affliction with the people of God, than to enjoy the pleasures of sin for a season." In the records of the first church in Plymouth we find a very noble tribute to his memory, probably written by Secretary Morton. Speaking of his embassage, in his early manhood, to the Low Countries, with Mr. Davison, Mr. Morton writes,

"He received possession of the cautionary towns; and, in token thereof, the keys of Flushing being delivered to him in her majesty's name, he kept them for some time, and committed them to his servant, who kept them under his pillow on which he slept, the first night, and, on his return the States honored him with a gold chain, which his master committed to him, and commanded him to wear it when they arrived in England, as they rode through the country until they came to the court.

"Afterwards he went and lived in the country, in good esteem among his friends and the good gentlemen of those parts, especially the godly and religious. He did much good in the country where he lived, in promoting and furthering religion, not only by his practice and example, and encouraging others, but by procuring good preachers for the places thereabouts, and drawing on others to assist and help forward in such a work, he himself commonly deepest in the charge and often above his abilities. In this state he continued many years, doing the best good he could, and walking according to the light he saw, until the Lord revealed further unto him.

"And, in the end, by the tyranny of the bishops against godly preachers and people, in silencing the one, and persecuting the other, he, with many more of those times, began to look further into particulars, and to see into the unlawfulness of their callings, and the burden of many anti-Christian corruptions, which both he and they endeavored to cast off, as they also did.

"After they were joined into communion he was a special stay and help to them. They ordinarily met at his house on the Lord's day, which was within the manor of a bishop. With great love he entertained them when they came, making provision for them to his great charge, and continued so to do while they should remain in England. And when they were to remove out of the country, he was the first in all adventures. He was the chief of those who were taken at Boston, in Lincolnshire, and suffered the greatest loss, and one of the seven that were kept longest in prison, and after bound over to the assizes.

"After he came to Holland he suffered much hardship, after he had spent the most of his means, having a great charge and many children. And in regard to his former breeding and course, not so fit for many employments as others were, especially such as were toilsome and laborious. Yea, he ever bore his condition with much cheerfulness and content. Towards the latter part of those twelve years, spent in Holland, his outward condition was mended, and he lived well and plentiful ; for he fell into a way, by reason he had the Latin tongue, to teach many students, who had a desire to learn the English tongue. By his method they quickly attained it, with great facility, for he drew rules to learn it by after the Latin manner. And many gentlemen, both Danes and Germans, resorted to him, as they had time, from their other studies, some of them being great men's sons.

"But now, removing into this country, all these things were laid aside again, and a new course of living must be framed unto ; in which he was in no way unwilling to take his part, and to bear his burden with the rest, living many times without bread or corn, many months together ; having many times nothing but fish, and often wanting that also; and drunk nothing but water for many years together, until five or six years of his death. And yet he lived, by the blessing of God, in health until very old age."

Elder Brewster was an accomplished gentleman, a genial friend, an eloquent preacher, and a fervent Christian. History has transmitted to us the record of but few characters so well balanced in all energetic, harmonious, and lovely traits. He died as he had lived, tranquilly, peacefully, in the enjoyment of all his faculties. His sickness was short, confining him to his bed but one day. He could converse with his friends until within a few hours of his last breath. About ten o'clock in the evening of April 18th, 1644, he fell asleep.

"Asleep in Jesus, blessed sleep!
From which none ever wake to weep."

CHAPTER XV.

Removal to Duxbury.

Friendship Between Captain Standish and Mr. Brewster.—Character of Mr. Brewster.—His Death and Burial.—Mode of Worship.—Captain's Hill.—Difficulty with the Narragansets.—Firmness and Conciliation.—Terms of Peace.—Plans for Removal from Plymouth.—Captain Standish's Home in Duxbury.—Present Aspect of the Region.

It is greatly to the credit of Captain Miles Standish, the puritan soldier, that his life-long friend was William Brewster, the puritan divine. Their farms in Duxbury were side by side. The scene upon which this noble Christian man looked, in the evening of his eventful life, must have been one full of peaceful beauty, as he stood, staff in hand, upon the threshold of his lowly, yet comfortable cottage. His peaceful home was situated about three miles across the bay from the village of Plymouth. By land it was a roundabout route of nearly eight miles. His farm was on a picturesque peninsula shooting out southerly into the placid waters of Plymouth Bay. In his life of fourscore years and four, he had witnessed the long reigns of three of the most remarkable of the English sovereigns.

The days of his early manhood were passed through

scenes of persecution and suffering, whose vicissitudes were painful and agitating in the extreme. His mental energies had been strengthened by the discipline of adversity and severe afflictions. As an exile, he had encountered poverty and had been exposed to the most severe deprivations and toils. He had landed, with a feeble band, in this New World when it was but a howling wilderness, and where the utmost courage and prudence were requisite, to save the little colony from utter extinction by a savage foe.

He had lived to see the colony securely established, to see the Indians to a very great degree conciliated, and not a few of them brought under the influence of Christian example and instruction. From one little settlement, of seven log huts, he had seen others springing up all around, till eight flourishing towns were established, with eight churches, under eight pastors. He had seen the colony reduced to but fifty souls men, women and children. And, ere he died, the census reported a population of eight thousand, with a well-defined government, a free constitution and established laws. Infant colonies were rising in various points to a vigorous manhood, and were uniting in a confederacy, already sufficiently powerful to repel all native foes, and which gave promise of being able, ere long, to maintain independence against the machinations of all foreign ene mies.

A system of common schools was established which even then was the glory of New England Harvard University, modelled after the renowned university of Cambridge in England, was already beginning to train young men for the highest offices in the church and the state. Thus freedom, education and religion were walking hand in hand. In the retrospect of his path through life, this thoughtful, devout and hopeful man could contemplate the stern conflicts, the cruel errors, and the heroic deeds of one of the most important eras in the world's history. Though he had sown in tears, he could hopefully look forward to the time when his children, and his children's children should reap in joy. In speaking of the death of this eminent man, Governor Bradford writes, under date of the year 1643: *

"I am to begin this year with that which was a matter of great sadness and mourning unto them all. About the 18th of April died their reverend elder and my dear and loving friend, Mr. William Brewster, a man who had done and suffered much for the Lord Jesus and the gospel's sake, and had borne his part in weal and woe with this poor persecuted church

---

* There is a little uncertainty whether Elder Brewster died in the year 1640 or 1644.

above thirty-six years in England, Holland, and in this wilderness, and done the Lord and them faithful service in his place and calling. And notwithstanding the many troubles and sorrows he passed through, the Lord upheld him to a great age. He was near fourscore years of age, if not all out, when he died.* He had this blessing added by the Lord to all the rest, to die in his bed, in peace among the midst of his friends, who mourned and wept over him, and ministered what help and comfort they could unto him, and he again recomforted them while he could.

"His sickness was not long, and till the last day thereof, he did not wholly keep his bed. His speech continued till somewhat more than half a day, and then failed him. About nine or ten o'clock that evening he died, without any pangs at all. A few hours before his death he drew his breath short, and some few minutes before his last he drew his breath long, as a man falling into a sound sleep, without any pangs or gaspings, and so sweetly departed this life unto a better. I would now demand of any, what was he the worse for any former sufferings? What do I say— worse? Nay, sure he was the better, and they now added to his honor. 'It is a manifest token,' saith the apostle,'of the righteous judgment of God, that

* Morton says, "He was fourscore and four years of age."

ye may be accounted worthy of the kingdom of **God,** for which ye also suffer ; seeing it is a righteous **thing** with God to recompense tribulation to them that trouble you ; and to you who are troubled, rest with us when the Lord Jesus shall be revealed from heaven with his mighty angels.' What though he wanted the riches and pleasures of the world in this life, and pompous monuments at his funeral, yet the just shall be blessed, when the name of the wicked shall rot, with their marble monuments."

A very pleasing account is given by Prince, of the mode in which public worship was conducted by these Christians, who were anxious in all things to be conformed to the habits of the disciples in apostolic days. The customs they observed have been transmitted to the present times in our meetings for conference and prayer. On Thursday, the 25th of October, 1632, Governor Winthrop, with Mr. Wilson, who was pastor of the church in Boston, with several other Christian friends, made a visit to Plymouth. They were received with great hospitality. Governor Bradford, Rev. Mr. Brewster, the ruling elder, and several others of the prominent men of Plymouth, came some distance out from the village to meet their friends **who** probably travelled on foot. They were conducted **to** the house of Governor Bradford, where most of them were entertained during their stay. They were, however, every day invited to dinner parties at the houses of the more opulent of the villagers.

On Sunday the Sacrament of the Lord's Supper was administered, in the morning. The service occupied the whole time. In the afternoon devotions, the service was opened by Mr. Roger Williams, who propounded a question of theology, or of conscience, upon which he made sundry remarks. Rev. Mr. Smith, pastor of the Boston church, then spoke briefly upon the subject. Mr. Williams again spoke, quoting freely from the Bible in explanation of the question which he had proposed. Then Governor Bradford, who had studied Hebrew, and was familiar with all scriptural antiquities, expressed his views upon the subject. He was followed by Elder Brewster. His reputation, as a man of profound learning, caused all to listen attentively when he spake. Then, by special invitation from the Elder, Governor Winthrop spoke upon the question, followed by Mr. Wilson, pastor of the church in Boston. Deacon Fuller, who was also the physician of the colony at Plymouth then called for the contribution for the support of public worship and of the poor. The Governor, and all the rest of the congregation rose from their seats and went to the deacon's seat to deposit their gifts The exercises were closed with the benediction.

This peculiarity of having various members of the
15

church speak in public worship, one after another, they brought with them from Holland, such having been the practice adopted by Rev. Mr. Robinson, founded on the primitive practice of the church at Corinth, as recorded by St. Paul, in chapter xiii. of the Acts, 14th and 15th verses. But, as the community advanced in intelligence, it was found that study was essential to the teacher who, Sabbath after Sabbath, would interest a congregation. It was also remembered that such a practice was peculiarly adapted to the age of inspiration which had passed away. Thus the practice was gradually laid aside for the mode of worship now adopted by all the churches descended from the Puritans. The highly educated preacher, in the stated services of the sanctuary, brings from his treasury things new and old for the benefit of the church and congregation. But in frequent meetings for conference and prayer, all the brethren of the church have an opportunity of expressing their views upon all questions of faith and practice.

There was probably no more sincere mourner, at the grave of Elder Brewster, than his life-long companion and friend, Captain Miles Standish. As we have mentioned, their farms in Duxbury were side by side. They had gathered around them several men of congenial spirit, among whom we find the name of

John Alden. From whatever direction one approaches the homes of these illustrious men, he sees looming up before him the remarkable eminence known as "Captain's Hill." It is an oval-shaped mound, rising to the height of about one hundred and eighty feet. This hill was on the farm of Captain Standish. From its summit, scenery of landscape and water was presented, in a calm summer's day, such as can scarcely be surpassed in beauty in any country.

In a clear atmosphere one can discern, in the far distance of the eastern horizon, over the bay, the outline of the sand-hills of Cape Cod, with its sickle bend forming in the extreme north the harbor where the Mayflower first cast anchor; and where for five long weeks their shattered bark rested while the Pilgrims were in vain seeking for a home. Almost at one's feet is to be seen the whole expanse of Plymouth Bay, with the entrance through which their storm-shattered shallop passed through the foaming breakers on either side. There was then no light-house on Gurnet's Point to guide their endangered keel. Just before you is Clark's Isle, under whose lee, in the midnight tempest, the Pilgrims found shelter, when every moment in danger of being submerged by the waves; and where they passed the ever-memorable Sabbath.

From the summit of the hill, all the land to the

south belonged to Captain Standish. On the east, spreading out to the water's edge, including what is called the Nook, were the acres allotted to Elder Brewster. Near the site of the humble house which he reared and occupied, are still to be seen the gray and decaying remains of a farm-house, and its outbuildings, erected by some one of his immediate successors. It was from this spot that the remains of the Elder were conveyed, in long procession winding around the western shore of the bay, to their final resting-place on Burial Hill.

It was in the midst of these peaceful scenes that Captain Miles Standish passed the evening of his days, mainly engaged in agricultural pursuits. But whenever serious trouble came, his energies were immediately called into requisition.

When the English commenced their settlements on Connecticut River, Uncas, sachem of the Mohegan Indians, acknowledged a sort of feudal submission to Sassacus, the powerful chief of the Pequot tribe. This chieftain had, as we have mentioned, twenty-six minor sachems, who paid him feudal homage. Uncas was a very ambitious, energetic man, and he was gradually bringing minor tribes under his sway. His territory was situated east of the Connecticut River and north of New London, Stonington and Norwich. Uncas, though a friend of the white men, was bitterly hostile to the introduction of Christianity among the Indians. Some occasion of war arose between the Narragansets and the Mohegans, and a very large force of the former fell upon Uncas, and slew a large number of his men, while they wounded more. This was in the year 1645, two years after the death of Elder Brewster. Many of the Narragansets had obtained muskets. Being superior in numbers to the Mohegans, and more powerfully armed, they gained an easy victory.

The English were not willing to see their friend and ally thus destroyed. They were bound by treaty to defend him, and sent to the Narragansets a remonstrance. The Narragansets, having engaged the co-operation of the Mohawks, and flushed with victory, returned an insulting and defiant answer. The Connecticut colonists immediately despatched forty well-armed men, for the protection of their ally, while commissioners from the several English colonies met, at Boston, to decide upon what further measures to adopt. Three messengers were sent to the Narragansets and to the Mohegans, calling upon both parties to appoint commissioners to confer with the English upon the points in dispute, and thus to settle the question by diplomacy and not by butchery. If the Narragansets refused to accede this proposal, which they were bound, by previous treaty, to respect, they were to be informed that the **English** had already sent forty armed men to **Uncas**, and a definite answer was demanded to the question whether they intended to abide by the treaty of peace, into which they had entered with the English, or whether they intended to make war upon them also.

To this perfectly just and friendly message, the Narragansets returned again a contemptuous and threatening reply. At the same time Roger Williams, who dwelt in the near vicinity, almost in the midst of the Narragansets, and who was familiar with all their operations, wrote to the Governors of Plymouth and of Massachusetts, stating that the war would soon break out far and wide, with great violence, and the whole country would be in flames. This was alarming tidings to the English. By the arts of peace alone could they be enriched, and for peace and friendship their hearts yearned.

The Narragansets were not far from Plymouth. The fiend-like warfare of the savages, with their hideous yells, tomahawks and firebrands, would first fall upon the scattered farm-houses of that colony. An immediate convention was called of the magistrates, elders and chief military commanders of the **Massachusetts** and Plymouth colonies. They came unanimously to the following decisions, That they were bound by treaty, to aid and defend Uncas; that this aid was not intended merely to defend him in his fort, or when attacked in his dwelling, but also to enable him to preserve his liberty and his estates; that this aid must be immediately furnished or Uncas would be overwhelmed and ruined by his enemies; that the war against the Narragansets being so manifestly just, the reasons for it ought to be proclaimed to the world; that a day of humiliation and prayer should be appointed to implore the Divine guidance and blessing; that three hundred men should be immediately sent to the aid of Uncas, of which Massachusetts should furnish one hundred and ninety, Plymouth forty, Connecticut forty, and New Haven thirty; that, considering the immediate danger of Uncas, forty men should be instantly sent to his succor from Massachusetts.

In accordance with the promptness which has ever characterized the Massachusetts colony, scarcely an hour elapsed, after the tidings reached Boston, ere the men were on the march. Governor Bradford, speaking of the insolent tone adopted by the Narragansets writes,

"They received the English commissioners with scorn and contempt, and told them that they would have no peace with Uncas without his head. They also gave them this further answer,—that it mattered not who began the war, they were resolved to follow it up, and that the English should withdraw their garrison from Uncas, or they would bring down the Mohawks upon them. And withal they gave them this threatening answer, that they would lay the English cattle on heaps as high as their houses, and that no Englishman should step out of his door but that he should be shot."

The English commissioners needed guides to lead them through the wilderness of the Narraganset country, to communicate the reply of the Narraganset chiefs to Uncas. They refused to furnish them with any guide. At last, in scorn they brought forward a poor, old, decrepit Pequot woman saying, with derisive laughter, that they might take her if they pleased. In addition to all these indignities the commissioners were seriously menaced with personal violence. As their interpreter was communicating his message to the sachems, three burly savages came and stood behind him, brandishing their tomahawks in the most insulting and threatening manner. The friendly Indians, who had accompanied the English, were so alarmed by this conduct of the Narragansets that they fled in the utmost haste, leaving the commissioners to go home alone.

"Thus," writes Governor Bradford, "while the commissioners in care of the public peace sought to quench the fire kindled among the Indians, these children of strife breathe out threatenings, provocation and war against the English themselves. So that unless they should dishonor and provoke God by violating a just engagement, and expose the colonies to contempt and danger from the barbarians, they cannot but exercise force, when no other means will prevail to reduce the Narragansets and their confederates to a more just and sober temper."

The Plymouth colonists were as prompt in action as those of Massachusetts. Captain Miles Standish was of course placed at the head of the command. With rapid steps his little army of forty men traversed the forest to the appointed rendezvous at Seekonk, now Rehoboth. Having a much shorter journey to take, he was encamped upon the spot before the Massachusetts men reached it. The Connecticut and New Haven forces also soon arrived. Quite a large number of friendly Indian warriors also joined them. They were armed with muskets, and placed under the command of Captain Standish.

All these measures were adopted with the greatest energy and promptness. The sachem of the Narragansets had, a short time before, sent a present to the Governor of Massachusetts. It was intended either to blind him as to their hostile designs, or to bribe him not to interpose in behalf of the Mohegans. But the Governor was not thus to be duped. He frankly informed the messenger that he was not fully

satisfied respecting the friendly intentions of the sa
chem of the Narragansets,—that he could not, therefore, immediately accept the present. He would not
however refuse it, but would lay it aside to wait the
levelopments of the future.

The military bands being now all assembled at
Rehoboth and ready to march into the territory of the
Narragansets, the Governor of Massachusetts, before
commencing hostilities, sent two commissioners, with
an interpreter, to return the present to the Narraganset sachem, and to inform him that he had already
sent forty men for the protection of Uncas, and that
another armed force was on the march to defend him.
They were also directed to inform the Narraganset
sachem that the English troops had express orders to
stand only upon his and their own defence; that they
should make no attempt to invade the Narraganset
country; and that if the sachem would make reparation for the wrongs which he had already inflicted
upon the Mohegans, and would give security for his
peaceful conduct in future, he would find that the
English were as desirous of peace, and as reluctant
to shed Narraganset blood, as they ever had been. In
conclusion, this messenger, seeking only peace, said:

'If, therefore, Pessecus and Innemo, with the
other sachems, will, without further delay, come to
Boston, they shall have free liberty to come and re-

turn without molestation, or any just grievance from the English. But deputies will not now serve; nor may the preparations in hand be now stayed, or the directions given recalled, till the forementioned sagamores come, and some further order be taken. But if the Narragansets will have nothing but war, the English are providing for it, and will proceed accordingly."

These wise measures accomplished the desired results. The Narraganset sachems had sufficient intelligence to perceive that they were arraying against themselves forces which they were but poorly able to withstand. Three of their most prominent chiefs, with a large array of warriors, after a few days visited Boston, and entered into a treaty of peace.

The Indians agreed to pay to Massachusetts two thousand fathoms of good white wampum, in payments extending through two years; to restore to Uncas all the captives, men, women and children they had taken, and all the canoes, and to pay in full for the corn they had destroyed or carried away. They also agreed to meet the commissioners from the several colonies at New Haven, and submit to their arbitration those grievances which would otherwise result in war. There were one or two other articles in the treaty of a similar nature. Four children of the sachems were, within fourteen days, to be surrendered as hostages to the English, to be tenderly cared for by them, until the terms of the treaty should be fulfilled. Thus happily this menace of war was dispelled.

A little while before the events which we have above recorded, a serious design was entertained of abandoning the location at Plymouth and removing to some place where they would find richer soil. Not only was the soil at Plymouth so barren that it would scarcely repay cultivation, but the harbor was incommodious and shallow. Several general meetings were held, and the subject was very thoroughly discussed. Many had already moved to other locations, and the church had thus become seriously weakened.

" Some," writes Governor Bradford, " were still for staying together in this place, alleging that men and women might here live, if they would be content with their condition. And it was not for want of necessities so much they removed, as for the enriching of themselves. Others were resolute upon removal, and so signified that here they would not stay ; that if the church did not remove, they must; insomuch that many were swayed, rather than that there should be a dissolution of the church, to condescend to a removal, if a fit place could be found, that might more conveniently and comfortably receive the whole, with such accession of others as might come to them, for their better strength and subsistence, and some such like cautions and limitations."

A committee of the church was chosen, by advice of Governor Bradford, to select a place to move to. They repaired to Nauset, on Cape Cod, where is now the town of Eastham. The report they brought back was so much in favor of the place that the large majority of the church consented to remove there. But it was soon found that they had by no means improved their condition by the removal. The result is graphically described by Governor Bradford:

"Now they began to see their error, that they had given away already the best and most commodious places to others, and now wanted them themselves. For this place was about fifty miles from here, and at an outside of the country, remote from all society. Also it would prove so strait as it would not be competent to receive the whole body, much less be capable of any addition or increase. Thus, in a short time, they would be worse there than they are now here. The which, with sundry other like considerations and inconveniences, made them change their resolutions. But such as were before resolved upon removal took advantage of this agreement, and went on, notwithstanding; neither could the rest hinder them, they having made some beginning. Thus was this poor church left, like an ancient mother, grown old and forsaken of her children, though not in their affections, yet in regard to their bodily presence and personal helpfulness. Her ancient members being most of them worn away by death ; and these of later times being like children translated into other families, and she, like a widow, left only to trust in God. Thus she that had made many rich became herself poor."

It required sleepless vigilance and the wisest measures to keep peace with the Indians. There were now, in the several colonies, many individual white men who were totally unprincipled. No power of law could restrain them from insulting and abusing the Indians. The ignorant savages had very inadequate conceptions of justice, and avenged themselves upon any white men who fell into their hands. One of these miscreant white men, who was running away from Massachusetts, was killed by an Indian, in the woods between Fairfield and Stamford. No one knows whether the Indian had any provocation to commit the deed. The murderer was demanded by the Massachusetts authorities. The sachem of the tribe promised to deliver him to the English, bound. Ten Englishmen were sent to receive the prisoner. The Indians, who were in charge of the captive, as soon as they came in sight of the English party, cut his bands and he fled like a deer into the woods. Upon this the English seized eight of the Indians, including two sachems, and held them in close captivity for two days, until they received, from the chiefs, satisfactory promises that the murderer should be delivered to them.

About a week after this, a wandering Indian came to a lonely hut in Stamford, and finding a woman alone, killed her, as he supposed, and robbed the house All the Indians in that region seemed angry, sullen, and often insulting. It was not deemed safe for the English to travel, unless well armed and in some strength. A vigilant watch had to be kept night and day. This was a very uncomfortable state of things, but no remedy could be devised for it. So many had moved from Plymouth that the little village was quite in a state of decay. Duxbury, where Miles Standish had taken his farm, was, as we have mentioned, at a distance of eight miles from Plymouth. Francis Baylies, alluding to the place in the year 1830, writes:

"The extensive pine forest, the certain evidence of sandy and barren soil, which even now almost skirts the ancient town of Plymouth on the south and the west, prevented any extension of population in that direction, and on the east the ocean was its boundary. So unconquerable is the barrenness of this region, that even now the wild deer makes his lair in the same place where deer were hunted by our forefathers two centuries ago, and a few wretched Indians inhabit the primeval woods in which their ancestors disdained to dwell." *

Fear of the Indians, with whom hostilities were liable at any time to break out, prevented the colonists from selecting farms far inland. The strong settlements on Massachusetts Bay induced the Plymouth people to extend their settlements along the ocean shore in that direction. The second church of the Plymouth colony was established at Duxbury.

The house which Captain Standish occupied here during the long evening of his eventful life, was situated on the southeastern part of the peninsula, where the remains of the cellar, which he probably dug, are still to be seen. The house in Duxbury, now called the Standish House, was built by his son, Alexander, partly it is supposed from timbers taken from the old house. This fact seems to be substantiated from the appearance of the beams, which bear the traces of a peculiar saw, which was used before the introduction of saw-mills. The hearthstone also, as well as the doors and latchings, were doubtless used in the paternal home. It was by the side of that fireplace that the heroic captain sat and mused, while the storms of a New England winter shook his dwelling. The timbers are of oak, and very sound and strong.

* Memoir of New Plymo th, by Francis Baylies, part i, p. 277.

Upon the south side of Captain's Hill there is a large rock, called the Captain's Chair. Near this spot the original barn was erected. The farm comprised about one hundred and fifty acres, and contained some of the most fertile land to be found in the county of Plymouth. Other parts of the town are sandy and unproductive. Clark's Island, where the explorers of Plymouth Bay passed their first Sabbath is said to possess, in some parts, a rich soil, which can scarcely be surpassed in any country. "While the northern and western sides offer the most desirable qualities for pasturage and grain, its southern and eastern declivities present a perfect garden, abounding with trees, through whose foliage, even during the summer's hottest months, stir the breezes from the sea."

The historian of Duxbury describes the scene now witnessed from the summit of Captain's Hill, and endeavors to give expression to the emotions which the view must awaken in every reflective mind. He writes:

"Select, should you visit it, the closing hours of a summer's day, when the burning heat of the declining sun is dispelled by the cooler shades of approaching evening, and ascend to its height. Now as the retiring rays of day form on the heavens above a gorgeous canopy of variegated hues, so on nature's face below all brightens into richness, and the verdure of her covering softens into mildness; the shining villages around, and the village spires towering against a background of unfading green, add gladness to the scene. The glassy surface of the bay within, with its gentle ripplings on the shore beneath, the music of the dashing waves on the beach without, give quiet to the mind and peace within.

"Before you, in the distance at the east, appear the white sand-hills of Cape Cod, shining beyond the blue expanse, and seeming to encircle by its protecting barrier a spot dear to the heart of every descendant of that Pilgrim band. Still nearer, at your feet and before you, are the pleasant bays of Plymouth, Kingston, and Duxbury, enlivened by passing boats, and sheltered by the beach from a raging ocean, crowned at its southern extremity by a lighthouse, and with the extending arm of Saquish enclosing the Island of the Pilgrims; turning your eyes to the south, they fall in succession on the promontory of Manomet; on the ancient town of Plymouth, rising beneath, and—as if under the protection of the mound beyond, the resting-place of the Pilgrim's dead—on the villages of Rocky Nook and of Kingston.

"Extending your eye over the extent of forest to the northwest, you see the Blue Hills of Milton, ascending far above the surrounding country; while nearer, at the north, are the villages of Duxbury and Marshfield, scattered over the fields, whose white cottages, shining in the sun, offer a pleasing contrast to the scene. Below you and around you once arose the humble abode of the Pilgrims. Who can gaze upon the spot which marks the site of the dwelling of Standish, without feelings of emotion? who can but give thanks that that spirit—

> ' A spirit fit to start into an empire
> And look the world to law '—

had been sent amongst them, to be their counsel in peace and their protection in danger? Who can but admire its ready adaptation to a sphere of action so totally different from the school of his youth? Here also arose the dwellings of Brewster, who having followed in his youth the retinue of kings and princes, preferred a solitary retreat in the western wilds, and there to worship his God in peace. Here, too, was the abode of Collier, who, under every circumstance of danger, strove with unceasing toil in the discharge of every duty necessary to the welfare and prosperity of the colony. Here, too, can be seen the spot whereon the habitation of Alden was, whose prudent counsels and whose rigid justice attained for him a rank in the estimation of the colony, alike an honor to himself, and a subject of pride to his descendants.

Turn your vision as you may, and you will feel that you are gazing on a scene of more than ordinary interest, full of the most grateful recollections, and of a nature the most agreeable and pleasing.

> " 'Scenes must be beautiful, which daily viewed
> Please daily, and whose novelty survives
> Long knowledge and the scrutiny of years,—
> Praise justly due to those that I describe.'

"Rose, the first wife of Myles Standish, died at Plymouth, January 29, 1621, about a month after the landing. She was among the first to succumb to the privations of that terrible first winter. He married a second wife (Barbara), who survived him.

"To his house on Captain's Hill, Standish removed after his second marriage, and here he drew around him a devoted class of friends, among whom were the elder Brewster, George Partridge, John Alden, Mr. Howland, Francis Eaton, Peter Brown, George Soule, Nicholas Byrom, Moses Simmons, and other settlers of Duxbury.

"The Indians also loved as well as feared him, and the faithful Hobbomak ever kept near to minister to his wants, and was the faithful guide in his travels. This devoted Indian died in 1642, having faithfully served his master twenty years, and is supposed to have been buried on the south side of Captain's Hill, near the great rock called 'The Captain's chair.'

Tradition fixes his wigwam between two shell mounds on the shore near the Standish place, till taken home to the house of Standish, where he became an inmate till his death."

CHAPTER XVI.

The Standish Monument.

The Will of Captain Standish.—His Second Wife—Captain's Hill. - The Monument.—Letters from President Grant and General Hooker.—Oration by General Horace Binney Sargent.—Sketch of his Life.—Other Speakers.—Laying the Corner Stone.—Description of the Shaft.

None of the particulars of the last hours of Captain Standish have been transmitted to our day. So far as is known he enjoyed good health until his last sickness. His will was dated March 1st, 1655. In it he expressed the wish that, should he die at Duxbury, his body should be buried by the side of his two dear daughters, Lora Standish, and Mary Standish, his daughter-in law. One-third part of his estate he bequeathed to his dear and loving wife, Barbara Standish. The following extract from his will indicates the devout character of the man:

"I do, by this my will, make and appoint my loving friends, Mr. Timothy Hatherly and Captain James Cudworth, supervisors of this my last will; and that they will be pleased to do the office of Christian love, to be helpful to my poor wife and children, by their Christian counsel and advice; and if any difference should arise which I hope will not, my will is that my said supervisors shall determine the same, and that they see that my poor wife shall have as comfortable maintainance as my poor state will bear, the whole time of her life, which if you my loving friends please to do, though neither they nor I shall be able to recompense, I do not doubt that the Lord will."

There is a tradition that Captain Standish's second wife, Barbara, was a sister of his first wife, Rose. When the Mayflower sailed, she was left an orphan in England. She afterwards reached the colony a full grown woman, and became the wife of the Captain.

Captain Standish died the 3d of October, 1656. But his character and achievements were such that for two hundred years since his death, his name has been one of the most prominent in our retrospects of the Pilgrim days. His descendants are very numerous. For some time it has been, by these his descendants, in contemplation to rear a monument to his memory. On the 17th of August, 1871, there was a very large gathering of these descendants at Duxbury, to consecrate the spot on Captain's Hill, where the monument was to be reared. Many others of the most distinguished men of our land were also present, who wished to unite in this tribute to the memory of one of the most illustrious names in American annals. President U. S. Grant wrote, regretting his inability to be present:

"I am heartily with your association in sympathy, with any movement to honor one who was as prominent in the early history of our country as Miles Standish; but my engagements are such that I regret I am unable to promise to be present in August."

In the reply from General Hooker to an invitation to attend the celebration, he writes:

"I regret to state that my engagements for the month of August are such as to render it impossible for me to join you on that memorable occasion. It is unnecessary for me to say that I deeply sympathize with the object of your meeting. I have been an admirer of the character of Myles Standish from my boyhood up, and would like to be identified with any body of gentlemen engaged in commemorating his great virtues. To me, his civil and military character towers far above his contemporaries, and they, if I mistake not (when history shall be truthfully written), will be made to appear to be the most remarkable body of men that ever lived. Viewed from our present standpoint, in my opinion, they are now entitled to that judgment. It will be a graceful act on the part of our friends, to erect a monument to his memory; but it must not be expected to add to his fame or immortality. Industry, valor, and integrity were regarded as the cardinal virtues of our forefathers, and I hope they will never be held in less estimation by their descendants. One of our gifted poets has happily named 'Plymouth Rock' as the corner-stone of the nation. The superstructure promises to be worthy of the foundation. With great respect, I have the honor to be your friend and servant,

"J. HOOKER, *Major-General.*"

Replies of a similar character were returned by Generals Sherman, Sheridan and Burnside, and by W. C. Bryant. General Horace Binney Sargent delivered the oration on this occasion. It was very eloquent in its truthful delineation of the character and career of the illustrious Puritan Captain. Every reader will peruse with interest the following grapic sketch from its pages:

"About the time that all Christendom was in mourning for the murdered Prince of Orange, and deploring in his death the overthrow of the bulwark of the Protestant faith, a little fair-haired child was playing among the hedge-rows of England, who was destined to learn the art of war in the armies of that king's more warlike son, Prince Maurice, then a boy of seventeen, and to be a tower of defence to the unsoldierly Pilgrim colony of Protestant America.

"That child—whose bones, after nearly fourscore years of toil and war, were laid somewhere on this hill-side, perhaps under our unconscious feet—was Myles Standish, the great Puritan Captain ! He was born about the year 1580, of English ancestry, dating back to rank and opulence as far as the thirteenth century. Of his childhood, little is known. To defeat the title of his line to lands in England, the rent-roll of which is half a million per annum, the hand of fraud is supposed to have defaced the page that contained the parish record of his birth.

"Unjustly deprived of these vast estates, as he avers in his will, in which he bequeaths his title to his eldest son, it seems probable that he went to Holland near the time of his majority. Queen Elizabeth signed his commission as lieutenant in the English forces, serving in the Netherlands against the cruel armies of the Inquisition. As she died in 1603, about two years after his majority, it is not improbable that we are indebted to that first disappointment, which may have driven him, in his early manhood and some despair, into the army.

"From 1600 to 1609, the year of the great truce between Prince Maurice and the King of Spain, the contest was peculiarly obstinate and bloody. In this fierce school the Puritan captain learned the temper and art of war.

"From 1609 to 1620, a period of truce but not of civil tranquility, the Low Countries were inflamed by those theological disputes of the Calvinists and Arminians which brought the excellent Barneveldt to the scaffold, and drove the great Grotius—a fugitive from prison—into exile. In this school, perhaps, Myles Standish learned some uncompromising religious opinions, which brought him into strange sympathy and connection with the Pilgrim church in Leyden. Both periods seemed to leave their impress on his character. The inventory, recorded with his will, mentions the Commentaries of Cæsar, Bariffe's Artillery, three old Bibles, and three muskets, with the harness of the time, complete. His Bibles were old. A well-worn Bible for every musket; and, thank God, a musket, not an old one, to defend each Bible!

"The schedule of his books, some forty in number, records nearly twenty which are devotional or religious. With the memory of one act of singularly resolute daring, when, in obedience to the colonial orders to crush a great Indian conspiracy, he took a squad of eight picked men into the forests, and deemed it prudent to kill the most turbulent warrior with his own hands, we may imagine how the Pilgrim soldier, friend and associate of Brewster, disciple of the saintly Robinson, rose from the perusal of one of the old Bibles, or of "Ball on Faith," "Spasles against Heresie," or "Dodd on the Lord's Supper," to stab Pecksuot to the heart with his own knife; a giant who had taunted him with his small stature, in almost the very words of Goliah in his insulting sneer at David, long before; and to cut off the head of Watawamat, which bloody trophy the elders had ordered him to bring home with him. We can imagine him on the evening of that cheaply victorious day, taking more than usual pleasure in the exultant psalms of the warrior David, and in a chapter of Burrough's "Christian Contentement" and "Gospell Conversation," especially as he had his three muskets with bandoleers, and Bariffe's Artillery, close at his hand. One can feel the unction with which the valorous Pilgrim would religiously fulfil the colonial order to smite the heathen hip and thigh, and hew Agag in pieces before the Lord.

"Not originally, and perhaps never, a member of the Pilgrim church, and possessing many traits which might have belonged to the fierce trooper, in an army whose cavalry was the legitimate descendant of Cæsar's most formidable enemies,—the Batavi, celebrated for cavalry qualities, and long the body-guard of the Roman emperors,—the appearance of the somewhat violent soldier, in the saintly company of Parson Robinson's church, is an anomaly.

"It has been proven many a time, from the days of Bannockburn, when the Scottish host sank on its knees to receive the benediction of the Black Abbot of Inchaffray, even to our own late day, when many of the best fighting regiments were blessed with the most earnest chaplains, that men never tender their lives more gallantly to God and mother-land than when they are fervently preached to and prayed for.

"Yet the all-daring contempt for peril, the roughness of temper, the masterly economy with which Standish saved human life by consumate indifference to personal homicide upon prudent occasion, his power of breathing his own fiery heart into a handful of followers, till he made them an army able to withstand a host in the narrow gates of death, would lead us to expect such a colleague for the saintly Brewster as little as we should expect to see Sheridan—

"'Cavalry Sheridan,
Him of the horses and sabres we sing'—

prominent among the Methodists.

"In truth, with the poem of our sweetest and most cultured bard in our minds, and with the memory of those fierce monosyllables with which our great cavalry leader rolled back defeat upon the jubilant rebel host, and rescued victory at Winchester, fancy can depict the foaming black horse pressed into the rush of the shell-shattered guidons by the iron gripe of knees booted in "Cordovan leather," and imagine that little Myles Standish rode that day in the saddle of little Phil. Sheridan.

"To the genealogist, who believes that names represent qualities and things, it is not unpleasing to find in the family record of Standish and Duxbury Hall, in the parish church of Chorley, Old England, the name Milo Standanaught. To stand at nothing, in the way of a duty commanded by the civil authority, seemed the essence of character in Myles Standish; and thoroughness stamps the reputation of the name and blood to-day.

"The materials for personal biography are scanty. His wife, Rose Standish,—an English rose,—whose very name augurs unfitness for a New England winter on an unsettled cape, died within a month of the landing. A light tradition exists that his second wife, Barbara, was her sister, whom he left an orphan child in England, and sent for. She arrived a woman grown, and the valorous captain added another illustration to the poet's story, that Venus and the forger of thunderbolts were married.

"From the first anchorage, Captain Standish, as the soldier of the company, was charged with all deeds of adventure. At first, certain grave elders were sent with him for counsel. But ultimately his repute in affairs, both civil and military, was such that he was fo many years the treasurer of the colony, and, during a period of difficulty, their agent in England. As a soldier, he was evidently the Von Moltke of the Pilgrims They invested him with the general command. Even in extreme old age—the very year that he died "very auncient and full of dolorous paines"— he received his last and fullest commission against new enemies, his old friends, the Dutch.

"It is singular that among the primitive people, who must often in the later Indian wars have missed his counsel and conduct, as the poet describing Venice, sighs,—

"'Oh! for one hour of blind old Dandole.'

no clear tradition has descended of the place where the war-worn bones of the soldier-pilgrim lie. Sent, like Moses, to guide and guard a feeble people to a promised land of power that he might never see, no man knoweth his burial-place until this day.

"More than one hundred years ago, the following paragraph appeared in the Boston "News-Letter," dated Boston, January 22, 1770: "We hear from Plymouth that the 22d day of December last was there observed by a number of gentlemen, by the name of the Old Colony Club, in commemoration of the landing of their ancestors in that place."

"The fourth toast on that occasion, a hundred and one years ago, was, "To the memory of that brave man and good officer, Capt. Miles Standish."

' Over the graves of the guests at that dinner,—

"'For fifty years the grasses have been growing.'

But the principle of public fidelity shares the immortality of God and Truth. Reverence for it never dies till the decay of nations. And to-day we come together, the dwellers in the city and the dwellers on the shore, men of every age and all professions, to dedicate one spot of this parental soil for an enduring monument to the same Myles Standish of the same unfaded record. The sunlight of near three hundred years, that has shone fatal on many a reputation since his baby eyes first saw the light of England, has only brought out the lasting colors of his fame.

"Believing, as I firmly do, that he was a useful, a necessary citizen, because he was 'that brave man and good officer' at a time when soldierly qualities were essential to the very life of the infant colony, it seems to me providential for the colonists that one of their number was, by temper and training, unable to sympathize with that soft tenderness for human life which is wont to characterize saintly-minded men, like the Rev. Mr. Robinson, who, when he heard of the marvelous conflict where Standish, with three or four others, in a locked room, killed the same number of hostile chiefs that were gathering their tribes to exterminate the English, uttered these sorrowful words: 'Oh! that you had converted some before you had killed any!'

"The soldier practised that terrible piece of economy which no saint of the company would have dreamed of doing with his own hand. To borrow the diction of the time, the gauntlet of the man of wrath was the fold of the lambs of God It was fortunate for us who believe in Plymouth Rock, that one trained soldier, who had faced war conducted by the Duke of Alva, came out in the Mayflower.

"Myles Standish represented the true idea of public service, vigorous fidelity, and trained fitness for his place. In his single heroic person he presented the true idea of the army,—skilled military force in loyal subordination to the civil authority. The confidence that the colony reposed in him to execute their most difficult commands as a soldier, seems to prove that he revered, in the words of Mr. Robinson's farewell sermon, 'the image of the Lord's power and authority which the magistrate beareth.'

"To be the founders of states is the first of glories, according to Lord Bacon. The career of our Pilgrim hero is a beautiful illustration of an education fitted to the great mission for which he seemed peculiarly, strangely ordained.

"In grateful memory we consecrate this spot of earth to a monument of the great Puritan Captain. May its shadow fall upon his grave! For two centuries the stars have looked upon it. At what moment of the night the circling moon may point it out with shadowy finger, no mortal knows. No mortal ear can hear the secret whispered to the night, 'Beneath this spot lies all of a hero that could die.'"

Several other eloquent addresses were made upon the occasion by General B. F. Butler, Dr. Loring, and other gentlemen of the highest social standing The community is deeply indebted to Stephen M. Allen, Esq., one of the prominent citizens of Duxbury, for the time and money he has devoted to furtherance of this good enterprise. As Corresponding Secretary of the Standish Memorial Association, he has been one of the most efficient agents in pushing forward the truly patriotic undertaking.

On Monday, the 7th of October, 1872, the corner stone of the Standish monument was laid. It was indeed a gala day in the ancient town of Duxbury. It is estimated that ten thousand people were present. The Ancient and Honorable Artillery Company, of Boston, acted as escort to the procession. Several Masonic Lodges, with their glittering paraphernalia took part in the imposing ceremonies. As the long procession wound up the slope of Captain's Hill, thousands of spectators lined their path on either side A memorial box was deposited under the corner-stone with a metallic plate which bore the following description:

THE CORNER STONE

OF THE

STANDISH MEMORIAL,

IN COMMEMORATION OF THE CHARACTER AND SERVICES

—OF—

CAPTAIN MYLES STANDISH,

THE FIRST COMMISSIONED MILITARY OFFICER

OF NEW ENGLAND,

Laid on the summit of Captain's Hill, in Duxbury, under

the Superintendence of

THE ANCIENT AND HONORABLE ARTILLERY COMPANY

OF MASSACHUSETTS,

In presence of

THE STANDISH MONUMENT ASSOCIATION,

BY THE

M. W. GRAND LODGE OF FREE MASONS,

OF MASSACHUSETTS

M. W. SERENO D. NICKERSON, GRAND MASTER

ON THE SEVENTH DAY OF OCTOBER, A. D. 1872.

Being the Two Hundred and Fifty-second Year since

the First Settlement of New England

BY THE

PILGRIM FATHERS.

SITE CONSECRATED AUGUST 17, 1871.

ASSOCIATION INCORPORATED MAY 4, 1872.

ASSOCIATION ORGANIZED, AND GROUND BROKEN, JUNE 17, 1872.

CORNER OF FOUNDATION LAID AUGUST 9, 1872.

This fine shaft rises one hundred and ten feet from its base, and is surmounted by a bronze statue of the

Captain, in full uniform, twelve feet in height, and is said to be a truthful likeness. The diameter of the shaft, at its base, is twenty-eight feet. The structure is of the finest quality of Quincy granite. I will close this brief narrative with the eloquent words of Gen. Horace Binney Sargent:

"High as the shaft may tower over headland and bay; deep as its foundation-stones may rest; brightly as it may gleam in the rising or setting sun upon the mariner returning in the very furrow that the keel of the Mayflower made, the principles of common-sense, a citizen soldier's education for a citizen soldier's work, the principles of moral truth, manly honesty, prudent energy, fidelity incorruptible, courage undauntable, all the qualities of manhood that compel unflinching execution of the states' behest,—are firmer and higher and brighter still. And to crown them all is reverence to the Supreme Executive of Earth and Heaven, who knows no feebleness of heart or hand, and whose great purpose moved the war-worn Pilgrim's feet to seek his home upon this rock-bound continent, where the unceasing waves of two unfettered oceans roar the choral hymn of Freedom."

THE END.

www.ingramcontent.com/pod-product-compliance
Lightning Source LLC
Chambersburg PA
CBHW020300240426
43673CB00039B/659